All Our Sisters

ALL OUR SISTERS

Stories of
Homeless Women
in Canada

SUSAN SCOTT

A GARAMOND BOOK

broadview press

This book belongs to all the women who so bravely told their stories in the hopes that they would give their more affluent sisters a better understanding of lives lived in dire poverty.

If you are going to help me
Please be patient while I decide
I can trust you
Let me tell you my story
The whole story in my own way
Please accept that whatever I have
Done whatever I may do
Is the best I have to offer and
Seemed right at the time
I am not just a person
I am this person unique and special
Don't judge me as right or wrong
Bad or good I am what I am
And that's all I got
Don't assume that your knowledge
Is more accurate than mine.
You only know what I have
Told you that small part of me
Don't ever think that you know what
I should do you don't I may be
Confused but I'm still the expert about me
Don't place me in a position
Of living up to your expectations
I have enough trouble with mine
Please hear my feelings not just
My words accept all of them
If you can't how can I?
I can do it myself, I know
I knew enough to ask for help didn't I?
Help me to help myself

—Karen Flett, Winnipeg

Library and Archives Canada Cataloguing in Publication

Scott, Susan, 1944 Oct. 3-
    All our sisters : stories of homeless women in Canada / Susan Scott.

Includes bibliographical references and index.
ISBN-13: 978-1-55111-759-1
ISBN-10: 1-55111-759-2

    1. Homeless women--Canada. I. Title.
HV4509.S43 2007   305.48'96942   C2007-901215-9

Broadview Press is an independent, international publishing house, incorporated in 1985. Broadview believes in shared ownership, both with its employees and with the general public; since the year 2000 Broadview shares have traded publicly on the Toronto Venture Exchange under the symbol BDP.

We welcome comments and suggestions regarding any aspect of our publications—please feel free to contact us at the addresses below or at broadview@broadviewpress.com.

North America
PO Box 1243, Peterborough, Ontario, Canada K9J 7H5
3576 California Road, PO Box 1015, Orchard Park, NY, USA 14127
Tel: (705) 743-8990; Fax: (705) 743-8353
email: customerservice@broadviewpress.com

UK, Ireland, and continental Europe
NBN International, Estover Road, Plymouth, UK PL6 7PY
Tel: 44 (0) 1752 202300; Fax: 44 (0) 1752 202330
Email: enquiries@nbninternational.com

Australia and New Zealand
UNIREPS, University of New South Wales
Sydney, NSW, 2052 Australia
Tel: 61 2 9664 0999; Fax: 61 2 9664 5420
email: info.press@unsw.edu.au

www.broadviewpress.com

Broadview Press acknowledges the financial support of the Government of Canada through the Book Publishing Industry Development Program (BPIDP) for our publishing activities.

PRINTED IN CANADA

CONTENTS

ACKNOWLEDGEMENTS

This book would not have been possible without the help of many people, most particularly the women who shared their stories, their insights, and their wisdom, and who allowed me to photograph them. Thank you; I hope the huge risks you took will not have been in vain.

I would also like to extend my appreciation to the shelters, drop-ins, and other agencies that opened their doors and hearts, in particular: CUPS Community Health Centre, Literacy Alberta, and the YWCA Mary Dover House in Calgary; Main Street Project and Agape Table Inc. in Winnipeg; Mavis/McMullen Place, Powell Place, Union Gospel Mission, New Westminster Drop-In Centre, and Women's Humanities Year in Vancouver; Centre 416, Nellie's, and the Yonge Street Mission Evergreen Centre for Street Youth in Toronto; Women's Emergency Accommodation Centre and Kindred House in Edmonton; and Cornerstone/Le Pilier in Ottawa.

Gratitude goes to: Jude Carlson and G.N. Ramu; Ashala, Aylah, and Mike Jovanovski and Rowan Lehmann; Dana Flavelle and Rick, Stuart, and Grace Orchard; Dave and Cecilia Humphreys; and Devin and Sheila Pratt for all their hospitality, encouragement, and prodding.

Thank you Kathy Houston, Tara Hyland-Russell, and Roberta Rees for nourishing the writing process; Rod Blank who managed the purse strings so ably; Fern Brooks for her vigilance; Nicole Moore who helped me keep in touch with many women; Annemarie Pedersen who was so willing to spread the word; Gillian Ranson for all manner of treats; Natalija Reljic for turning mountains into molehills; and Marilyn Wood for spring cleaning the grey cells at the appropriate moment.

Thank you Ashala Jovanovski, Grant Larson, Susan Mate, and Luke Shwart for assistance with photographs.

The generous financial support of the Alberta Foundation for the Arts and the Douglas-Coldwell Foundation was crucial to the research and promotion of the book.

Many people have been remarkably helpful in different ways and remarkably patient, especially my editors at Broadview—Anne Brackenbury and Betsy Struthers. Thank you for all your unique contributions: Mark

Agg, Joven Antolin, Brenda Bennett, Reta Blind, Nancy Bradley, Susan Brandt, Erynn Ceallaigh, Kim Chester, Lin Conover, Cindy Cowan, Marcia Davis, Paul Drohan, Petti Fong, Greg Gerrard, Laura Godfrey, Shawna Hohendorff, David Hulchanski, Bill Huntley, Luka Jolicoeur, Nadine Kernahan, Margaret Leslie, Tina Loo, Paul Malchow, Carol Martin, Jim McLaughlin, Donna McPhee, Lainie Neal, Kim Pate, Jake Pyne, Gillian Ranson, Capri Rasmussen, Joy Reid, Angela Robertson, Jan Rothenburger, Helen Sadowski, D.J. Scott, Trudi Shymka, Myra Skerrett, John Slavik, Mike Spence, Rita Spence, Kathy Stringer, The Websters, and W. who lost his knees in a good cause. Finally, I would like to acknowledge Lois Hole, friend and mentor, whose example illuminated the way and whose questions clarified my thoughts.

PREFACE

Doreen didn't look like a person you might think to find in one of Canada's tougher, larger homeless shelters. She was friendly, neat, and clean. She didn't use bad language, was never drunk, noisy, or violent. She helped out with the chores and always had a smile. She was gentle, if not genteel. In her late 50s, she stuck out like a beautiful thumb. Later she moved away from the shelter, saying that it was an unsafe place for her.

Doreen and I used to meet downtown, usually at a bus shelter, and then go for Sunday breakfast. One day, instead of Doreen and her cart, the shelter contained a drunken man sprawled on the ground. Doreen, who probably took this as an elaborate omen of doom, was nowhere to be seen. In subsequent days I searched for her and hung out at her usual haunts. No Doreen. There were insubstantial reports of her in the suburbs, but they were reports and nothing more. I miss Doreen—her stories, her sense of humour, her consideration for others, her generosity. I hope she's safe.

Then there was Sheila who, sitting in the passenger seat of my car, cheerfully informed me, between bouts of hacking, that she's incontinent when she coughs, but she doesn't like to ask male homeless shelter staff for pads. She and I were off for a meal at a cafeteria. She was very excited because she was going to choose exactly what she wanted instead of whatever the shelter had been donated that day. She missed her kitchen and fretted that she might lose her homemaking skills while living in an institution.

These two women were the immediate catalysts for this book; knowing them prodded me to think about what it means to be female and homeless in Canada. Some homeless women are very visible, but most are far from the public's eye. When they do surface, it is only to be labelled in cruel ways and to have impossible demands placed on them. When we look at what has happened in Canadian society over the last 30 years or so, it is easy to see why there are so many women without a safe place to lay their heads at night, and yet when we see a person panhandling or bottle-picking, it is alarmingly easy to blame her instead of recognizing her as someone we as a society have failed. Since I began this project in January of 2004 I have watched in dismay as the situation has only deteriorated for homeless women.

When we think of the homeless, we tend to think of men. It's almost a heroic image. If a man leaves home, it's in keeping with our mythology. Men are supposed to go on quests like Odysseus, travel the land like Forrest Gump, or live rough like Robin Hood. Women, though, are supposed to stay behind and keep the home fires burning. If a woman has the temerity to leave, we blame her for not being very womanly, and we say it's her fault if she finds herself in trouble like Little Red Riding Hood. In a society that still tends to judge women by their homemaking skills and elevates Martha Stewart to near-goddess status, home is part of our identity and our definition. Without a home, who are we? And, if our children are apprehended because we don't have a home for them, then our womanhood is eroded even further. Finally, if we lose our looks, the one sure way we can make money—prostitution—is also lost, or at least the financial return is reduced. Without home, children, and looks are we indeed women in our society?

Homeless women grieve for everything they have lost—from their children to the contents of their freezer. Ellie, in her early 60s, living in a shelter because of the physical abuse meted out by her husband, a former police officer, used to list the contents of her freezer. Somehow the litany of roasts conferred upon her respectability and an identity that she felt was sorely lacking in her current circumstances.

Once homeless, many women have to cope with a life that is extremely masculine. Sheila's reluctance to ask for sanitary pads is a poignant symbol of how the system is stacked against women from the outset. Our housing policy—or lack thereof—ensures that there is not enough housing for everyone in the lower income brackets, but, many politicians as well as shelters and the bureaucracy of social assistance do not make life easy for the destitute. Contrary to popular opinion, all this is not because the women won't pull up their socks. As one said, "We do not loll about all day eating bonbons."

I'm grateful to all the women who have opened my eyes and ears to their lives, particularly grateful to the 60 or so who gave me their stories for *All Our Sisters*. While not all their stories are included, they all informed the text in different ways. The title comes from Tonya, a 26-year-old Winnipeg woman, who briefly became very involved with the project. It bothered her that at that point the book had no title. She suggested a title that would reflect the universality of women's experiences and how homeless women are part of the greater community, how they are connected to us all: "Our mothers, our daughters, our grandmothers, our aunts, our nieces, our wives." This was a little long to fit a book cover, so we boiled it down to "All Our Sisters." When I last saw Tonya, she was in an addictions program and finding it heavy going, partly due to her devastating lack of self-esteem.

Beginning in January 2004, and financed by a grant from the Alberta Foundation for the Arts, I travelled from Vancouver to Ottawa, where the money ran out. (My apologies to Quebec and the Maritimes.) Wherever I went, women urged me to tell their stories in the hopes they could make a difference, if not for themselves, then for others. They also wanted me to tell Canadians how difficult it is to obtain the services they need and how alien and imperiled they feel in most mixed homeless shelters. They didn't want to be part of a study, they felt they had been studied to death to no avail, but they believed and desperately hoped that their stories might change the world at the gut—or at the heart—level. Some were quite rightly cynical that their stories would ever see the light of day; others were touchingly confident that they would be published and soon.

We laughed and cried together, and I came to admire their courage and humour in the face of all kinds of adversity. Few felt they were owed anything by the rest of us, even though our system lets them down so badly. The least we can do is see them as people and not as problems. Most of us were shocked by the pictures of US troops torturing Iraqis at Abu Ghraib, but equal cruelty and degradation happens in Canada to women and children on a daily basis. Most of us are aghast at the numbers of women who have disappeared off the streets of our cities, but while we continue to support the status quo and remain silent, every one of us contributes to the pain and the murder of Canadian women.

INTRODUCTION

Before looking at homelessness, it is important to understand what its opposite, "home," means. For most of us, home is a word loaded with emotional, spiritual, and heartfelt emotions, which run deep and evoke cherished memories, fondest hopes, and almost sacred feelings. Home is where we can be ourselves—where we don't need to wear a dressing gown to go to the bathroom at night, where we can put a knife down the ketchup bottle to scrape out the reluctant last drop, where we can squabble with our nearest and dearest. Home is the place that says who we are and, for women in particular, that expresses our identity by what we choose to display—our pictures, our books, our music—and what we have stored away—important papers, baby's first lock of hair, grandmother's tablecloth. Home gives us choices: we can choose what to eat and when, who to invite in and who to exclude, what clothes to wear, and when to go to bed. Home fortifies us to go out into the world and provides a retreat from the world's clamour. Above all, home is about safety.

Someone who is homeless is deprived of not just four walls and a roof, but of all these less tangible things. Added to that loss are the epithets freely used to describe homeless women—"lazy bum," "slut squaw," "crack whore," "trash." Even worse than the name-calling is the violence that poverty inflicts upon the women in its clutches. Such violence is legion and various: not being taken seriously by the police, having children forcibly removed, suffering indignities at the hands of authority figures, and physical attacks. Who in their right mind would want to forfeit their home and all that it provides from status to sanctuary? Not many of us. Yet, we continue to believe that being homeless is a choice: you have a roof or you don't.

For women there are many ways of being homeless, besides living on the street: staying with a violent partner because she can't afford to leave; being bound to a pimp or a dealer; couch-surfing from one relative to another; or living in unhygienic and unsafe buildings and/or over-crowded conditions with cockroaches in the fridge and two families squeezed into a one-bedroom apartment. While all women living in these situations have a roof, none has the kind of place where most of us would feel "at home."

Canada is one of the few countries in the Western world without a social housing policy; the result is suffering for people at the lower end of the economic spectrum. Some women find it impossible to find housing. Others have a place, but they live in constant fear of homelessness because welfare payments or minimum wages are not enough to cover rent, food, and utilities. They come up with solutions like sleeping with the landlord or sharing the space with an abusive man to help pay the rent cheque. "A woman is only a man away from the streets," say women who have learned the hard way that females are still a financially disadvantaged group in Canada. These precarious conditions constitute what is sometimes called the "continuum of homelessness" (Kappel Ramji 2002) because the people living in them are so close to the edge that one change— like the need for an over-the-counter medication or an increase in the cost of utilities—can push them out.

Through a combination of women's stories and a brief examination of some of the many complex issues entwined with homelessness and poverty, *All Our Sisters* gives an overview of the situation in Canada and shows why certain beliefs about homeless women are, in fact, constructions to help the affluent turn a blind and complacent eye to people in desperate straits.

The first such myth is the enduring and strong belief that many people on the streets are there by choice. For the women interviewed in this book, there is no choice in the usual sense of the word. They are fleeing sexual or physical abuse; are unable to cope because of brain damage caused by such disorders as fetal alcohol spectrum disorder (FASD); are too poor to afford even inadequate housing; or are unable to make good decisions because they are mentally ill and unmedicated. They have lost everything, their possessions and their self-esteem. To think they would do so willingly is simply not believable.

A second strongly held belief is that because we don't see them, there are very few homeless women and children in this country. In fact, we have no way of knowing how many are without a safe place or who have some kind of place but cannot afford the other basic necessities of life. Officially, there are 100,000 Canadians with no homes and another 1.7 million unable to afford adequate, suitable shelter. But if women are suffering the blows of a vicious partner because they can't afford to leave, they are not counted as homeless, nor will they show up in the statistics if they are sharing a condemned house with several other families. In other words, most of the situations in which women find themselves homeless, or close to being without a home, are not covered by official counts, partly because it would be very difficult to locate them. This book includes interviews with women in these situations as well as those who are outright homeless, because it is important for us to know what it is like to live in fear of losing everything, including one's children.

The third myth is that it is easy for homeless women to pull up their socks, find work, and set themselves and their children on the high road to prosperity. It would be really nice if life worked liked that! Although this belief lets the more affluent off the hook of responsibility for the plight of the poor, this book will show how the system is stacked against women in poverty at every turn. Canada has a shortage of safe, cheap housing, and social services are frequently inadequate and difficult to access if a woman has no phone, no bus fare, and no address. So not only is it inevitable that some women will be homeless, but also once they have reached that state, it is very difficult to dig themselves out.

Homelessness is a complex issue. Some of the factors that contribute to this condition relate to Canada's social policies, while others come out of the individual's background, health, and life experiences. It is all too easy to blame the women for their situation, and while it's not productive to see them as victims, we won't be able to help them unless we are fully aware of all the issues and factors contributing to their plight. For example, how can we talk about a woman "choosing" to hang onto her addiction when we learn that detox and long-term rehabilitation oriented toward a woman's needs are so hard to access? One of the amazing things about almost all the women I met when doing the interviews for this book was their optimism. Most of them should have been dead long ago given how hard and brutal their lives have been, but they were still trying to protect their children as best they could and looking forward to the day when they could finally find themselves a home and reunite the family. When asked what they wanted for the future, almost all said they dreamed of a home where they could live in safety with their children and of holding down a job so they would not be dependent on social services. Despite everything, they were able to laugh at life, love others with tenacity, and extend a helping hand to those even worse off than themselves.

Most of us take for granted that we have friends and acquaintances who will listen to us. One of the great losses on the street is that stories are almost always heard through the distorting prism of someone else—and that person is not necessarily friendly or even benign. To women in poverty, social workers, shelter workers, police officers, truancy officers, doctors, and child welfare workers often appear to be nothing more than upholders of red tape and frustrators of good intentions. Nor do the homeless have the luxury of their stories being heard from beginning to end, as they would like to tell them. This is especially true of homeless women as opposed to homeless men. Women are more likely to have to tamper with facts so that they comply with shelter or social service rules or so that they blend with their male partner's version. Many times I have been told by a woman in an interview, "He's a good man," then later in the conversation she lets slip the number of bones the "good man" has broken during their relationship.

As a result, I have tried to present these stories as the women would like to tell them because I believe that it is important to hear what the women have to say, even if this means including some details I believe might be inaccurate. In order to help, we must understand how the women perceive their situation, how they feel about it, and what they believe is blocking them from getting help. Does it make a great deal of difference if they say that they have been waiting for social housing for ten years when it's actually been seven? Either wait is still too long. Nor have I tried to make their stories fit a particular social theory because these tend to wax and wane over the years, depending on the state of research and the latest fashion in ideas. Unless we see the situation from the women's (disad)vantage point, it will be difficult to find acceptable solutions or at least solutions that they see as acceptable and that they are willing to put their hearts into. For example, social workers often believe that they have given mothers ample warning that their children will be apprehended if certain things don't change, but if the mothers don't hear that warning, as many seem not to, it's not much good. Or, if the mother can't effect those changes because she doesn't have sufficient resources, what is she supposed to do? We need to hear the women's version of reality and work with that, rather than imposing what is easiest for a stressed-out system.

The stories are snapshots in time although some of the women have stayed in touch with me. Barb is in the process of leaving the streets, building a new community of friends, and forging several creative interests. Carol is working in a fish-packing plant, although she is almost the last person I could imagine in such an environment. Naomi died in May 2005. Distance and lack of access to a phone or a computer have meant that news about some of the women I interviewed comes second-hand or has completely faded away. I shall forever wonder about them: how are they faring, are they still alive, did they get that home they so desperately wanted?

Violence is the constant and universal theme of the stories. Unbelievable violence occurs against children both in their birth homes and in foster and adoptive homes; it often continues throughout their lives at the hands of partners both male and female, landlords, police, johns, family, and, occasionally, shelter staff. Mixed shelters, it must be said, are perceived as very dangerous places, which is one of the reasons that women are reluctant to use them. The violence—rape, name-calling, beatings, and so on—leaves its legacy: self-esteem so low that women cannot look in a mirror for the horror of seeing themselves, crooked noses, burn scars, and/or a permanent limp. Some have contracted AIDS, and many have undiagnosed cases of post-traumatic stress disorder. Because violence is such a huge issue, the names of the women, their partners, their children, and other significant people have been changed to protect them. Two, however, were adamant they wanted their real names used: Carol M. because she is proud of her achievements and is truly comfortable with who she is today, and Ginger because she wanted to make her story as authentic as possible.

Because trust is the crucial element in obtaining the women's stories, I worked with shelters, drop-ins, and other organizations in Calgary, Edmonton, New Westminster, Ottawa, Toronto, Vancouver, and Winnipeg rather than approach women on the street. This shortened the time taken to build a relationship, important when doing research on a limited budget. However, it also eliminated those who were severely mentally ill or too afraid to connect with shelters. Another reason for going the shelter route is that I have witnessed homeless people telling tall stories to researchers, reporters, and others who have approached them without an introduction. My connection to the women varied from place to place and woman to woman. In some cases, staff effected the link; in others, I hung out or assisted staff with chores such as serving meals until people volunteered to talk. My purpose and intent was always declared up front, and often women would chat with me for a while before making up their minds to go on record. When they did decide to tell their story, there was usually no holding back, except for those who had had their children apprehended. It was exceedingly hard for these women to put their enormous sorrow into words. Even if the seizure had occurred years ago, the experience was frequently too raw for them to handle. In some deep way, their lives had ended at that point.

At the start of the interview, I explained that my purpose was to help the general public understand what it is like to be homeless. I told the women that if they were having trouble expressing something, they could stop and we could work on the wording together; they had control over how much information they gave me or didn't give me. The object was not to make their lives more difficult. For many the experience appeared to be very positive, and frequently they would return to thank me. I was very careful to leave each woman on as upbeat a note as possible, since I was worried that reliving some very dark days might precipitate a new crisis.

I tried to remain, as far as possible, in the role of an amanuensis, but because the women ranged over territory peppered with the emotional equivalent of land mines, it was impossible, indeed inhuman, to remain impassive to their narratives. Depending on the woman's fluency, I might ask questions either to complete the picture or to clarify some of the more elusive details. With some women bonds developed quickly; with others, never. However, I always attempted to support both the woman and her story, believing it is important to give the voiceless a voice because usually they have to listen to experts telling them what to do. As George Orwell observed in *Down and Out in Paris and London*: "It is curious how people take it for granted that they have a right to preach to you and pray over you as soon as your income falls below a certain level." After transcribing the interviews, I tried very hard to find the women and let them read their stories and to make changes if they wanted. The changes were all minor and mainly revolved around safety issues.

Many of the women I interviewed were not homeless in the literal sense, but they were without a home because they did not have a place where they were secure, let alone comfortable. Although I stayed with hospitable friends in various cities where I was made most welcome, I still longed for my own bathroom, my own kitchen, my own bed, and to make a phone call without anyone else knowing about it. Some of the supposedly "housed" women I interviewed were living with violent men to obtain a roof; some spent almost all their welfare money on rent; others had homes occasionally. I chose to include all of them because they are part of the same large picture. For some, it is anyone's guess when the front door will bang behind them, leaving them to live under a bridge, in a shelter, or couch-surfing.

Because I'm a story-teller rather than a sociologist, I consider the women's stories the heart and soul of the book. Before we open our mouths to cast blame or suggest solutions, we must understand—not just with our heads, but with our hearts—what it's like to be in these women's shoes; we must leave the safety of our homes, our families, and our jobs to experience the frustration of trying to pull a life together from nothing. The need for a view from the bottom up was underlined for me when I read a newspaper story about one of the women I interviewed. The article was a long litany of name-calling and sneers with very little, if any, point to it; had the reporter been interviewing a businessman after an alcoholic lunch, I doubt such language would have been used. Such liberties imply that women in poverty are somehow less important and have fewer human rights than the rest of us; it is the same mentality that allows serial killers to get away with murder on the strolls of our cities. It is, therefore, very important to see disadvantaged women as people with the same hopes, fears, rights, aspirations, and feelings as the rest of us.

Listening to the women, I came to see life from their perspective and came to identify with their view of the world. In Winnipeg I was outraged by the violence in the cheap local hotels, while recognizing that at least they provided some kind of shelter. In Vancouver, I was infected with the women's optimism that they could change the social order and that, if they stood together, they could be a powerful voice. In Toronto I raged about the fact that gentrification ousts the original inhabitants of an area. In Edmonton I absorbed the prostitutes' fear that they would be the next murder victim, and in Calgary I wondered why there are so few services specifically for women. I felt—and still feel— angry, helpless, and deeply disturbed by the systemic oppression that very few people question. I hope that I have reflected the women's intentions accurately and in such a way that people who have never been down and out will feel a connection to them.

The stories, though, need some background material, or connective tissue, to put them in perspective and to give the reader an idea of how they fit into the bigger Canadian scene. Therefore, each chapter begins with an introduction, which, however, is not meant to be a definitive discourse; indeed, each issue deserves a book of its own. However, the introductions will give readers a generalized picture and a springboard to do further research, if they are interested in delving deeper. For instance, the few women I interviewed who have found good, affordable housing have also found a place where they can work on their other problems: their experience shows that the difference between being housed and not housed can be dramatic. When I mentioned this to a senior person in the federal National Housing Initiative, she was very struck that, after years in the field, she had never heard it before, and yet it is only common sense. So, the book begins by looking at housing policy and how it has affected Canadian women. This is followed by a chapter on violence, because violence is something with which the women have contended all their lives and is a common thread in the narratives. So, too, is poor health, both physical and mental, which is often self-medicated and thus leads to addictions; this is the subject of Chapter 3. Succeeding chapters deal with FASD, parenting, prostitution, and two groups who have a particularly hard time—Aboriginal peoples and the gay, lesbian, bisexual, and trans community. Finally, I look at problems specific to women in poverty and some solutions that have changed the lives of our sisters, but unfortunately not all of them—yet.

I hope that *All Our Sisters* will assist readers in two ways. First, that it will give them an emotional understanding of what it is like for the women who find themselves without a place where they can sleep unmolested, where their children are safe and their treasures secure. I hope that this knowledge will prevent further cruel labels from being used to describe these women so that our dealings with them and our conversation about them will be illuminated with greater sympathy. Second, I hope that this book will provide a better intellectual awareness that, for the most part, it is the political system that creates poverty and homelessness, preventing women from changing their lives. As a result, rather than endorsing band-aid solutions such as food banks, we will tackle the roots of the problem, however deep we have to dig. It is all too easy to get ourselves off the hook by blaming the poor for the ills that we have all had a hand in creating and have a vested interest in maintaining.

Source

Kappel Ramji Consulting Group for Sistering. 2002. *Common Occurrence, The Impact of Homelessness on Women's Health.* June. <http://www.sistering.org/issues.html>.

CHAPTER 1

HOME SWEET HOME

To have and to have not—that's the system
—Graffiti in London, England

Forests of trees are felled and prodigious numbers of civil-servant hours are consumed producing numerous reports, complete with pie charts, diagrams, and promises, explaining why so many women and children are homeless. These reports, at all levels of government, show what is common knowledge: there are increasing numbers of men, women, and children living on the streets in Canada. And the reports all come to the same conclusion: there is not enough affordable housing, or wages simply are not high enough for people to rent the housing that exists. This is the same beast looked at from different angles: the gap between income and the cost of accommodation means that inevitably some Canadians will be homeless. And yet no one lifts a significant finger or spends a substantial dime to alleviate the situation. The root causes are ignored, while temporary solutions—for instance, shelters or houses for the fortunate few built by groups like Habitat for Humanity—are sought, and piecemeal social assistance takes the place of coherent overarching policy. In the 1970s Canada had an internationally recognized housing program, but over the last 20 years it has declined into a situation described as "an area of shared neglect" (Carter and Polevychok 2004), because so many levels and departments of government have backed away from it.

While no one knows for sure how many homeless people there are, a report, *Housing, Horizontality, and Social Policy* (Hay 2005) put out by the Canadian Policy Research Networks says that 100,000 Canadians have no homes at all while another 1.7 million (almost 16 per cent of the population) are in need of core housing. Not counted in these figures are the "hidden homeless," many of them women who do not have what we think of as a home. Some have decided to stay with an abusive partner rather than face the impossible task of finding an affordable place; others couch-surf from friend to relative; some shack up with pimps; some hang out in bars looking for a man to take them to bed for the night; and others hide so well that no one realizes that they and their children are sleeping in a car or in the bushes. Many women avoid mixed shelters at all costs, finding them dangerous, or perceiving them to be an admission of failure. Few of these women and their children show up in homeless counts, and yet they have no home.

In February 2004, former Prime Minister Paul Martin asserted that "A society that can't house itself is simply dysfunctional." Yet, little meaningful has been done to prevent more people from becoming homeless or to help those who are already on the streets. In fact, the United Nations (UN) has reprimanded Canada a few times for its poor record. In 1966, the International Covenant on Economic, Social, and Cultural Rights stated that "The States Parties ... Recognize the right of everyone to an adequate standard of living ... including adequate food, clothing and housing, and to the continuous improvement of living conditions." Since signing the covenant, Canada has back-pedalled fast and furiously on the home front. This explains, in part, why there is such a long line-up at local shelters every mealtime. In 1998 the UN Committee on Economic, Social, and Cultural Rights urged Canada to address the problem as a "national emergency," suggesting a number of measures, including a national strategy. The following year, the UN Human Rights Committee said, "The committee is concerned that homelessness has led to serious health problems and even to death." This should have been embarrassing to Canada, a long-time advocate of human rights elsewhere, but we hardly blushed.

The right to housing is nowhere enshrined in Canadian law, although the Charter of Rights and Freedoms guarantees fundamental rights for all. When the Charter was drawn up in 1982, food banks hardly existed and the visible homeless were, for the most part, a small number of transient men; perhaps that is why it did not seem necessary to include adequate housing as a fundamental right. Yet since 1993—the year the federal government froze almost all its funding for social housing—adequate housing for all has been denied. At the same time the income and wealth gap between renters and homeowners has been increasing, leaving the former group unable to pay the rents commercial developers require to turn a profit (Hulchanski 2004). In other words, although the average income has been rising, polarization has occurred—the rich are getting richer and the poor are getting poorer. Using Statistics Canada figures, Hulchanski shows that in the 15 years between 1984 and 1999 the median income gap between renters and homeowners went from $19,800 to $22,500 and that it rose by 1 per cent a year. The wealth gap—that is, the gap between the net worth of the two groups —increased from $112,900 to $143,000 over the same period. "There are two very different types of Canadian households in terms of income and wealth—and housing tenure represents the divide between the two," says Hulchanski, pointing out that renters find it increasingly difficult to cross that divide and own a home or to pay rent in a society where owners get most of the breaks. He continues:

> Homeowners receive a tax subsidy to assist in their ac-
> cumulation of household wealth. Capital gains from the
> sale of a principal residence are not taxed and first-time
> buyers can use their tax-sheltered registered retirement
> savings as a down payment. There are no related tax con-
> cessions for renters.

With cash in hand and money in the bank, those who can buy a house look much more attractive to developers, so there is no incentive to create affordable rental accommodation. Gentrification has also taken its toll, repopulating inner-city areas with affluent, upwardly mobile residents. In Calgary it is estimated that 1,000 rental units are lost every year as apartments are turned into more profitable condos. Therefore, in the rental sector, there is high demand but precious little new supply. This is all too apparent in the conditions in which many of the poor live: in a room without windows in a Vancouver rooming house; with a fridge full of cockroaches in Edmonton; in a room in Winnipeg the size of a bathroom with only a broken hot plate to cook on and a shared filthy toilet; or with several families crowding into a one-bedroom apartment.

Back in the 1970s tenants' rights were relatively strong, but they have become so weakened that security of tenure is problematic for many low-in-come families. Sharing a bathroom or kitchen with the landlord may exempt the tenant from protection, as does staying week-to-week in a motel. Women and children can be evicted from apartments when the male partner's name is on the lease and he leaves. The presence of children can make it difficult for mothers to take any accommodation that happens to come up in the right price bracket. They have to think about safety, accessibility to schools, grocery stores, bus routes, and other amenities—if the landlord accepts children in the first place. Landlords can disqualify potential renters if the rent comes to more than 30 per cent of their income, even though for large numbers of people—mostly single mothers, young families and newcomers to Canada—this is the reality. There are 60,000 evictions a year in Ontario alone. That's the size of a small city. At the same time as the social housing policy was being dismantled, three significant developments in federal and provincial policies exacerbated the situation.

1. In 1996 the federal government revoked the Canada Assistance Plan Act, a pillar of the right to an adequate standard of living. It ensured that those in need received enough assistance to cover necessities, including housing and food. The result is that now families on social assistance pay rents that are maybe only $100 less a month than their entire cheque. It is sobering to realize that welfare rates almost everywhere have been cut back to levels below what Statistics Canada deems to be the Low Income Cut Off (LICO), the level at which an individual or family spends a significantly higher amount of their income on food, clothing, and shelter compared to similar-sized households and communities across Canada. In other words, the LICO identifies those who do not enjoy the quality of life most Canadians take for granted.

It should be noted that one of the problems in Canada is that there is no agreed way of measuring poverty and therefore no official poverty line. LICO statistics, usually accepted in most government work, have been collected since the mid 1960s and are readily available, but there are at least two other measurement tools. The Fraser Institute, a right-wing think tank, takes a tough line, defining poverty as the inability to purchase even subsistence levels of shelter, food, and clothing. More recently, the Market Basket Measure has been developed by various levels of government; it is based on the "necessaries" required to rise above subsistence levels but not enough to reach the levels of "social inclusion." Some people see problems with this last method, because it depends on what is included in that basket. The Fraser Institute, for instance, would probably put much less in the basket than someone in charge of a homeless women's shelter.

"Governments are supposed to look after the interests of *all* Canadians, but they always seem to find ways of excluding those Canadians who are forced to rely on welfare when all other means of support fail," says the National Council of Welfare (2003). A biting indictment of welfare from coast to coast, *Welfare Incomes* says that while everyone else in Canada is protected from increases in the cost of living by various mechanisms like annual increases to the Guaranteed Income Supplement in line with the Consumer Price Index, provincial and welfare benefits are typically frozen year after year and are even reduced from time to time.

2. In 1998, federal and provincial governments came up with the National Child Benefit for low-income families. However, in many provinces this tax benefit is clawed back from social assistance recipients with children, so that

the people who need it the most aren't eligible for it. "Families with children are the focus of much flowery government rhetoric, but most governments also go out of their way to deprive families with children who have the bad luck to be on welfare" (National Council of Welfare 2003).

3. Dramatic changes to the unemployment insurance system in 1997 also served to put many families out on the edge of the precipice. Re-titled Employment Insurance (EI), the effect was to disqualify many vulnerable people from benefits. It's now much more difficult for part-time workers, 80 per cent of whom are women, to qualify for EI benefits.

To sum up, cheaper rental properties disappeared from the market at the same time social assistance and other services were cut to the quick. The result is more homeless people, more people at risk, deeper social problems, and more difficulty finding help. In 2004 the Federation of Canadian Municipalities estimated that a million Canadians needed housing assistance, but Joe Fontana, Minister of Labour and Housing, had only $1.5 billion to spend over five years. With some nudging from the New Democratic Party (NDP), the 2005 federal budget put $1.6 billion into housing, but Canada still has a long way to go.

Why is housing policy of particular relevance to women? One out of 10 women in Canada has insufficient savings to sustain herself and her family for even one month if her usual source of income dries up. Almost half of the female-headed households in Canada are spending 30 per cent, or more, of their income on housing. The Coalition for Women's Equality says we are witnessing the highest rates of women's poverty in two decades. In 2004:

+ one in five Canadian women lived in poverty (Morris 2002);
+ 56 per cent of families with children headed by sole-support mothers were poor (Morris 2002);
+ 49 per cent of unattached women 65 or older had low incomes (Morris 2002);
+ in 2000 the average employment income for women working full-time was equal to 70.8 per cent of the average income for men (Coalition for Women's Equality 2004); and
+ in 1996, Aboriginal women earned only 45.6 per cent and visible minority women earned only 63.7 per cent of what the average man earns, underscoring the fact that these women, along with immigrant women and women with disabilities, live in even worse conditions than white women (Coalition for Women's Equality 2004).

In sum 2.8 million women live in poverty, and some urban women report waiting 10 years for social housing. With figures like these, we can see how women are extremely vulnerable to rising rents and housing shortages. When utilities go up or some emergency happens, the best budgeting in the world won't allow a woman to survive on social assistance and remain in her home.

A good indicator of the situation is the rising number of people unable to feed themselves. In October 2004, the Canadian Association of Food Banks (CAFB) issued a report, *Hunger Count 2004*, which stated that the number of Canadians using food banks had increased by 8.5 per cent from the previous year. The shameful total was 841,640 people, including 317,343 children, a figure that exceeds the population of Winnipeg. "With over three-quarters of a million people using a food bank in a month, we have never seen numbers like this before," said Charles Seiden, Executive Director of CAFB, who also pointed out that this has happened despite Canada's re-endorsement of the 1996 Rome Declaration on World Food Security in 2002.

Toronto's Daily Bread Food Bank fingers high rents as the culprit. The food bank's numbers have gone up substantially over the last four years despite fairly stable unemployment rates. To figure out what was causing this increase, Daily Bread ran a statistical analysis comparing rents and food bank numbers between 1990 and 2004 and discovered that higher rents have a much closer correlation than unemployment with the rising figures. This became especially apparent after the Ontario Tenant Protection Act loosened its controls in 1998, allowing rents to increase. "Food bank clients require real, effective protection from excessive rent increases," concluded the report update in November 2004.

Ironically, it appears that the heavy, and understandable, emphasis on child poverty has blinded everyone to the obvious: children are poor because their mothers are poor. This is a situation that will continue to deepen because of the obstacles women have finding secure, full-time employment. Barriers include:

1. lack of education and job skills—many marginalized women have learning disabilities and low education levels, while an unknown number have FASD and/or other brain injuries resulting from childhood trauma;
2. lack of affordable child care;
3. the continuing proliferation of low-paid, non-unionized, part-time jobs so that employers don't have to pay benefits;
4. the fact that although men can often pick up labouring jobs, temporary work for women is more difficult to come by because most

unskilled jobs, like waiting table, require a neat, clean appearance and a certain standard of wardrobe, not always available on the street;

5. increasing pressures on women to do other kinds of care-giving that compromise their ability to work.

Women are less likely to have a decent wage, less likely to have a secure job, and more likely to have children with them, so they are more at risk in the national rental squeeze. Women have reported sleeping with the landlord or allowing him to sleep with their daughters so that he will waive payments. When a woman and her children are hungry and desperate, good solutions seem far away and bad solutions all too evident.

Most homeless women fantasize about the home they don't have right down to details of the furnishings and the exterior. However, their dreams are very modest; they don't want a mansion, they just want somewhere safe for themselves and their children. How can we help make that dream a reality? Simplistic though it seems, there has to be more affordable, safe housing on the market in locations suitable to raise children. More new social housing, refurbishing present accommodations, supported housing for those who require some assistance with day-to-day living, rent supplements, leases in the name of the woman and not her male partner, more damage deposit programs, and welfare payments that cover the actual costs of daily living including utility bills—all these would go a long way to make the right to housing a reality for many currently homeless people. Hulchanski (2002) points out that market forces will not produce the rental housing that women so desperately need for themselves and their families, but that implementing most of these programs would only cost about another 1 per cent of our annual federal spending.

While the event that precipitates women onto the streets may be associated with violence, addictions, mental health, sexual abuse, divorce or job loss, the fact that there is so little appropriate, affordable housing offsets everything. It is very hard to address issues on the streets or in a shelter. A home is more than just a roof, as John Howard Payne, waxing in a sentimental vein, captures in his famous lines, written in 1822:

> Mid pleasures and palaces, though we may roam,
> Be it ever so humble, there's no place like home;
> A charm from the sky seems to hallow us there,
> Which, seek through the world, is ne'er met with
>   elsewhere.
> Home sweet home!

We now have second-generation homeless people in Canadian cities, people for whom this verse is totally alien. Children running around shelters, rubbing shoulders with addicts, dining on donuts, attending school sporadically, and catching all the infections are evidence that Canada has become, as Paul Martin put it, a dysfunctional society.

Suzanne

Suzanne, now 46, stayed with her violent boyfriend because he could offer her a respectable address. It was only after she moved into a tiny but attractive subsidized apartment in Vancouver's Downtown Eastside that she found the security to leave the abusive relationship and to clean up her heavy addictions.

Very neat, Suzanne's apartment is filled with nice furniture and beautiful things that she has collected over the last few years. The cat basks in the sun while she works away at the computer.

Life is a far cry from the days when Suzanne could be found on the sidewalk, passed out due to a surfeit of drugs. "When I got my own place I started to clean up and told Jeff to hit the high road. It was the first place I wasn't ashamed of." Jeff, her boyfriend of five years, had a nice house, but he treated her very badly, and in those days Suzanne considered that an "okay trade-off." Moving into her new apartment got her thinking: "I can live the rest of my life going downhill, or change around. It won't hurt to change, but it will hurt not to…. I was always passed out by the Carnegie (Library). It was so sad. So sad. I really relate to them when I see girls like that, and the saddest part is that whatever you say to them won't change things."

Suzanne should know. At one point she was so deeply addicted to Valium that Jeff told her to pick out her own funeral plot; the ambulance crews used to look for her before they were even called on Welfare Wednesdays, the day the cheques are issued; and a doctor told her she had been taken to St. Paul's Hospital Emergency Department more times in one year than any other individual. She knew all the staff by name.

Life didn't start out like that. Suzanne's father was a physicist who developed a product that was mass-marketed to the US and Europe. Eventually, he headed up the company until it was sold to the Japanese. The family travelled back and forth to the US, living alternately in both countries.

However, Suzanne hated the US schools, calling them blackboard jungles. Her mother, although very artistic, didn't work and suffered from depression after her daughter's birth. "She always told me she would kill herself and that I shouldn't be afraid of death," Suzanne says, believing it was her mother's way of preparing her for what was to come. As an adult, Suzanne, too, suffered from deep depressions caused, she believes, because she felt too ugly for her husband or her subsequent boyfriends.

While she lived, Suzanne's mother was the life and soul of the clan. Suzanne recalls her giving $20 bills to the homeless on Toronto's Yonge Street.

"Mum, you know they will just buy booze," protested her brother.

"Good, if it makes them happy," her mother replied.

When Suzanne finished Grade 12, she returned to Canada to go to college. Her boyfriend Joe, who unbeknownst to her was a heroin addict, followed and moved in with her, much to her parents' dismay. However, he couldn't find a job, so the two returned to Erie, Pennsylvania, where they married. Suzanne's father promptly cut her off. "I was so in love with Joe, it was all I cared about. When they say love is blind, it sure is." She still dreams about him, and he will always be the one and only for her. "There was no one like him. He was wonderful. Others are not even close. He was the funniest, intelligent, and loved to listen to women."

One night when Joe was away, a man came to the door. He had unscrewed the porch light bulb, and in the dark Suzanne thought it was her brother-in-law who liked to play practical jokes. The man pinned her to the floor, tying her hands and blindfolding her. Her mind went blank while he raped her. When she came to, she told him her purse was upstairs, and while he was looking for it, she was able to break free and run naked through the snow to the neighbours.

Joe, who was into cocaine, had found another job as a car salesman in Texas, so they moved there, never believing the rapist would be caught, but he was. Suzanne, who was mixing codeine and Doriden to obtain a heroin-like high, had to return to testify. She straightened up for the trial and was happy to see her torturer found guilty. Ten months after the rape, she was diagnosed with an advanced case of cervical cancer—the worst the doctor had ever seen. "I did something very unusual for an agnostic, I prayed." Treatment and prayer appear to have worked as she is now cancer-free.

Suzanne had also become anorexic, weighing and reweighing her 90-pound body up to 20 times a day. She would go to K-Mart and surreptitiously stand on the store scales to make sure the ones at home were correct. "I got such a high when I lost another pound. It was a willpower thing," she says, comparing it to an addiction. Crystal meth was her drug of choice because it helped her to starve herself and kept the blues about her putative defects at bay.

The couple moved to Tucson, Arizona, to be closer to her parents who had moved there. Suzanne had just about had enough of Joe's escalating and costly habit. "He no longer loved me; he loved cocaine, and he didn't say no. It was me, Joe, and his needle, and it was always scary. He must have been desperate to want to get this high. We no longer slept together." In the end, despite her growing addiction to crystal meth, she kicked Joe out.

It was Suzanne, however, who was caught by the police with $10 worth of drugs on her and sent to jail for a year. As she says, "It might be one of my saving graces." During that year, she turned around, throwing herself into rehabilitation, making friends with other inmates and the guards. She was happy. "How could I be happy in jail?" she wonders, but she was and figures the experience came in good stead when she did kick her various habits 10 years later.

Her father never missed an opportunity to visit, so Suzanne finally realized that in his own way he loved her. Her mother, however, committed suicide during that year, which might explain why Suzanne went straight back to her old life of alcohol and drugs as soon as she was released. "If death is good enough for my mother," she reasoned, "I don't want to be here either."

Finally, the law caught up with her again and, because of the drug sentence, dumped her off at the Canadian border where the authorities couldn't have been nicer. When they looked at her papers, they said, "Do you know what we do to people like you in Canada?"

"No," said Suzanne, dreading what was coming next.

"A slap on the wrist," they replied. "Don't tell anyone you were deported because you have a clean record in Canada. You are only 35 years old, you can do anything."

Suzanne got a job at a racetrack but soon, under the influence of another man, started shooting heroin and cocaine (speedballs), not to mention swallowing 10 Valium pills at a time. She lost the job because of painful shin splints and went into methadone treatment. Very depressed, she moved in and out of shelters for abused women, staying the maximum permissible time. The way she saw it, she could choose to have no place, a dingy room, or live with Jeff. She chose Jeff, preferring his abuse to the streets. Her way of coping was to overdose with Valium and to drink to the point of alcohol poisoning, ignoring the doctors who told her she would surely die. "I don't understand why, or what it was that made me feel so desperate. Why was I so desperate to disintegrate, to die a slow death? If there was a reason, I can't think of it," she says. Ironically, she believes it was the Valium that prevented her from committing suicide by taking her mind off the mental pain. "It is not a good thing to be addicted to drugs, but if one has to say one good thing about them, they sometimes serve a purpose and with me it was staying alive, because I couldn't shake the blues and they were dragging me down."

The apartment building where Suzanne lives is another of her saving graces. It gave her a safe place where she could deal with her addictions. "I was still messing up, but knew to go off things slowly." She concluded that men, alcohol, and drugs just don't work for her. "I would rather just be me and see if I drive myself to drink. Once men were out of the picture, I started cleaning up."

Although she doesn't believe in counting the days, Suzanne has been sober for two years, using a program called Rational Recovery rather than Alcoholics Anonymous, which she terms a "great cult.... I just believe one should take responsibility for one's actions because one cannot change one's bad behaviour if one doesn't admit fault, and AA has a tendency to say that it is not your fault, it is the disease."

Suzanne's father and her stepmother have rallied, giving her financial and moral support. They pay for her phone and her computer, and this helps her stretch her social assistance which is supplemented by a few extra dollars a month because she has hepatitis C, the result of a tainted blood transfusion given to her after an accident more than 10 years ago. She is proud of the fact she is able to save a little bit every month to enable her to visit her English aunts.

Suzanne strokes the cat before closing down the computer and leaving to pick up her daily methadone prescription. On her way, she will pass the people who have taken her place on the sidewalk. How does that feel? "When I see people passed out, I don't wish I was doing it again. I just feel sorry for them."

❖ ❖ ❖

Marie B.

Marie B. spent a good proportion of her first 20 years couch-surfing and in shelters. Now that she's a mother, she's inspired to stabilize her life, but she still needs a huge amount of help to give her baby a fighting chance because it's hard for anyone, let alone a single mother, to find affordable rental accommodation in Toronto.

*We meet in a street clinic where she has brought her baby
girl, who is ill with a fever.*

Marie B.'s teenage parents got married when they realized she was on the
way. Her mother, who was in Grade 10, seems never to have forgiven her
oldest daughter for ending her youth. Marie B., however, sees her own
pregnancy differently: becoming a mother has straightened her out. She is
not such a paragon of virtue that she isn't wistful about abandoning her
contemporaries and her education for a life of diapers, formula, teething,
and midnight crying jags, but all this is balanced by the gift of McKenzie:
"She's everything. My whole life. The whole reason I got my stuff together
is because of her."

Marie B.'s stuff was seriously untogether a few years ago. She's no stranger to the streets of Toronto and to the youth drop-in centre. Her childhood
was difficult. Her parents argued at dinner over which one would get which
child if they separated. Her father, a tow-truck driver with a Grade 8 education, wanted Marie B., her mother put dibs on the second daughter, and both
claimed the third. The truth of the matter is that they would never have split
up, because "Mom could never leave dad, she's never worked a day in her life."

Marie B. has few, if any, happy memories of her mother, who did her
best to drive a wedge between her and her father. Things deteriorated as
she entered puberty and her mother tried to shut her off from friends as
well. Inevitably Marie B. began rebelling, staying out late and not calling
home. She was in and out of school, living with friends or her aunt, and not
returning for days. Fed up, her mother told Marie B. not to come home. The
girl was devastated. Although she had been running away, this wasn't the
outcome she really wanted. "I felt lost. I remember walking around and I
didn't know what to do." She went to the police who called her parents and
then took her to a Toronto shelter for teenagers. It was a month before her
sixteenth birthday. She had never been popular at home or at school and
was amazed that suddenly everyone at the shelter wanted to be her friend. "I
couldn't understand why. My mom thinks everyone has a hidden agenda. It
must have rubbed off."

That year, Marie B. was drunk most of the time. She finished Grade 10 in
a couple of months, found an apartment, was quickly evicted because it was
a haven for "too many crazy people," and was kicked out of the teen shelter
several times for drinking. "I didn't see any problem with it. I was a totally different person. I would drink anywhere with anyone. I wasn't stupid, but pretty
bad." Then she moved in with Debby, a friend of her aunt's. The good thing
was that it was a place; the bad thing was that there were a lot of problems.

Marie B. quickly began drinking with Debby's son and watching the rivalry developing between Debby's husband and the man who rented the basement. When Debby's husband discovered his wife was having an affair, he retaliated by putting sugar in the lodger's gas tank and crazy-gluing his locks. Debby would get annoyed with Marie B. for minor things, but the situation was never like the hassle of living with her mother. "[Living in Debby's house] was nothing too extreme. It felt normal. It wasn't like a big deal, and I didn't really know any different. If my parents didn't want me, why would anyone else?"

Marie B. moved into her aunt's house and started school again, but that didn't last long because she preferred going to the youth drop-in to meet Don, a boy she knew from the shelter, and her other friends. When she became pregnant, she moved back to the shelter for a while until Debby, who had married the lodger and was back on an even keel, offered her a home again. Marie B. accepted and started to get her life in order. She had already quit drinking and began to think about which of her street friends would be okay to have around a baby. At the same time, she and Don went looking for their own apartment.

On a limited income it was difficult for the teenagers to find a place; it was mere days before McKenzie was born when a kindly landlord took pity on them. The labour was long and draining, and Marie B. was completely overwhelmed. Tears well up as she speaks about seeing McKenzie for the first time. "Finally, I saw my daughter. I didn't want to hold her because I thought I would drop her. I couldn't feel anything. I just cried." However, this isn't a case of everyone living happily ever after. Don has his own problems that have now become Marie B.'s. His mother ran away to Florida when he was a child, leaving him with an abusive father, and he spent his later childhood ping-ponging between shelters and his father's place. Now 20, he has severe depression and has never shouldered responsibilities, so debts have piled up. When it suits him, Don can be a delightful father, but it's Marie B. who changes the diapers and gets up in the middle of the night.

Don has announced that he's leaving Marie B., who is pregnant again, and this both pleases and frightens her. She thinks her small family will have more stability without him, but she also worries about loneliness. Being a young mother is very isolating, especially as her own mother doesn't want any part of her grandchildren. "I was hurt. I don't think she should punish McKenzie for the problems we had."

Marie B. worries about money and talks about the cavalier way the system treats women like her. For example, using her recently acquired cellphone, she placed a call to her social worker, who put her on hold for 20 minutes, eating up precious time on her card. At the same time, she knew if she hung up that it would take three days for the worker to call her back. "There needs to be less judgement and more support."

While her contemporaries comb the malls for new clothes, Marie B. makes do with second-hand items. She used to skimp on groceries, but now that McKenzie is starting adult food, she tries to buy things like milk and fruit. She feels she should start to become independent of the youth drop-in but finds it hard to move on when it offers so much of what she needs: companionship, food, health care for her and McKenzie, a phone, a nursery, parenting advice, Internet access, help with housing. "I think I would be lost without it. I'm here at least once a week."

The paradox for Marie B. is that while McKenzie's birth has stabilized her and given her hopes for the future, she has to play a waiting game to capitalize on that maturity. She would dearly like to finish high school and go to university to study psychology and sociology. "I'll just have to wait. My life is on hold."

Jen

Originally from the Caribbean, Jen thought she was coming to the promised land. Fired from her low-paying job when she became pregnant, she is one of the many immigrant women on the streets of Toronto who perform menial work with no job security and who have trouble finding housing.

Jen's never forgotten the time she was found by her aunt chatting with a group of young people. It wasn't so much the chatting that was memorable, but rather the conclusions her aunt drew and the steps she took to discipline the teenager. Always considered the "black sheep" of the family, Jen was in real trouble after this incident because her aunt figured she had gone off willingly with the guys and been raped, thus bringing shame on the family. "When I got home, my aunt beat me, my cousin beat me, and my aunt's good friend beat me," she recalls. Her skin was broken, she couldn't move her hands, and her lip was swollen, but that wasn't the worst of it—they also put pepper in her vagina to deter her from any further sexual activity. "And nothing had really happened."

Jen was born into an extended family in Guyana. Her father took off, leaving her mother to do the best she could. She had to leave the house early in the morning with 50 pounds of bread on her head to sell in a nearby town to try and make enough money to look after her four daughters and three sons. The mother's female cousins, whom the children called aunts, rallied around, but it was a harsh existence. "Any aunt and uncle automatically beat you."

Kids were "licked" if they asked questions, butted into adult conversation, or, worse yet, corrected adults. Their mother was slightly different in her approach, saving up a number of grudges for one big licking, all the while listing off the child's misdemeanours. When she was really angry, she lined up all seven children and "really beat" them. "She only did what she knew. If you don't know any different, you can't do it better." Jen herself would never treat her own little boy badly, nor would she let anyone else take a hand to Ezekiel, aged 2½.

When Jen describes herself as "the black sheep," she is being almost too literal. In Guyana, she says, the lighter the skin the better. "If you are dark like me, you didn't matter." Her grandmother was of Portuguese descent who had married a man of Chinese origins; in other words, they were desirably fair-skinned. Jen's mother married a black-hued man from Grenada. "My grandmother always said us children would be no good, that we wouldn't turn out to be anything. Basically, most of them wanted their kids to be fair. If you were ugly, but light, you had opportunities to get the best jobs." At an early age, her grandmother started calling Jen a little whore, and, as a result, no one wanted to hang out with her. She always felt as though it was her fault: "I grew up thinking I was a bad girl and I actually nearly believed it too."

School began well, then for reasons she can't figure out, the teachers started to call her a stupid dunce and her achievements gradually matched their expectations. She became very angry, ceasing to care. "I actually became bad." She started to run away to other family members, often just showing up on their doorstep. As no one had a phone, there wasn't much her mother could do. Jen would help her aunt with housework until her mother caught up with her and hauled her home. When Jen was raped by a neighbour's husband, she was told not only was it all her fault because she must have pushed herself onto him, but also, because she was still able to walk, her family was "thinking you have been sexing all along ... I always came out of the end of the day feeling you have done something wrong. It's not a good feeling."

In her late teens Jen got a job as a sales clerk at the tailor's counter in a store selling suit lining, buttons, and other similar items. With no reading skills, she had to memorize everything, learning the fabrics by their textures. She saved what she could to take a hairdressing course, but most of her money was handed over to her family. Her father's sister came to visit from the US and saw how Jen was being pilloried, so she sent her to her father in

Grenada. Jen lived there with another aunt, who found her a hairdressing job, because by this time her father had moved to Jamaica. Unfortunately, the job was with a woman who was good at the theory of hairdressing but, unlike Jen, was ham-handed at putting it into practice. "So I was considered to be a hair butcher, too."

Jen, who could spell her name and stumble through the alphabet, desperately wanted to learn to read. She knew it was the key to any kind of advancement. So far, she had made her way depending on her memory and her ability to ask the right questions. No one in Grenada knew that she was guarding a secret, nor that she was plotting a big change. "I knew I had to go somewhere where I could re-invent myself. In my country if you can't read and write, people automatically think you are stupid."

At 21, she made the decision to come to Canada, where she had yet another fairly close relative.

> I knew I needed to learn, and I knew I wanted to be somebody. The one thing pulling me back was you needed an education. I didn't want anybody there [in Guyana and Grenada] to know the situation. I was so accustomed to being ridiculed and degraded. I wanted to be somebody so badly. I didn't want to go back to being a nobody. In Grenada I was given a fresh chance and a fresh chance made me want to try a fresher chance.

It didn't quite work out that way. So keen was Jen for an education that when her relative didn't send her the visa forms to fill in, she sold her hairdressing equipment and spent all her savings on a flight to Canada. On arrival she was told she would have to go back home to fill them out. "I wasn't a millionaire, so I decided, okay, I'll just stay."

Jen also discovered that her family reputation had preceded her, but by now she had acquired some self-esteem and wasn't so willing to let her relatives call her names and take advantage of her. With the help of her aunt in the US, who sent money and warm winter clothes, she found a room and in four months had a job in a restaurant, earning $200 a week, working six eight-hour days. Even though her rent gobbled up $85 a week, she still managed to send cash back to her family.

A friend told her about an agency that paid people $7.50 an hour to do various factory jobs. "She told me it was really hard, but it wasn't as hard as she said." Jen subsequently went to work in shipping and receiving for such diverse products as gloves, small electrical items, plastic cups, and in a meat-packing plant, where, working in frigid temperatures, she suffered constantly from colds and developed asthma. In the evenings, though, she began to learn to read and write at the Toronto YWCA.

Jen ended up working in a car-parts plant, but she became pregnant and very sick. When she began to throw up on the job, the agency discovered her condition and fired her because, they said, they would be liable if anything happened. "I had to use my savings for hospital and my rent. Eventually, there was no more. Just nothing and I had to go to a shelter." She lived in a shelter until Ezekiel was born, all the time worrying how to afford a place that would be large enough to placate authorities who frown on raising a baby in a rooming house. Unable to get onto social assistance, she did manage to finance a home for a while by doing bits of cleaning and other odd jobs where she could take the baby. Most of the time she had enough to feed the little boy, but not much for herself.

So busy was Jen making ends meet and looking after Ezekiel that she wasn't able to put things in motion to become a landed immigrant, and eventually the authorities caught up with her and issued a removal order, holding her in a hotel. The owner of the restaurant where Jen first worked bailed her out for $1,000, and she returned to the shelter where she is preparing her case for an immigration hearing to stay in Canada on humanitarian and compassionate grounds.

Jen is hoping that the fact she has almost always been self-supporting, doing jobs that are too poorly paid for most Canadian-born workers to consider, will stand her in good stead. She knows that most people won't see her achievements, but when she looks back, she's pleased. "I have really come a long way, even though I am in a shelter. I really surprised a lot of them by getting this far. I was supposed to be a little whore and a prostitute, but I had my first child at 25, and I don't have 10 or 12 children around me. I proved them wrong." Now that she can stumble through her Bible, one of her favourite passages is Psalm 27. Jen feels she has been given the strength to create a good world for Ezekiel, a happy, playful little boy who prefers to sit down with a book or a puzzle than watch television. A major component of this good world is Canada. "Hopefully, with God's help, we'll get to stay."

Note

Special thanks to David Hulchanski, PhD, MCIP, and director of the Centre for Urban and Community Studies, University of Toronto, for information and suggestions in this chapter.

Sources

Amdur, Reuel. 2004. "Housing In Crisis for 1.7 Million Households." *Straight Goods*. 6 December.

Axworthy, Thomas A. 2004. "Enough Talk: Homeless Must Become a Priority." *Toronto Star* 9 August.

Canada Mortgage and Housing (CMHC SCHL). 2003. *Family Homelessness: Causes and Solutions, Research Highlights*. Socio-economic Series 03-006. July. <http://www.cmhc-schl.gc.ca>.

——. 1999. *Women on the Rough Edge: A Decade of Change for Long-Term Homeless Women*. Socio-Economic Series Issue 54. <http://www.cmhc-schl.gc.ca>.

Canadian Association of Food Banks. 2004. *Hunger Count 2004: Poverty in a Land of Plenty: Towards a Hunger-Free Canada*. Press release. 15 October. <http://www.cafb-acba.ca>.

Carter, Tom, and Chesya Polevychok. 2004. *Shared Neglect: Canada's Housing Policy*. Canadian Policy Research Networks. 3 December. <http://www.cprn.org>.

Coalition for Women's Equality. 2004. *Still in Shock*. <http://www.canadaelection.net/shock6.html>.

Daily Bread Food Bank. 2004. *Housing Report Update: Rising Food Bank Use Linked to Tenant Protection Act*. 2 November. <http://www.dailybread.ca>.

Hay, David. 2005. *Housing, Horizontality, and Social Policy*. Canadian Policy Research Networks. 11 March. <http://www.cprn.org>.

Hulchanski, David. 2004. *Social Housing and Homelessness*. Course outline. Toronto: University of Toronto.

——. 2002. *Housing Policy for Tomorrow's Cities*. Canadian Policy Research Networks. December. <http://www.cprn.org>.

——. 2001. *A Tale of Two Canadas: Homeowners Getting Richer, Renters Getting Poorer*. Centre for Urban and Community Studies, Research Bulletin No. 2. Toronto: University of Toronto.

Morris, Marika. 2002. "Women and Poverty." Fact Sheet. Ottawa: Canadian Research Institute for the Advancement of Women. March.

National Council of Welfare. 2004. "Welfare Incomes 2003." *Report 121* (Spring).

Porter, Bruce. 2003. *The Right to Adequate Housing in Canada*. Centre for Urban and Community Studies, Research Bulletin No. 14. Toronto: University of Toronto.

Scott, Susan. 2003. "Nowhere To Run." *Alberta Parent* (Spring).

United Nations. 1999. Human Rights Committee Concluding Observation on Canada.

——. 1998. Committee on Economic, Social, and Cultural Rights. *Report*.

CHAPTER 2

THE PAIN AND THE SHAME

Hands are not for hitting
—Sign at a shelter

Violence pervades all homeless women's lives, in some cases from before the cradle—if their mothers were beaten up while pregnant—to the grave, often an early one. It is so pervasive that it becomes part of the order of things and, therefore, unremarkable, so that many of those in the helping professions cease to think about the implications and merely pay lip service to the havoc it wreaks.

Violence is no respecter of class or race. What women on the street experience is also endured by women in all other walks of life, only they have more resources to cover it up, for one of the pernicious things about violence is that somehow it becomes the shame of the person who has experienced it and not the perpetrator's ignominy. Women are reluctant to report rape, and women who are abused by their partners wonder what's wrong with them, not what's up with the abuser.

There are many kinds of violence and neglect—emotional, physical, sexual, financial, verbal. Often it's not just one, but several forms that are un-leashed by people who know no other way of negotiating their way through life. It can take place in the home, on the streets, at work, anywhere, and women are the most vulnerable. In 2001, male partners committed 80 per cent of Canadian spousal homicides, and in 2002, 85 per cent of the 34,000 victims of domestic violence who reported incidents to the police were women. If a woman is disabled, from an ethnic minority, poor, or lesbian, bi-sexual, or trans, violence becomes even more than a gender issue; race, class, and homophobia are also involved.

Violence has deep-seated consequences for the person on the receiving end. It affects body, mind, and spirit. This translates into a number of be-haviours, which vary from person to person, including depression, poor self-esteem, being easily distracted, lack of concentration, fear of risk, unkempt appearance, short fuse, bullying or being bullied, sullenness, manipulativeness, anxiety around loud noises and shouting, attention seeking, fatigue, physical problems, and bizarre actions. The sum of violence and its results can kick a woman out of her home and into poverty, as well as inflict scars on body and soul. A history of rape, violence, and sexual abuse can explain why she is frightened to seek help at mixed shelters or why she is anxious about going to a doctor.

Thanks to Roméo Dallaire and his book, *Shake Hands with the Devil: The Failure of Humanity in Rwanda* (2003), we are beginning to recognize post-traumatic stress disorder (PTSD) in war veterans, but we have not yet begun to come to grips with it on the home front. Reverend Susan Brandt, who has worked with homeless people in Ottawa and Calgary, said in a 2004 interview that PTSD goes unrecognized and undiagnosed on the streets. It occurs after experiencing or witnessing an event like sexual assault (including sexual abuse as a child), natural disasters, combat, and terrorist attacks; and it results in flashbacks, nightmares, difficulty sleeping, and feeling estranged. It frequently manifests itself prior to substance abuse, depression, self-mutilation, and other mental and physical health problems.

Given that violence for so many women on the street began when they were children and continues unrelentingly, it makes sense that many of them would have PTSD, but frequently this diagnosis doesn't factor into treatment for alcoholism and other addictions. Yet, when the numbing effects of self-medication wear off in recovery, the symptoms of PTSD often reappear and, if left unaddressed, may lead to relapse. It is, therefore, important to deal with the trauma and the addiction concurrently. According to Brandt, 91 per cent of homeless women report being assaulted at some time in their lives, and 42 per cent of long-term homeless women report an assault in the last 12 months. Out of fear, newly homeless women often attach themselves to a man, even though their part of the bargain usually includes yielding to his demands for sex and to beatings. In the macho street culture, it is better "to stay with the man you know than the predator lurking around the corner." Many women say defensively, "He's a good man, he only hits me when...." The excuses include "when's he's drunk" and "when I deserve it."

Another effect of violence that keeps women in poverty is the diminishment of their ability to learn. Coping skills that have enabled them to survive, such as mentally removing themselves from a situation, while useful in abusive partnerships, do not contribute to academic performance. If they have learned to operate from crisis to crisis and find that comfortable, it may be difficult for them to concentrate in a calm classroom. Almost all the women interviewed for this book said they had been abused as children, often by fathers, stepfathers, brothers, uncles, and other male relatives, and almost all of them, although obviously intelligent, had not done well at school. Lack of success at school means that one is less likely to hold down a well-paid job, more likely to lose it than people with better education, and probably unable to benefit from training programs. Not only that, health problems are likely to compound the issue, because having difficulty under-standing verbal or written materials makes it more difficult to take care of oneself. Children, too, are affected because their mothers may not have the skills or the resources to deal with the school and health care systems on their behalf.

Is violence against women institutionalized in our society? Let us con-sider what happens to women who flee an abusive home. Although many women leaving a dangerous situation do not consider themselves homeless, they quite literally no longer have a home of their own, and once they leave the domestic violence shelter, they may never have a safe place again. Not only do they leave most of their material possessions behind, but many, without skills or resources, are also entering a life of poverty so dire that they return to the abuser, or they become effectively homeless, sleeping on friends' and relatives' floors. In Alberta in 2003 Stacey, a single mother of a nine-year-old boy, who had recently fled a violent partner, received $750 a month in welfare. The rent for her tiny one-bedroom apartment was $575 a month, leaving $175 for everything else. She considered herself fortun-ate to have a roof. With low welfare rates and high housing costs across the country, this situation plays out repeatedly. As Gunhild Hoogensen (interview 2004), political scientist at Tromsø University, Norway, said, we should be paying these women, not penalizing them further. Ignoring the consequences of violence is, in effect, accepting it.

Violence has more and much longer-lasting ramifications than a black eye or a broken rib. It affects everything from the way women conduct themselves in the world to the way the world treats them. Until we under-stand this and act on it, we cannot help. As Brandt (2004) says, "Without an understanding of the psychological harm resulting from physical and sexual trauma, treating the homeless is impossible."

Teele

Advised by a priest, Teele repeatedly forgave her husband for abusing her, but forgiveness was an ineffective shield. When she finally left, she was plunged into poverty and will never

be comfortably off again, even though she is fortunate enough
now, at the age of 58, to have secured safe, affordable housing.

Teele is on a mission. She wants the visitor to see the Ottawa monument raised in honour of the 14 female engineering students slain by Marc Lepine at Montreal's L'Ecole polytechnique in 1989. She approaches the statue reverently, head bowed, yet somewhat anxious the guest won't understand how much it means to her. It's a warm Sunday in early summer. Young men sun themselves in the Ottawa park, drinking coffee and reading the newspaper. Teele stands in silence. Very quietly, she says, "My sister was found dismembered in a Montreal park. They needed three body bags for all the pieces."

Teele is no stranger to violence and poverty. Of French and Aboriginal ancestry, she talks readily about her childhood in a small Ontario town where her father owned the candy store that, naturally, she loved to visit. School wasn't so good, because she and her siblings were the only francophone Catholic children and were subject to a lot of bullying. The teachers also hit the students. Summers were spent happily with grandparents in Quebec. One of her grandmothers was only four feet tall and had a gift for connecting with children and animals. Squirrels would sit on her head, so that at a casual glance she looked like she was wearing a fur hat. She could also whip up doll's clothes in minutes. When a male relative tried to rape Teele at the age of seven, she was sent to this grandmother to recover. "She taught me to learn to live with what had happened. I was very lucky I had her," Teele recalls. Her grandfather, too, cherished her, feeding her ice cream and licorice. "There were three rocking chairs in her kitchen in Quebec and we would each sit in one. He would tell stories and feed me chocolate and the three of us would rock." The summer she was 14, Teele hung out at her other grandfather's lakeside lodge. According to her, it had the best of everything—swimming in clear water, dancing, and French chefs. She clearly recalls the blue dress she was wearing when a handsome guy drove up on a motorbike and asked if she would like to go for a ride. She hopped on, and they departed. Eventually the police found them and returned Teele unharmed to her worried family.

Fast-forward several years, and Teele has become a hostess dressed in a bunny suit in a club in Hull, Quebec. One night she went over to the second-floor window to surreptitiously rest her aching feet. Looking out, she saw a guy gazing up at her. He pointed to his watch. She nodded, and when her shift was over, they went for coffee. Coffee graduated to drinks, and they started dating. One night while they were waltzing and chatting, they suddenly realized they had met before—he was the guy with the motorbike.

Their first date was in August, and they were married in November. "I had so many dreams that day. It snowed and the snowflakes were like diamonds; you pretend sometimes."

The marriage lasted 19 years during which time she learned many unpleasant things. In her innocence, she thought he drank water for breakfast, dinner, and supper. It turned out to be gin, and when she objected, he said, "Fuck you, I drink what I want, when I want." He owned a limousine service, useful for dealing drugs, and often partied with the passengers. He also beat her. She consulted a priest, who had no understanding of violence against women and advised forgiveness. She forgave him 77 times, which is why she now "walks like a crooked, old lady and can't straighten out for three hours in the morning." After the police were called—yet again—an older officer sat her down, made her coffee, and told her that there wasn't much more they could do. "You have to go to court and ask for a divorce," he said.

At about the same time, the place where Teele had worked for almost 24 years went bankrupt, and all the employees lost their jobs. "It was a traumatic experience. I got my divorce, lost my job, and hit menopause all in the same day." After her divorce, Teele's former husband continued to shadow her and their son, stalking them to a shelter and waiting outside while they cowered inside behind bars. Because her son was unable to sleep, Teele felt she had to leave.

She went to work as a housekeeper for a wealthy man who had escaped from the Soviet Union. "There was nothing sexual; he loved me like a daughter. He looked like a gorilla, but he had a beautiful soul. He had no concept of social graces, so I would educate him. He tried to teach me Russian, but it didn't work out. Through him I met some really good people and he gave me a fighting spirit. He was like my dad re-incarnated."

After that job ended, for more than five years Teele says she lived on a welfare cheque of $199 a month, out of which she also had to pay rent. She wore out all her underwear, her winter boots lasted seven years, and her purse 20, with a little stitching now and then. She couldn't afford a phone for nine years and didn't go to a film for 25. If someone asked her whether she'd seen the current blockbuster, she would say, "Oh, yes, it's not quite my type of movie." She knows what it's like to turn down an invitation for coffee because she didn't have $5 in her pocket and says she learned to live on water and that she "had a beautiful bill following her every month—the hydro." At one point the power was cut off, so that she couldn't take a bath or boil water. The provincial government helped her pay the $950.49 bill, plus the reconnection fee, because she was receiving radiation treatment for cancer in her throat and brain. She was so nervous about radiation that she had a heart attack. "I saw my father and he winked at me. The doctor hit me in the chest and brought me back. 'Why did you do that? I hate you,' I said. He said, 'It's not your time, Teele.'"

Teele has been cancer-free now for more than five years and lives on a disability pension of $649 a month in an apartment for abused women, visiting places where she can find free food and clothes. She has also become a fierce advocate for marginalized women. "When you have no money, you have to shut up and take what they give you." She talks passionately about a woman who was arrested for going barefoot in the dead of winter. "We are treated like common slaves or dirt," she adds, saying that food donated to shelters is often crawling with animal life and full of hairs. "I don't think women should be eating garbage."

Like many women in her situation, Teele would like to be able to hold down a job again, not just for the wages, but also for the respect that goes along with employment. "I worked hard by the sweat of my brow in all kinds of weather. I want you to remember that I once, too, I had a job and that I may come back one day and be the manager. And I don't think that you'd like that. I may have holes in my shoes, but I walked to get them. I walked the streets for three years looking for a job. Please don't laugh at women with broken shoes. She may be your mother."

As the visitor is about to leave, Teele says, "Can I ask you something?" She doesn't request cash; she wants something for all impoverished women. Second-hand underwear is a big problem, she explains. No one really wants to wear it, and often it doesn't come in the right sizes. "You may have noticed that some of the girls have given up and don't wear bras any more; they can't get anything to fit. And if they are big, if you know what I mean, that's not nice. Can you find someone who would donate a whole load of bras and panties in all different sizes? It would make a lot of women happy."

Willow

Willow was neglected and abused from an early age and now has trouble handling some very big issues in her life. Without a safe place it is unlikely that she will be able to attend to her medical needs and fulfill her dream of going to university.

We go to a nearby White Spot Restaurant because it's where Willow's mother used to take her for treats and so she has good memories there. It's a place where she feels comfortable enough to talk. However, she breaks off our interview when her story becomes too intense and she feels that she is going to break down.

Willow sits at a busy Vancouver intersection panhandling. Her head is deep in a couple of university textbooks. In the evenings, she is taking a course on the history of dissent that covers such icons as Mahatma Gandhi and Rosa Parks. Sometimes she sleeps all the way through class; at other times she asks the most intelligent questions of the group. She wants to go to the University of British Columbia (UBC). She's bright enough; what's keeping her back is a lack of stability. She's evasive about where she lives—it could be a squat or a single room in a sleazy hotel. The rain comes in around the window, there's vermin in the room, and the water in the tap isn't drinkable. Her stylish clothes come from trashcans.

She probably has a drug habit to support, and her boyfriend is currently in jail. Although 29, she has the vulnerability of a lost teenager, with huge eyes in an elfin face. At times the same face can be distorted with anger, the source of which she says is a mystery to her, although she has much to be angry about.

Willow grew up in the Vancouver area. She can't remember her birth father because her parents divorced when she was two. Her mother was "messed up mentally and unstable. She was kinda crazy. She had nice clothes, a nice house, but she starved us. We were all hungry. Everything was counted and locked away." Her two full brothers and three stepbrothers eventually went to live with their fathers, leaving Willow with her mother who never let her play with other kids, have birthday parties, or any of the other things that are generally taken to be a part of childhood. Once she was sent shopping for some wool and returned with the wrong kind, so her mother locked her out of the house. "I didn't know how weird it was," says Willow, adding that she couldn't relate to other children. At school she was shy, quiet, and timid. The teachers, however, liked her and considered her to be a bright child.

One day she found a pamphlet on normal families and read it avidly. It included a checklist of what was normal and what wasn't. Willow did her own little evaluation and concluded, "Oh, wow, we are crazy."

Her mother married again when Willow was nine, this time to a Polish sailor who had jumped ship. It was not a good situation for the child. "He whipped us every fucking night." One day when Willow was 10, her stepfather came to pick her up from school and took her to the Vancouver

General Hospital. Her mother had overdosed. Willow wanted to see her before she died, but the nurses wouldn't let her. "She had it all planned out," says Willow, who was supposed to live with her grandparents. "She wrote each of us a letter." However, not all went to plan. In the middle of the night, her birth father came with the police and took Willow to his home in Enderby, BC.

If Willow's mother was bad, her stepmother was worse. "I have nightmares about her. I couldn't look people in the eye until I was 20. I was terrified of people that they would judge me. Everything was for his boys. I was never allowed to eat. I would go at 2 a.m. to the kitchen to steal an Oxo cube. I had to do all the chores and baby-sit." Willow now understands that she probably posed a threat to her stepmother, but that doesn't ameliorate the pain. The family moved to Alberta where she was made to do a paper route to pay for her winter coat. Pushed to the limit, she ran away. She can't remember whether it was to Calgary or Edmonton, but she met some people who took care of her and with whom she felt "totally safe." Feeling better, she phoned her father and ended up returning to the family, taking not much with her except the happy memories of the family who had once cared for and about her.

Naturally, life did not improve. Just to get away from the house, Willow would tell her parents she was going to non-existent sleepovers, then lurk unseen in the backyard. Her only outlet was the writing that she started when she was seven; it is still both a joy and a relief from the oppression of her life.

In Grade 8 at school in Lethbridge, Willow tried to kill herself, the first of many suicide attempts. "I took a bunch of pills in the stairwell. I got scared and the counsellor took me to hospital. They called my dad who got mad at me. He wasn't worried. I don't remember any help, ever, for anything." She talks desolately about her bad memories of other suicide attempts, of waking up in hospital, of walking around Lethbridge in freezing temperatures so that she wouldn't have to go to school.

Willow was raped, and as a result she has AIDS. That's all she can say about this episode, except that she's very angry that she's been robbed of a future, that she doesn't have a lot of time left to get her act together and go to UBC.

Willow can't talk any more. She wants to leave the restaurant before she breaks down completely. "I want to tell you, I really do," she says and makes arrangements to meet a couple of days later at another panhandling site. She doesn't turn up at class, but she is panhandling again where and when she said she would be. "Did we say today?" she asks distractedly. "Okay, okay."

She gets up and walks to a coffee shop, but her attention span barely gets her through adding cream and sugar to her mug. She's agitated and looks ill; her eye make-up is smudged. This isn't the day to press for more information. She drinks her coffee and leaves.

❖ ❖ ❖

Parveen

Subjected to financial and physical abuse by her husband, many years later Parveen's life is still scarred by the untreated trauma caused by the repeated attempts on her life.

Before Parveen was married at the age of 16, her grandfather checked out the prospective groom; nothing but good reports came back. Those reports turned out to be lies.

Born in Pakistan to a professional, land-owning family, Parveen was well educated and held a good job before following her husband to Toronto where she and their two children stayed with his family before they found their own place. Wanting to be a dutiful daughter-in-law, she brought gifts of clothes, food, and toys for her husband's family as well as $20,000 US. "What is this garbage?" her mother-in-law asked inspecting the garments, although she was happy enough to scoop them up when no one was looking.

Parveen's husband, who had a drinking problem, owned a number of stores where she worked too. "He had a very bad temper, he beat up the children and he beat up me. He didn't want the children to go to school because he was money hungry." He thought the children, especially his daughter, should work in the stores from the age of five. He didn't see that forfeiting their education, not to mention breaking the law, was a problem. On top of everything else, he gave Parveen only $10 a week to feed the family—even in the 1970s, she couldn't stretch it far enough.

The mother-in-law, who delighted in being a troublemaker, at times urged her son to beat Parveen. If Parveen offered her tea, she would say, "No thank you; I think I would like a cold drink," so Parveen would dutifully get her one. When her son returned, he would ask his mother how she was. "Oh, I've got a headache because I haven't had any tea today," she would reply, giving him all the licence he needed to hit Parveen with his heavy shoes. Other times, because Parveen was busy, she left her mother-in-law's food ready so that she could serve herself. The woman didn't consider this adequate and would tell her son she hadn't eaten all day. The result was another beating.

One day, Parveen's son arrived home accompanied by his teacher. He had gone to school covered in bruises, and the teacher was concerned about his safety. When Parveen opened the door, the teacher said, "Oh, my God." Parveen, too, had a black eye and other bruises.

"Why are you living with him?" blurted out the teacher.

"Because he told me he'd take the children if I left."

The teacher helped Parveen pack a few things and take the children to a shelter for abused women. When her husband realized she was gone, he called the police to say that she had stolen everything, although she had packed nothing of value, not even her dowry jewellery, which somehow found its way into the hands of her sisters-in-law. The husband hounded her, hiring people to try and push her under subway trains, to garrote her, and to attack her both verbally and physically. Once her youngest brother-in-law lay in wait for her outside the welfare office and beat her up on the sidewalk as she was leaving.

Parveen still fears for her life, constantly looking behind her and monitoring her phone. Although the beatings are long over, they triggered severe arthritis, aggravated by the fact that she cannot afford good shoes and walks around in flimsy sandals. Her son, now 39, still limps from the beatings he received as a child.

Despite the disruptions and violence, Parveen's children have done well. She loses her agitation when she speaks of them, saying, "I'm proud of them and thankful to God." Her son, who is a computer expert, ignores the fact his doctor would like him to take long-term disability because of arthritis in his spine. Her daughter is studying to be a doctor. It is significant that neither child has married.

Proud she was never on welfare, Parveen worked as a sewing machine operator and as a homemaker, but then her arthritis got the better of her, and now she's on a disability pension and does what she can to help out at a women's drop-in centre. Sometimes when she can't walk, they send food to her apartment.

Parveen feels her losses keenly. She has lost her birth family, her health, her looks, her jewellery, her gorgeous clothes, and what money she had. When she and her husband split up, he hid his assets so he has never paid her any support. "Canada should get better treatment for women," she says, indignant that her husband managed to hoodwink the courts.

Parveen seems to have been immobilized by the trauma, but it is hard to imagine what it is like living under the constant shadow of violent death. Even though the threats weren't made yesterday, she still lives with the pain of blows inflicted 25 years ago—a constant reminder of the man's capabilities. "I am always scared," she says.

Louise

Suicide was the only solution Louise could find to deal with her husband's physical, sexual, and emotional abuse. Her waning self-esteem was bolstered artificially by crack cocaine. What saved her was an arrangement she negotiated with Children's Services to place her daughter in temporary care, giving her a chance to go for treatment.

Louise is an inspiration and role model to the clients at the family resource centre where she works in Calgary. It's no secret that she was once a frightened, homeless addict and that she lost her children to Children's Services (CS). People who knew her then say admiringly, "Now, look at you." What they see is a kindly, cheerful woman of 38. She's a wife and mother and holds down a demanding job as a floor manager at the centre used by homeless and nearly homeless families. "Now I can do almost anything," she declares.

It wasn't always like that. Louise became pregnant at 17 and married the father. Her marriage was a classic case of isolation and abuse, starting with a broken nose on her wedding night. In five years, her husband broke her nose two more times, her arm twice, her ribs once, split her head open, and beat her body and her spirit repeatedly. He would rather throw the phone at her than let her answer it, and he locked her in the house, only allowing her two minutes to shop at the corner store. He told Louise that their son wasn't his and soon started to beat the little boy. Although she learned to protect him with her own body, it was harder for her to deflect the hot dinners he hurled at the toddler. She became pregnant again when her husband raped her. Deprived of friends, she didn't know what to do, believing that she was a "waste of skin."

Her husband alternately blamed his tantrums on his epilepsy and on Louise for not living up to his impossible and ever-changing standards. "I tried to be good. I was like a little robot; I didn't breathe until I was told to. After being with him for a while, I thought I should be hit."

While pregnant, she became so despondent that she figured out a way of killing herself and her son. She noticed that a truck drove by at regular intervals, so she decided to jump out of her apartment window in its path, dragging the child with her. She even marked a red spot on the pane where she was going to leap through. As she was preparing to jump, there was a knock on the door. It was one of those very rare times when a friend ventured by.

Shortly afterward, a group of friends turned up to challenge Louise's belief that her husband had the right to beat her. There and then, they helped her call the police and leave. But it wasn't the end. Even after the divorce, he stalked her around Ontario, sometimes kicking her front door down. Finally, she decided enough was enough, sold everything except the car and, with $2,000 in her purse, drove her two boys to Calgary. After a five-day trek, they arrived in that city with nothing except 10 cents and some food. At first they slept in the car, then they connected with Social Services, which attempted to send them back to Ontario. Aghast, Louise explained her circumstances, and they helped her re-establish herself. She was astonished when a few days after the boys started school, several parents arrived with clothes, furniture, dishes, toys, and even pictures for the walls. Odd, she thought, but very nice.

Louise met another man who became the father of her daughter, Chelsea. He turned out to be an alcoholic. "He didn't know I existed. He was never sober. He didn't know what sober was." The relationship didn't last long. Louise was too busy being a mother, holding down jobs, and getting counselling to regret his departure, although she's sad Chelsea doesn't know her dad.

At one point Louise worked in construction, relishing the physical labour and getting dirty. "The men didn't like it. They were very upset a girl could do the job, but if you like what you are doing, it's easy." It ended when her employer's wife issued an ultimatum: "Fire her, or I'll leave you." She also worked in home care, looking after elderly people, which she enjoyed until she was sent to care for a man dying of AIDS. She didn't know much about the condition and received no education or training about how to look after him, so quit because she didn't want to expose her children to the disease.

For a while, Louise was on social assistance, receiving $800 for her and the three children. Rent was $650. Thanks to food banks, the children were never hungry and, in fact, probably never realized what desperate straits they were in. Louise, however, was very ashamed.

Then she met her present husband, the single father of one son. They married after they had been together for two years. Although they have split up a few times, Louise says this relationship was made in heaven; she characterizes Paul as a good father and a hard worker. He's also helped restore her confidence. In the beginning, both Paul and Louise were fairly abstemious by nature; neither of them did drugs and did not drink much alcohol. Then acquaintances introduced them to crack cocaine, telling them nothing would happen. "I didn't want to be a party pooper, so I tried it. It was a large mistake. I was addicted there and then." The couple dived deeper and deeper into the drug. Soon the neat-freak mother was letting the housework go and, even worse, neglecting her children. They lost jobs and homes, sometimes spending up to $1,400 a night on their habit.

Louise financed the crack by pawning much of what she had and then by prostitution. She phoned telephone sex lines. After talking with a man for a few minutes, she offered him sex at her place for $80. It was pathetic, she says, but she felt better about doing it at home than on a street corner. After a while, all three boys were apprehended, and the two parents and Chelsea were on the street. The situation was compounded by a social worker who didn't have a good word to say about Paul because of his Aboriginal heritage. She also blamed Louise for her stepson's troubling tantrums, which were much more to do with the fact that he has FASD and ADHD (attention deficit, hyperactive disorder). Louise requested and luckily obtained a more enlightened worker.

Being on the streets with a young daughter was extremely frightening. Every evening the three checked in at an agency that sends clients out to different church basements for the night. "My daughter was petrified. She went into herself and wouldn't talk or move. If you moved, she'd freak out. She missed a lot of school. It was very rough. It was not a good place to be." There was a wide range in standards and volunteers at the churches: "Some were nice; at other churches, the volunteers didn't care. It was eat your dinner and shut up."

Louise decided she wanted to quit crack, so she went to a women's emergency shelter and from there to a friend's house, only to discover the friend was a closet crackhead. She was soon back on the drug. In the meanwhile, Paul had got his act together. One day he showed up and told her she had to stop. It pulled Louise up short. Normally she weighed 120 pounds, but by then she was down to 84; she was petrified that Chelsea would be apprehended too. "I realized what I was doing when my child had to ask for dinner and I was missing my husband. It was like a part of my life was gone and I wanted it back."

After much thought and very frightened that she would never see her again, Louise took Chelsea to the CS and signed a six-month agreement so that she could go into treatment. She entered a short-term detox centre and then a long-term residential recovery program.

Since then Louise has had her relapses, but Cocaine Anonymous and her sponsor help keep her clean. She knows she cannot pretend that one hit will be okay, because it won't. On 23 December 2002 at 6:15 p.m., seven months after Paul and Louise found a one-bedroom apartment, Chelsea was restored to them and her files were purged from the system. It was the best Christmas gift they could have imagined.

Louise's boys are doing well. The oldest, at 18, is out of the child welfare system and working. He's sweet-natured, kind to his girlfriends, and has resisted the temptations of drugs. The younger one is still in care and wants to become a corporate lawyer. Paul's little boy is also in care, handling his FASD as well as can be expected. As for Paul, a construction worker, things are tougher. He was injured when a brick wall fell on top of him, so he has a desk job with a social agency. He's not used to being inactive, nor to the small paycheque, but it hasn't kept him away from his 12-step program nor from continuing to support Louise emotionally. When they first met, she agreed with everything he said. Now, she is so confident that she sometimes has to remind him that it was he who gave her permission to speak.

On behalf of the homeless, she says the system stinks because people can't get a place to live without money and yet without an address, they can't obtain financial assistance. "They need to give some leeway." She says the catch-22s in the system drive people to lie and to commit fraud. "You can't snap your fingers and have money show up and you can't snap your fingers and have a home show up. You can't get out of it because you can't, unless someone is willing to help." Some people, she says, make $700 and pay $650 rent. The question of how they pay for everything else hangs in the air. "The rental situation sucks big time," she says, adding there is a four-year waiting list for subsidized housing in Calgary. She and Paul moved up the line, thanks to letters from CS, her children's therapist, and two agencies.

Although her income still isn't huge, Louise is fulfilled by her job. "Knowing I've helped someone totally, absolutely makes me feel good," she says, cutting the interview off so that she can dash back to her clients and their children.

Sources

Brandt, Susan. 2004. *Trauma and Homelessness*. <http://www.streetlevelconsulting. ca/newsArticlesStats/>.

——. Undated. *What is Post Traumatic Stress Disorder?* <http://www.streetlevel consulting.ca/newsArticlesStats/>.

Braun, Tracey, and Julie Black. 2003. *It Shouldn't Take an Inquest: A Review of the Literature Examining Links Between Domestic Violence and Homelessness.* Violence and Education Centre. <http://www.viec.org>.

Dallaire, Roméo. 2003. *Shake Hands with the Devil: The Failure of Humanity in Rwanda.* Toronto: Random House.

Literacy Alberta. 2003 (Updated). Literacy Fact Sheets. <http://www.literacy-alberta.ca>.

Metropolitan Action Committee on Violence Against Women and Children. 2001. Statistics Sheet: Violence Against Women Partners. <http://www.metrac.org/new/stat_vio.htm>.

Morrish, Elizabeth, Jenny Horsman, and Judy Hofer. 2002. *Take On the Challenge.* <http://www.worlded.orgs/TakeOnTheChallenge.pdf>.

National Centre for Post Traumatic Stress Disorder. *PTSD Information for Women's Medical Providers.* Washington, DC: Department of Veterans Affairs. <http://www.ncptsd.org>.

Norton, Mary (Ed.). 2004. *Violence and Learning: Taking Action.* Calgary: Literacy Alberta.

Sharkansky, Erica. n.d. *Child Sexual Abuse.* Washington, DC: Department of Veterans Affairs. <http://www.ncptsd.org>.

Whealin, Julia. n.d. *What is Post Traumatic Stress Disorder?: PTSD and Problems with Alcohol Use.* Washington, DC: Department of Veterans Affairs. <http://www.ncptsd.org>.

Interview

Hoogensen, Gunhild. Associate Professor, Department of Political Science, University of Tromsø, Norway. 2004.

CHAPTER 3

A SICK SYSTEM CREATES
SICK PEOPLE

This is Wednesday. We are in a meeting. Please call back
next week.

—Vancouver woman commenting
on her mental health worker

Ask any homeless woman about her health and, depending on her stoic-
ism, she will probably list a number of conditions that might include
heart problems, fibromyalgia, sore knees and feet, breathing difficulties,
hepatitis C, depression, osteoporosis, HIV/AIDS, and diabetes, to name
but a few. Although most will not even bother to mention it, many also
have severe gum and dental problems that are not only painful but that also
contribute to heart disease, diabetes, breathing difficulties, and premature
births. Of course, not everyone has all these problems, but health issues take
their toll. Conditions are so bad on the street that at least one social housing
complex on Vancouver's Downtown Eastside has lowered the qualifying age
for a senior to 45 because homeless women at that age are in the same kind
of physical shape as their middle-class sisters at 65.

In 2004 Angela Cheung and Stephen Hwang released a study on the
mortality rates of homeless women in Toronto. It showed that in the 18-44
age bracket, they are 10 times more likely to die than women in the general
population and that they are dying at about the same rate as homeless men
of a similar age, losing women's universal advantage of greater longevity. No
one should have been surprised; the wonder is that homeless women aren't
dying even faster.

One problem is the quality and quantity of the food; scarcely a broccoli
stalk is to be spotted in shelters where donuts are donated by the dozen.
Another, as we learned in the last chapter, is violence. There is the exhaus-
tion that comes from walking to numerous appointments in ill-fitting,
second-hand shoes and the stress that comes from not having a home and

from fearing the children will be taken away by social services. Some feel they have no choice but to give or sell their bodies in return for a bed or for cash to support a drug habit—and then there are all the risky behaviours associated with that. It's difficult to take meals and medication regularly when one is constantly on the move and has no safe place to store pills or insulin syringes. Without a fixed address, it's almost impossible to find a family doctor and the women are often reluctant to make appointments. And it's easy to pick up lice, colds, flu, tuberculosis, and other diseases in the crowded conditions of many shelters. This situation is exacerbated now that hospitals release people so much earlier, never enquiring whether the patient has a home to go to and the means to get there. They stumble back to shelters where bed rest is impossible, and then they proceed to infect everyone else.

On average, homeless people have eight to nine concurrent medical illnesses, says Dr. Martin Donohoe (2004). He lists dermatological conditions, respiratory infections, tooth decay, foot problems, vision problems, sexually transmitted infections, hypertension, asthma, diabetes, and mental illness, in particular depression, schizophrenia, PTSD, and personality disorders. He says that in the US, mental illness is reported in 30 per cent of homeless people, rising to 50 to 60 per cent in women. In conversation, staff at shelters across the country put that figure even higher, arguing that homelessness can trigger depression. It's tempting to separate mental health from physical health, because there is so much to say about both, but on the streets the two are even more obviously entwined than in the rest of the population.

Some of the factors that make it hard to treat homeless people include more vulnerability to crime and violence, prolonged standing, excessive outdoor exposure, overcrowding, risk of being robbed of medication, limited access to showers and dental care, inability to follow complex regimens, lack of privacy, and social isolation. On top of this, there may well be tobacco use, sleep deprivation, dehydration, drug use, and extreme long-term stress that creates physical and hormonal changes and physical and emotional trauma. Homeless women have little access to the media to learn about good nutrition and healthy lifestyles; even if they have such knowledge, it takes cash to buy fruit and a fitness club membership.

Homeless women are less likely to have a family doctor than other women, so they are apt to turn up at emergency departments after their situation has deteriorated into a medical crisis. They cite a number of reasons why they don't visit doctors regularly. They are ashamed of not having an address and feel intimidated; they don't have the bus fare or the phone money to make an appointment; they are unable to find a doctor; and, if they have been sexually assaulted, they fear flashbacks. Medical visits during pregnancy, or for mammograms and Pap smears (to prevent cancer of the cervix, more prevalent in women with multiple sexual partners), are all likely to trigger strong reactions in women who have been sexually abused. "It's heartbreaking because I know the fear they go through," says Cori Keating, a Vancouver outreach worker who has helped develop Pappaloosa, a program designed to make Pap smears less terrifying.

Women view health as a private matter, so it is very embarrassing for them to give physical details to receptionists in busy waiting rooms full of men also hoping to see the doctor, or to give personal information in front of a crowd waiting to enter detox. Once with a doctor or counsellor, women are reluctant to answer questions like: "Were you ever sexually abused?" unless a rapport has been built up, which is difficult to establish during a brief assessment. Because there is no family doctor to monitor their health care, nor even a regular pharmacist, homeless women are very likely to be prescribed medications that react badly with each other or with street drugs that they might be taking, thereby compounding their problems.

In recent years many psychiatric beds across the country were closed down with the admirable aim of supporting people with mental illness "in the community." Those supports have failed to emerge in either sufficient numbers or in ways that are always helpful to consumers, as mental health patients are often called. Without a safe place, it is hard to deal with schizophrenia, bi-polar disorder, and depression, and many street workers say there just isn't the help available to deal with the deep trauma affecting many homeless women. Women also report that while they may be quite prepared and happy to stand by their man should he run into problems, they don't find the support is reciprocated. Men tend to disappear fast, often moving on to another relationship and leaving the woman at an even higher risk of becoming homeless. If their partner vanishes, the system seems at best ineffective and at worst downright harmful.

"The popular image of a person sitting on a couch receiving therapy makes me laugh. It's not therapeutic. It's about diagnosis, prescribing and monitoring," says a woman with a long experience of dealing with the mental health system, adding that visiting a psychiatrist is like "putting your head in a lion's mouth and expecting to be made well." She reported having to stand in line for the bathroom and for medication at psychiatric facilities and of being jumped on by guards, stripped naked, and locked in a room. Because she has never gone to hospital willingly, she also has the word "violent" attached to all her files. "If women are angry, it's a problem; there's more tolerance for men if they are angry," she says.

The physically sick, too, find there's one system for the rich and another for the poor. Some hospital staff and addictions workers seem to believe that the homeless are not entitled to confidentiality or respect like anyone else. Women recall hearing nurses say things like, "Don't worry, she's just a hooker." Toronto street nurse Kathy Hardill says one of the problems is that the current medical model does not look at patients as people nor at the context in which their illness occurs; therefore, homeless women are blamed for their poverty and when they inevitably become ill, they are blamed for not taking care of themselves even though the situation was not of their making.

As middle-class women strive to swallow their vitamins and to exercise regularly, it is worth reflecting on the huge body of research that clearly demonstrates that the greatest predictor of a healthy life is a decent income. In other words, poverty makes you sick. According to York University professor Dennis Raphael:

> The strong link between income and disease is one of the most well-established findings in the health sciences but the least publicized by health care and public health workers, and the media. The link occurs across a wide range of diseases, but the strongest association is with cardiovascular disease. It has been demonstrated time and time again—in Canadian, United States, and United Kingdom, and other studies—that the illness-producing effects of low income swamp the influence of medical and lifestyle risk factors such as cholesterol levels, hypertension, tobacco use, quality of diet, physical activity, and body/mass index among others. Yet, all we hear about from the medical and public health communities is about cholesterol screening, drug therapies and lifestyle changes. (Raphael 2002)

Raphael says it goes even further, that childhood poverty haunts one for life; the poor are much more likely to die at a younger age than people who were raised in comparatively wealthy homes. Poor families have much higher than average infant mortality rates and more low birth weight babies, frequently resulting in chronic problems. Poor children frequently lack nutritious food, and although their needs are greater, they make fewer visits to doctors, dentists, and other professionals. They can suffer stunted physical and mental development and have a low resistance to infection, often living in areas where there are environmental hazards like traffic emissions or lead paint. In addition, there is the shame of not being able to participate in organized sports or group activities, not having a lunch to take to school, wearing second-hand clothes, and not having the same books and toys as the other kids.

However, middle-class people should not be complacent that their bank accounts will enable them to lead if not the good, then the healthy life. The poor are the canaries of society: societies with higher levels of poverty have higher mortality rates. Raphael (2000) cites a study that shows that, after years of increasing economic polarization, the richest people in Britain now have higher adult male and infant mortality rates than the poorest people in Sweden, a cautionary tale for Canadians as our poor become even poorer.

❖ ❖ ❖

Naomi

Naomi was left to fend for herself on the streets of Winnipeg because of her severe psychiatric condition. It wasn't until she met an outreach worker willing to support her on an ongoing basis that she finally found and was able to keep a home. In May 2005 she was silenced forever. Like so much in her life, the cause of death was not made known; it was speculated, however, that it might have been caused by an accidental overdose.

Naomi walks into the filthy hotel coffee shop and greets the waitress boisterously. The greeting is not reciprocated. Naomi's noisy and erratic behaviour has caused her to be barred from many similar hotels on Winnipeg's Main Street that are happy to accommodate drunks, addicts, pimps and prostitutes, but not her. She is very loud, and the two or three other people in the coffee shop perforce listen in on the interview. She has recently returned from a hitchhiking trip to British Columbia and, as a result, has missed a couple of the monthly shots that keep her schizophrenia from swinging out of control.

Naomi, who is 48, wants to talk about Tony, her boyfriend. No one, apart from Naomi, has seen Tony—"he's shy, you see"—but her life revolves around him. She consults Tony before every move and does nothing unless it meets with his approval. Whether he is, or was, a real person, or a fantasy that has subsumed her is an open question. That he is important to Naomi is in no doubt. Like it or not, real or imagined, he comes first in her life and in her heart. Naomi says they met at the Salvation Army, although Tony has his own home. Sometimes she locates it in the country; at others it's in a different part of Winnipeg. At times she waffles on details, especially when pressed by social workers; at others she is very precise—his birthday, for instance, is February 26. She says that they meet daily for coffee or at a soup kitchen, and he gives her advice, frequently contradicting her outreach worker, although sometimes he can be in complete agreement with the caregivers.

Naomi's childhood was spent on a farm in Ontario. The first time she tells the story, she had a good childhood, but several versions later she says her mother spent most of her time in bed, emerging from her room only for meals. However, when she took Naomi and her sister to the cottage, she was just fine. It may be significant that her father was not present on these trips. Naomi's mother wanted to work but was forbidden to do so by the father. When she did eventually leave him to go to Toronto and a job, her fatigue disappeared and she thrived.

Naomi appears to have got along for the most part with both parents and is grateful to her father for instilling in her various interests. She makes frequent references to watercolour painting, singing in a choir, and most of all cooking—Thai food, cabbage rolls, blueberry cake, and a chicken dish with mint and almonds. In fact, many of her hopes for the future revolve around creating the home she doesn't have and cooking for herself and Tony.

Naomi left school in Grade 10 because she couldn't concentrate and went to work in a Toronto bar where she says she did a variety of jobs from keeping bar to the night audit and cooking. It was while working there she met her husband. Although "a nice guy," the relationship lasted only a few months. Naomi left the bar, went to work as a teller at Green Road Race Track, and then trained as a chef, working her way up the culinary ladder to make good money in a three-star restaurant. She's glad she did it but wouldn't want to be in the food business again because the work is too hard for someone with multiple health problems.

At this point, her story takes a few confusing turns, involving several falls downstairs in which she seems to have broken her ankle at least twice. She rolls up her leggings to display the vicious scars where it was set with the help of pins. "I broke my ankle, hurt my back, and I'm incontinent, so they put me in a psychiatric hospital; they had to have a place to put me. I get needles now for my thoughts," she says, convinced that the hospitalization was all about her physical, not her mental health and that she ended up on a psychiatric ward because of a shortage of beds.

Naomi does recall some of the reasons why she is banned from so many of Winnipeg's cheap hotels, but in her version usually someone else started a fracas by pushing her or being lippy. She appears to have very little aware-ness of the effect of her penetrating voice and insistent conversational style, but for an observer it is easy to see how people lose patience with her and that she's not above losing patience herself.

After a lot of hunting, Naomi's outreach worker found her a small apartment where she seemed to be doing well. On a routine check, she found a note from Naomi saying she had left for Vancouver. This was considered progress, because previously Naomi would have gone with no communication at all. Naomi thumbed her way and lived at shelters while on the West Coast. Now that she's back, she wants her own room again before she and Tony move in together, but she's worn out her welcome at most of the places she can afford on social assistance. Finally, her outreach worker has found a cheap hotel with a manager who is warily willing to work with her to keep Naomi housed and stable.

The hotel appears quite clean, despite the drinking party going on in a nearby room at 10 a.m. The door is sturdy and the lock new. The bed is still unmade from the previous person; the toilet and the bath are down the hall. Naomi and her worker agree that it's better than many they have seen and decide to take it. The price, of course, is the maximum that welfare allows for a single person's rental accommodation. Tony will be okay with it, observes Naomi. The caseworker looks relieved. It's a sign that Naomi, too, will be okay with it. "Please, please let me know if you think she is running into trouble," says the outreach worker to the manager, "then we can head it off before anything happens."

Naomi is oblivious to their concerns. She's indignant that other places won't give her a room when she believes she is a model citizen. Her piece said, she turns to a practicum student working with the social worker. "You know Tony has a friend called Garry. Would you like to meet him? He's nice, and I've told him that you are single." When the student says that she's leaving, Naomi replies, "You will have to come back and stay with Tony and me. We are going to get a little house and I can cook for you. It will be really nice."

❖ ❖ ❖

Amy

Although Amy hasn't had an epileptic seizure in four years, employers are reluctant to give her work. Amy and her husband, who has a back injury, have a hard time providing for their children. They would much prefer to be employed.

I spoke with Amy and her two young daughters at a New Westminster drop-in centre.

It's spring break, and the family is at the drop-in because they have run out of food. They went to a food bank the previous day and, for two adults and two children, received two cans of soup, canned pumpkin pie filling, Rice Krispies, and some junk food. It was supposed to last three days. They don't blame the bank for the lack of nourishment, since they realize it can hand out only what comes in. At the same time, the food certainly wasn't enough to last three days, and no one even checked to see if they had a can opener.

Over the course of the week, the girls help out at the drop-in because Amy wants to make sure they grow up doing their bit for society. At other times she encourages them to draw pictures celebrating St. Patrick's Day and dresses them up in green, complete with shamrocks on their cheeks, to honour the Irish saint.

Amy's family arrived from England when she was three, but already she was plagued by ill health and required heart surgery. She also had something wrong with her eyes, which meant another operation a few years later. At school she was diagnosed with attention deficit disorder, but in the 1970s the family couldn't find help for her. She went to a vocational high school in Toronto where she took a hairdressing course.

Amy was the apple of her father's eye and the bane of her mother's life, and neither parent knew how to deal with a teenager who was testing them to the limit. Whenever there was a family row, her aunt and uncle jumped in too, compounding the situation. "I knew it all. My parents were wrong, they had never been there, never done it," says Amy, now wise at 32. "My parents didn't see I wanted to be a cool kid."

After a number of violent episodes, Amy made her break at 14. She hung out with bad kids and slept at friends' houses. She met her first husband, and they went to New Brunswick where she became pregnant. He then moved to Edmonton and Amy, 19, followed two weeks before the baby was due. There the beatings began. "In the beginning I thought it was my fault. I didn't know if it was normal or not. I phoned the police and they told me that he had to have a gun to my head before they could do anything."

Amy went to a shelter, but in a state of confusion and not knowing to this day if she was distraught or scared, she returned to her husband. At this point the authorities stepped in and took her daughter, fearing for the baby's safety. The father promptly blamed Amy for the loss. Devastated, Amy took all the Tylenol and penicillin in the house and then phoned for help. In hospital they told her that she was lucky to have survived because of her childhood heart surgery. "I was trying to find a way out, but that escape route didn't work."

Four months later, she met her second husband, Rick, and in two weeks had moved in with him. Her first husband saluted her departure with a volley of baseball bats and a hail of threatening phone calls to her parents. Moving in with Rick was a turning point in Amy's life. It wasn't the end of her problems, but it signalled a time of growth and maturation. Rick is warm, friendly, loveable, huggable, gentle, and has a lot of compassion; most of all, "he never beats me." In fact, she instructs her two young daughters, "that's what you'll look for in men—your dad; his qualities." Nonetheless, Amy did leave Rick once for another man. Rick looked after the girls and patiently waited until she was ready to return. She is desperately ashamed of this episode because the new man made her work as a stripper, but it wasn't until he became addicted to crack and started to beat her that Amy saw the light and returned to her family. "It still hurts to talk about it. I made a mistake and could have lost all three kids.... [Rick's] one in a million."

Health problems continue to plague Amy. She has had 29 surgeries, one abortion, 17 miscarriages, cancer of the cervix, and epilepsy. Although she hasn't had a seizure in four years, taking Dilantin to control the condition, it means she has trouble finding a job. She's become almost resigned to the situation, but it doesn't help the cash flow. "I've been turned down for four or five jobs because of the epilepsy. I don't care any more. I'm human, so what. I have a disorder. Big deal."

Currently Amy works on weekends as a dishwasher at a fast-food restaurant, earning $400 a month. In addition, the family receives $900 in social assistance and a $400 baby bonus. Rent is $680, leaving just over $1,000 a month for food, utilities, clothes, school supplies, and so on. They can't afford nutritional food, but most of the time they don't go hungry. There's not a big margin for emergencies.

Rick, who injured his back, is waiting to go back to school to retrain. The family hopes this will result in a lucrative job because, with the new British Columbia regulations, they will come off assistance in a year's time. Even if he does start to bring in real money, they don't know whether it will cover all the medication that Amy alone requires. There are many question marks in their future. Amy says there is an almost unbridgeable chasm between being on welfare and being financially safe and that it's very difficult to cross that divide because of the lack of support services. If she is ill and has to take a day off work, for example, all the family's calculations fall apart at the seams. "I want to get my life together and get off the system. My worker is really good and compassionate, but she does her job. We need more social workers who care about people instead of their paycheque. A lot just care about that cheque."

Amy sees increasing numbers of families hitting unacceptable poverty levels. Asked what she would do to change the system, laboriously she writes down this list:

- more family shelters;
- more training for parents-to-be;
- more support for kids so they can achieve their goals;
- action on domestic violence;
- the Canadian government has to put more money back into the community;
- social workers should come into homes to teach and to be a support system so children aren't apprehended as frequently;
- more subsidized day care.

"I'm not ashamed to say we are a low-income family. We get the free lunch program at school," says Amy who blames "the government" for not helping people. "They turn around and give the money to something else. Basically, they are not helping our country. I've been on the streets long enough to know."

If Amy's not ashamed of telling strangers about her financial difficulties, she is also not ashamed of telling it as it is to her daughters. "I would rather my daughters see what is really happening to us because this is reality, it's not the fantasy in which most Canadians are raised. It makes them both stronger, and it shows them they do need schooling, that they can't give it up. My mother gave up on me, but I'm not giving up on my kids."

Pandora

Pandora's mental illness catapulted her onto the streets, but she is one of the lucky ones who found help so that her life has taken several turns for the better. She has seen her share of chaos, but she defies every stereotype. It's worth noting that in the Greek myth the last quality released from Pandora's box was hope.

"By any medical definition, I'm nuts," says Pandora, "but I can talk, I can work, and I have a normal life."

Pandora, who is 21, does, indeed, look like a very together young woman. She has her own apartment and a job she likes, she volunteers and looks forward to a good future. It's hard to imagine that she was ever accused of setting fire to a school, that she was heavily into drugs, that she went through boyfriends on almost a daily basis, and that she chose her street name as a deliberate reference to the young woman in Greek mythology who unleashed chaos upon the world.

Pandora has a mental illness—bi-polar disorder. A year ago she was re-diagnosed with borderline personality disorder. She says she has been seriously misdiagnosed three times and that one of her medications has just about wrecked her liver, but she's here to tell about her life on the streets of Toronto in extremely lucid terms.

Her family has strong values that they tried to instil into her at an early age. By 10 she was doing the cooking and laundry and saving her allowance. When puberty hit at 13, Pandora's body rapidly developed. Her brain chemistry as well as her hormones went into overdrive. Pandora began to pay visits to the juvenile psychiatric ward. As well, the rules at home started to chafe. She ran away to the streets, morphing into a "twinkie"—street slang for a new kid on the Yonge Street block where she panhandled. At the time she was on probation for arson. "I was on Paxil that had thrown me into a manic spin. They claimed I set fire to the school—me and another person. She said it was me and I said it was she."

Pandora and three of her street friends decided to hitchhike to the West Coast. Everywhere they stopped, they looked for outreach offices and used the facilities until they felt the urge to continue their journey. She had stolen an art book from school and kept notes on the services in each city. "In Winnipeg, there weren't many; in Regina, none. In Calgary we stayed longer, so I called my mom." Her mother sent her some money, and Pandora continued westward with a new bunch of youngsters, having several adventures on the way. After one, the RCMP took her to an aunt in Kelowna, who bought her a bus ticket to Vancouver where she arrived just as the sun was rising, a magical sight.

Pandora spent two weeks on welfare, moving several times until she met a friend, Philip, who "saw a broken soul and wanted to fix it." He invited her to live with him, his wife, and children. It was an unusual ménage in that the parents were "polyamourous." It was, however, a safe haven for Pandora and, although she didn't have a relationship with him, she made good money working for Philip.

After 18 months, she decided to return to Toronto and called her mother to let her know. "Are you coming home or home-home?" she asked. They agreed that it was probably better for all concerned for Pandora to stay at a shelter, but her mother sent cash for a plane ticket. Pandora quickly moved into transitional housing and acquired computer graphic skills. Two years ago she progressed into her own apartment in a complex run by a non-profit housing society. She has a job as the personal assistant to a company president who understands her ups and downs. "There are days when everything makes me angry," she says. "I isolate myself on those days. I'll let you know if it's a bad day. If I'm really quite bad, leave me be. My boss is really good about it."

Her life now is a far cry from her teens when her time was spent getting high, trying everything "minus heroin and coke." Once she passed out at a club. When she came to, she found her arm was bleeding, and it looked as though someone had given her an injection. She went to be tested for heroin, and the results came back positive. She entered a clinic for treatment because she didn't want to become an addict. She still has flashbacks from the acid she dropped and says, "I don't recommend drugs to anyone."

Speaking as a reformed drug-user, she says it would be very helpful if there were 24-hour drop-in centres for street youth because most facilities close in the early evening, just at the hour when the kids start using chemicals. "If they don't have a shelter and they are wandering around, there is a tendency to get into trouble." However, the greatest danger to young women on the streets is men. "I don't care what anyone says, it's not love. It's a guy who has duped you until he's finished using you. A lot want to chase tail and be drug dealers." She's not saying there are no successful relationships, but she's sized up the situation pretty realistically.

Many young women lose themselves, their minds, and their money, ending up pregnant, infected, or dead. "Girls have to be careful or they get a very nasty reputation. It's very hard to lose, I know. Formerly I had a bad reputation. I played the guys' game against them. I switched guys as often as most people switch their underwear. I switched before they did and a couple I used as a personal punching bag."

Pandora has been lucky enough to find Jackie, a mechanic and "a guy not like the other guys." They have been going together for a year and a half. She says Jackie's been her rock, seeing her through a serious breakdown last year that led to the borderline personality disorder diagnosis.

Pandora takes many of the new street kids under her wing, briefing them on survival skills and the unwritten code of the streets. She has taken some of them back to her apartment to help them pull their lives together. She's had her successes and her failures. She notes that 50 per cent of street kids will stay on the streets, 30 per cent will make a go of life, but will only earn $20,000 a year or less, and 20 per cent will be "truly, truly successful. I want to fight for it [success]." She has her high school equivalency and is now working on college entry. Eventually, she wants to work with the deaf and dumb.

Few would suspect that mental illness has taken Pandora to the edge and back. She has also fought the prejudices and fears of the public about mental illness and about street kids. "They picture raving psychotics, the schizos, the worst-case scenarios. When it comes to homeless youths, they picture the dirtiest youth, the absolute worst."

❖❖❖

Barb

Childhood abuse and living rough on the streets have taken their toll on Barb's physical and mental health. She rarely complains about her conditions that include diabetes, a bad knee, dental problems, and dissociative personality disorder because she's too busy putting a new life together with the help of an array of professionals and her new friends.

A truly creative spirit, Barb writes the way most of us eat or breath; it's a necessity. She can carve out an "office" on a busy outdoor pedestrian mall or in a corridor while waiting for an appointment. Stories pop out of her mouth in everyday conversation. There is no curbing her imagination.

With a delightful sense of humour, a penchant for writing haunting children's tales, and her own idiosyncratic take on the world, Barb is not frightened to stand up for her beliefs. In fact, with multiple personality disorder (MPD), now known as dissociative identity disorder, she feels she's uniquely equipped to champion others: "I got 'alters' (alter egos) that do that. It's quite interesting."

Perhaps this sense of natural justice stems from the fact that Barb, 49, was routinely abused as a child. She is hesitant to talk about it because she's learning to live in the present and refraining from dwelling in the past. But occasionally the veil lifts, and she lets something fall—that her father offered her up to other men or that she didn't realize until she was an adult that it's not normal for a sister to have sex with her brother. At the age of six she revealed to her mother that her father was sexually abusing her. In retaliation, he beat her mother who, in turn, told her daughter not to be so silly: "Daddy says it's an awful thing you made up, but he will forgive you this time." Looking back, Barb says her father was a liar and her mother a manipulator who was quick to anger and equally quick to apologize without realizing that once the flower is picked "you can't put it back." In darker moments, she also hints at pedophile rings and ritual abuse. One of the scariest things about this is that her father was a school caretaker with plenty of access to small children, and, as Barb remembers it, she was far from being the only child who was subjected to his deviancy, although she and her siblings were not encouraged to play with other kids in the neighbourhood. Her sense of isolation, on top of everything else, still haunts her and, like many others, it wasn't until she started living on the streets that she felt safe and that she made friends. "I wanted to be part of another family so bad. Everyone wants to fit in somewhere."

Barb explains that the trauma she experienced as a child caused the MPD by providing safe places in her mind. With more than 50 alters, at times it was quite a cacophony, and not all of those personalities have been benign. There have been mornings when she woke up covered in blood because one of them has urged her to slash herself. On the other hand, there have been occasions when a couple of the alters have stepped in to relieve her of pain, most notably when she slipped and smashed her front teeth, or they have taken charge in frightening situations.

Some doctors dispute the MPD diagnosis and have given her other labels, like schizo-affective, but whatever they choose to call her condition, two things remain clear: childhood abuse has traumatized her deeply and, despite everything, she's putting her life together and is, once more, a contributing member of society with a new circle of friends, several of them fellow writers.

Many of Barb's short stories are about transformations or about loving parents. She keeps her writing in a big briefcase under her bed in her small downtown apartment along with a few other precious possessions. "Just in case there's a fire and I can pick it up and run." This is not such an unlikely fear in a building where many residents have mental illnesses or addictions. Her collection of seashells is displayed on a small table, and her numerous stuffed animals are dotted around the room.

For many years Barb had no home, moving from a park bench to a stranger's bed when it grew cold, finding it easy to pick up men when she was in need. "I was a step lower than a prostitute because I didn't get paid. I didn't know how to have a relationship with a man without sex. I think I was pretty sick. Scared? No, because God will look after me. It was what I was used to, remember?"

Before moving into this apartment, Barb lived in a hostel for women in transition where she felt safe enough to begin tackling her issues. She continues to move forward, but wonders why there are not more similar facilities for women, pointing out that women like her may need special kinds of assistance. "We need long-term help.... You just don't forget about it [the abuse]. We need lifelong help. We have got to find a new way, we've got to find new coping skills, and we need more shelters for women, but they have got to be safe, and you're not safe with guys."

Five years ago, Barb was a sullen, angry woman whose tougher alter egos were as likely to roar out of her mouth as she is to smile these days. If she spoke then, she talked only about the terrible things her parents had done and blamed them for her troubles. Or she would sit in a corridor, crying and staring into space. Now, she's much happier, describing her volunteer work with children, the university courses she's taking, and her stories that appear in local publications.

The change was slow, but she began to get help at various agencies, not just for her addictions and mental health problems, but also for her physical illnesses. Formerly when Barb was taken to hospital, it was always an emergency—an overdose, a suicide attempt, or a collapse; now it's more likely to be a scheduled test. Despite the fact some health professionals have refused to treat her, Barb did find people who were ready and willing to stand by her. A year ago she made a dramatic turn for the better with new medication and cut herself off marijuana. "I had to give the meds a chance." Booze and drugs are a way for street people to cope, she explains, not to defend her own actions, but to explain those of others and why it is so hard for people to move on. "You have to give us back the hope we may never have had."

Barb is slowly acquiring hope for the future, especially now that her parents have died and can no longer touch her. She is learning techniques to cope with the terrible flashbacks and "not to react so much." As childhood episodes return, she patiently deals with them with the help of counsellors. She is also learning that self-mutilation isn't effective at quelling demons, and, as for all those personalities, she's beginning to integrate them into her life. "You think I want to get rid of that? No way." Her object is to have all the alters working for her, so that she can run them like a team, under the leadership of Anne whom she considers to be her real persona—Barb being the front woman, as it were. She would prefer that even the evil ones like Roberta and Tara—"one wears suede and the other leather"—join in rather than go away.

Certainly they all come together to speak out on behalf of sexually abused children. "We need more awareness of what's going on. Kids are not to blame. I don't care what they do, or who they do it with." She observes that those who are against protecting children are often perpetrators of the abuse.

Once the street appeared to be a safe and caring place; now Barb realizes that although she went there to relieve her pain and to find community, it has exacerbated the losses and accentuated the hurts. The prospect of returning to that way of life has, in turn, become frightening. "I'm terrified of going to the street again because I would lose my identity."

Sources

Cheung, Angela M., and Stephen W. Hwang. 2004. "Risk of Death among Homeless Women: A Cohort Study and Review of the Literature." *Canadian Medical Association Journal* (April).

Dental and Oral Health, Calgary Health Region. 2001. <http://www.calgaryhealth region.ca/hecomm/oral/healthy.htm>.

Donner, Lissa. 2000. *Women, Income, and Health in Manitoba*. Winnipeg: Women's Health Clinic.

Donohoe, Martin. 2004. "Homelessness in the United States: History, Epidemiology, Health Issues, Women and Public Policy." *Medscape* (July).

Hurtig, Mel. 1999. *Pay the Rent or Feed the Kids: The Tragedy and Disgrace of Poverty in Canada*. Toronto: McClelland and Stewart.

O'Connell, James. 2004. "Dying in the Shadows: The Challenge of Providing Health Care for Homeless People." *Canadian Medical Association Journal* (April).

Raphael, Dennis. 2002. Interview. Sunnybrook and Women's College Health Sciences Centre. <http://www.womenshealthmatters.ca>.

——. 2001. "Increasing Poverty Threatens the Health of All Canadians." *Canadian Family Physician* (September).

——. 2000. "Addressing Health Inequalities in Canada." *Leadership in Health Services* (October).

Interviews

Hardill, Kathy. Nurse practitioner, Regent Park Community Health Centre, Toronto. May 2004.

Hwang, Stephen W. Assistant Professor of Medicine, Division of General Internal Medicine. St. Michael's Hospital, University of Toronto, Toronto. May 2004.

Keating, Cori. Outreach worker, Downtown Eastside Women's Centre, Vancouver. April 2004.

Ricciardi, Josie. Community health worker, Regent Park Community Health Centre, Toronto. May 2004.

CHAPTER 4

DROWNING IN THEIR SORROWS

> The only time I was sober was when I was in jail. In one
> month I lost 21 pounds withdrawing from alcohol, hard
> liquor. At times I tried different programs, but I usually
> gave up. I was in one for four months. I tried with all my
> heart, but anger and resentment crept up. There must be
> something wrong with me.
>
> —Edmonton woman in a shelter

Drowning in their sorrows is a phrase that takes on new depth of meaning when listening to the stories of homeless women. They drink alcohol; sniff solvent; and use crack, heroin, Valium, crystal meth, and anything else that will carry them to oblivion. Almost all of the homeless women addicts interviewed said they used various drugs so that they wouldn't commit suicide, that the drugs help them forget, even if briefly, the violence, loss, and grief in their lives. They don't like what they are doing and in many cases are ashamed of their addiction, especially if they finance it through prostitution. In a grim way their reasoning that it keeps them alive makes sense. They have chosen survival in the short term, although in the long term it is a slow way of dying, as many of them acknowledge.

Official estimates state that 30 to 40 per cent of homeless women have addictions; however, this figure may be far too low. Those who work closely with them sometimes venture to put the number of addicted homeless women as high as 90 per cent. What creates this discrepancy? The answer, in part, is that there is still much more of a stigma attached to a woman having an addiction than a man, so women become creative at concealing their habit. The other possibility, according to Reverend Jan Rothenburger, mission outreach pastor at Toronto's Yonge Street Mission, is that a number of women are on the streets for only a few months because they have the emotional wherewithal to re-establish themselves. Therefore, "The ones who will remain in that situation, 98 per cent of them have addiction/mental health problems" (Rothenburger interviews 2004).

Rothenburger points to another feature of addictions in women—that it is hard to look at addictions in isolation because violence, addictions, and mental health issues go hand in hand. Probably about 50 per cent of those using substances also have a mental illness and that doesn't count those who are depressed because, as one shelter executive director said, "living with an addiction sucks and the thought of giving it up (or trying to) causes anxiety disorders that become chronic" (Neal interview 2004).

Many homeless women revolve through treatment programs, but find that there are too many hurdles set too high, especially if they don't have a safe place to work on their issues. "Housing is so powerful. It sets the framework for recovery" (Bradley interview 2004). Also, it is now acknowledged that addiction treatment is based mainly on research done by men, on men, and for men, and yet there are many gender differences to take into account. Women have different physiology, different social circumstances, different attitudes, different needs, and different ways of responding, which add up to a need for different forms of treatment.

Physiologically, drugs and alcohol affect women faster and more severely than men. Women, for example, reach higher peak blood-alcohol levels than men from equal doses per pound of body weight. Thus, they have a greater risk of over-dosing and/or developing liver damage, hypertension, malnutrition, and gastrointestinal problems. Drugs and alcohol also have an impact on the female reproductive system. Women users run high risks of miscarriages, infertility, vaginal infections, and premature delivery. Pregnancy, menopause, and menstruation can all be affected by drug use. The one bright note is that many women of their own accord make huge efforts to reduce consumption or to stop using substances on learning they are pregnant. Centres like Toronto's Breaking the Cycle (2002) report that a supportive multi-faceted intervention, based on the harm-reduction model, can be highly effective at this time.

As far as attitudes are concerned, historically, women's use of drugs and alcohol has been associated with "loose morals" and is frequently discussed within a framework of blame, accompanied by a great deal of shame and secrecy. As late as the 1970s there was little research on the issues because it was thought that heavy drinking in women was minimal. For example, between 1970 and 1984, women represented only eight per cent of subjects in alcoholism studies. A Health Canada report stated "the emphasis on male substance-use patterns and treatment for men has resulted in a 'male as norm bias,' which has judged women who require treatment more harshly, and has limited the exploration of gender-specific treatment approaches" (Currie 2001).

Most women users have many interlocking issues to deal with beyond the addiction. Violence is high on the list. Mental health problems, including depression, PTSD, panic attacks, and eating disorders, are also seen more often in women than in men. The trick is to help each woman identify where to start unravelling her tangled ball, although it is important to note that nothing substantial can happen unless she feels safe both physically and emotionally.

Nelson-Zlupko *et al.* (1995) detail many other gender differences:

+ Women are more likely to use a combination of legal drugs and to use them in private, whereas men favour illicit drugs in bars and other social settings.
+ Many women report they began using drugs after a traumatic event like incest or rape.
+ 75 per cent of women in treatment report having been physically or sexually abused.
+ Women are likely to come from families where drug use is the only coping strategy.
+ Women are more likely to be in a relationship with a drug-user.
+ Women often have a history of over-responsibility.
+ Women have experienced greater disruption in their families than their male counterparts, who in the main do not support their partners in treatment.
+ Chemically dependent women are more likely to experience affective disorders, while men are more likely to demonstrate sociopathic behaviour and to engage in criminal acts.
+ Women in treatment who report criminal involvement usually cite shoplifting and prostitution, whereas men rely on robbery, con games, and burglary to support their habits.
+ Finally, women experience higher levels of guilt, shame, depression, and anxiety about their addictions than men.

As noted, women in the shelter system have traditionally fared poorly in drug and alcohol treatment programs compared to men. Rates of entry, retention, and completion of treatment are significantly lower, perhaps because programs in mixed facilities frequently use an aggressively confrontational approach designed to break the layers of denial often built up by men. Women come to treatment acutely aware of their shortcomings and their perceived failures, so this type of approach is often counter-productive. Programs in women's centres are now finding more positive ways to help women.

Women tell of huge difficulties put in their way when they do ask for help. Those with children are very unwilling to go into a program because they fear, often with foundation, that the authorities will declare them unfit mothers, even though they are seeking treatment in order to become better parents. It is especially difficult with long- and short-term residential programs if the woman has no one reliable to take care of her children while she is gone. Few detox and rehabilitation programs allow women to bring their children with them; if push comes to shove, mothers are understandably unwilling to lose their kids.

If a woman can get into detox—beds are not always available—that's the easy part, says Nancy Bradley, executive director of Toronto's Jean Tweed Centre, because afterward they need to deal with the harder issues: trauma, finding housing, lack of education, poverty, abuse, and, above all, creating a safe place for themselves. At Jean Tweed, which uses a harm-reduction approach, they find that tranquillizers and anti-depressants help many women stabilize so they can begin to address these issues, but not all programs permit women to use such medications, especially those where abstinence is the order of the day. Bradley (interview 2004) says, "It's important to meet them where they are at and then to start building."

Relapse should be seen as an inevitable part of the recovery process and can be used to explore the triggers so they can be addressed and avoided in the future. If the client perceives relapse as failure, she may quit trying and then suffer the repercussions of losing her children and her housing, until eventually she doesn't want to try anymore (Bradley interview 2004). Studies show women respond much better to programs capitalizing on their strengths, using their experiences as learning tools rather than turning them into sources of grief and shame. For this reason, harm-reduction programs that work toward abstinence by cutting back on risky behaviours and/or substituting less damaging practices—like smoking marijuana rather than using crack cocaine—often work better for women than all-or-nothing treatments.

Some women dislike going to, or refrain from attending mixed groups for fear of seeing their pimps, johns, or dealers. They speak, too, of the ribald, demeaning language they encounter at some groups that are led by willing amateurs with no training in what is appropriate and what is not, and of being hit upon by sexual predators seeking vulnerable women. They are also embarrassed to talk about sexual abuse in a mostly male group, so they quit. Women are more relational in their approach; therefore, when they lose their initial numbness, they want to open up, talk, and share, whereas men tend to be much more linear and to isolate their addiction from other circumstances in their lives. For all these reasons, mixed groups can be counter-productive to recovery in women.

Women see failure in treatment as a further sign of their inadequacies, not of the program's shortcomings. It's a novel and thrilling idea for them to question whether the treatment actually works and to think about what might be helpful for them. Most say success takes a long time and requires a great deal of support.

❖ ❖ ❖

Kelly

Kelly started using drugs to dull the pain of childhood abuse, but now she finds her life is controlled by crack, which threatens everything she has, including her career and her daughter.

Kelly says she was a problem child. In truth, she was a child with problems. The result of an affair, Kelly, now 26, has an avid curiosity about her birth father, by all accounts a rich, self-made businessman. His life is a far cry from where she is, sitting in a shelter just off Winnipeg's Main Street. She has never met him or her four half-siblings.

When Kelly was three or four, her mother left her first marriage and came to Winnipeg, finding shelter with Kelly's uncle and her three male cousins, all somewhat older. It wasn't long before one of the boys began touching her inappropriately. "I didn't know any better. I realize now it was wrong. At the same time I was abused by a neighbour, a girl of 16." The teenager made Kelly and a boy of about the same age try to have sex with each other and to touch her genitals. Kelly knew it wasn't right because a couple of times they were caught by older children who "freaked" and also because no one was supposed to find out. This continued for a year.

Her mother's second husband beat Kelly. "He would pull down my pants and get me over his knee. The worst part was that you knew it was coming. It was planned, calculated and it [the beating] was for nightmares, whatever—basically anything. I don't remember my [half-] brother being spanked." What hurts Kelly the most is that her mother never intervened and to this day denies that anything bad happened, either with the step-father or anyone else. "There wasn't any penetration was there?" her mother asks.

In Grade 2 an educational play about sexual abuse and the wrong kind of touching came to Kelly's school. At the end, the kids were told that if they had experienced such things, they could talk to one of the staff. So Kelly did.

Then she went home and told her mother. Her mother screamed, "Don't tell anyone, or they will take you away." The next day when a social worker turned up, Kelly felt compelled to deny everything. "It freaks me out now that she [her mother] didn't protect me. It affects me even now because I'm so over-protective of my daughter. I have been asking her for three or four years if anyone has touched her, and I know that that's not healthy."

Her mother was absent for long periods, working in bars until 4 a.m., leaving Kelly to look after her half-brother, take him to school, cook supper, and get him ready for bed. She began to resent him and started to beat him up. But underneath she was a frightened child who didn't know any better.

At school she let older boys look up her skirts, and at dances they had their way with her in unseen corners. "I was very sexual," says Kelly. "This made me feel wanted," as opposed to her stepfather who called her fat and ugly. At nine Kelly was caught shoplifting; at 10 she discovered the comfort of slashing her arms; at 11 she set the school bathroom on fire, fought with another girl, and drank for the first time; and at 12 she was stealing joints from her mother. Her first experience with getting drunk was with a couple of men in their twenties. She consumed a lot of rye and inevitably passed out. When she came to, one of the men was having sex with her. She vomited all over him, and he rolled off. It took her three days to sober up, but that didn't stop her from drinking and stealing the cash for it from her mother.

Kelly was acting out partly because she was angry with her mother, who had finally left her husband because he had started to beat her up instead of beating Kelly. "Why are you so special?" Kelly asked, puzzled her mother hadn't left much earlier. Six months later, her mother entered a new relationship with a very traditional man of Japanese descent, a situation designed for conflict. At first Kelly liked him because he had money, but he also had rules. When he refused to take Kelly on a family outing because she had flouted his authority, she ran away, and finally Child and Family Services was called. In theory, she remained in care until she was 18. However, that didn't deter her from a spectacular revenge when she heard the rest of the family was leaving for Mexico on her birthday. "I was so bad. I still had the key to the house. I broke in and let people steal anything they liked. They brought trucks and were taking furniture and paintings out and I put syrup on the paintings that were left. I kept myself drunk as he had boxes of liquor; we took all those too. They knew it was me because I wouldn't let anyone touch my brother's things. I was so angry; I was so sick of those men [all her ersatz fathers]."

Kelly was charged and sent to a youth centre. In five years she rotated through 30 group homes, drinking as she went. "Anything that's been put in front of me I've tried, except needles," she says. "It's always in excess." She frequently escaped to hang out in bars while she couch-surfed from friend to friend.

At 15, Kelly met Dave, who ran the "booze cabin" where she drank. He was big, wielded power, and had money. Dave told Kelly he loved her and that he wanted her to have his baby; he gave her cash and a place to live, all very seductive to a neglected teenager. She thought that she had finally found love. Suddenly, Dave stopped paying the rent, leaving Kelly alone with nowhere to go. A man whom she describes as her seducer's "Doormat" appeared and asked her to work for him as a prostitute. "He's right," she thought, "I don't have anywhere." She consoled herself with her first hits of acid.

The Doormat didn't prepare her in any way for the streets. Another pimp had to tell her where to stand and how much to charge. Everything she earned she gave to the Doormat in return for a few flaps of coke. A week later Dave showed up. "I love you," he said. "Why don't you work for me?" Kelly became one of eight girls working for him. Hoping to regain his love, she took all the customers the others rejected for whatever reason. Still in her mid-teens, she was the youngest prostitute in the area and had to negotiate her way through the street culture in which young women are bought and sold. She has had eggs, beer bottles, pennies, and taunts hurled at her from passing cars. Men who think it's amusing to beat up prostitutes have attacked her. And that's not counting the bad dates. "[The john] could probably be your husband. I've had guys whose wives are at work, with baby seats in the back of the car and rings on their fingers, or there are the guys who want a blow job before work."

The older women took pity on the teenager and so did the police who removed her from the streets at regular intervals. The last time they did so, she was taken to a juvenile lock-up for five months where she caused a riot and was sent to what amounted to solitary confinement. The only clothes she was allowed were her pyjamas. Incarceration didn't block her access to drugs; she took whatever came her way—crystal meth, acid, Tylenol 3s. Several times she ended up in hospital as a result of an overdose.

In her late teens Kelly began to use crack, a drug that she says makes you do "crazy" things. In her case she went to sleazy hotels with strange men and sat around naked all day and all night. "After the crack's gone you feel so depressed, so shitty about all the things you've done." When she was 18, she met Angel's father. Although he was a gang member, they never did crack while they were together. After a year of drinking and partying, Kelly discovered she was pregnant. Once she decided to have the baby, she quit using everything.

When Angel was born normal and healthy, Kelly was overwhelmed by an unexpected surge of intense love. It was inexplicable to her why Angel's father didn't feel the same way. "I'm grateful to him for having my daughter. He came with me through labour and was with us for the first month, but all of a sudden he started cheating." He packed his bags and departed, leaving her in the throes of post-partum depression with a baby who had trouble breastfeeding. Kelly moved back in with her mother. "I know I wasn't the mom I should have been," Kelly says, regretting she found solace in the bottle. However, she also started to pick up some high school courses, arriving at class with a hangover, but still achieving good marks. Finally, her mother told Kelly to move out.

Kelly was in touch with an inmate who claimed he was inside because he had been falsely accused of domestic violence. After his release, he moved in with her and stayed for four years. In two weeks, the romance was over in this "crazy-assed relationship." He was so jealous, he made her sit in her room all by herself. If she even made eye contact with anyone, he became violent. To someone as deprived as Kelly, it was all worth it for the honeymoon phases when she felt loved and wanted. He broke her nose five times, telling her that she was lucky to have him.

Miraculously, Kelly persevered with her education. She had wanted to be a veterinarian but, after Angel was born, decided nursing would suit her better. She finished three grades in two years at a school where teens can work at their own pace. She won an academic scholarship as well as one for outstanding citizenship and enrolled in college. But the trauma at home was taking its toll. Angel started emulating the adults, throwing her dolls around and pounding them into the floor. Kelly was allowed no contact with her friends and family, not even by phone. One day she turned up at her mother's sporting a goose egg. Her mother called the police, and the next day a CFS worker put Angel into her care. "That made me think," Kelly says. It took her 72 hours to make her choice: her man or her daughter. In the end, Angel won the day, although Kelly wasn't quite ready to bid her partner goodbye. But, as she says, it was a starting point.

Although Kelly deplores the behaviour of most of her partners, she is also very compassionate, pointing out that none of them had mothers or jobs. "They were very needy too," she says. It took her some time to figure out that she didn't have to put up with the ex-con; even when he spat in Angel's face, the truth didn't hit her. She did, however, begin to lay charges against him when he was violent, not that she ever followed through on them. She finally woke up to his painful and treacherous personality when he got another girl pregnant. Then, and only then, she left him. She still misses him.

In the summer of 2002, Kelly began to sell crack and to smoke it. In her depressed state, it didn't matter that it cost $200 a night. Because of drug-induced paranoia, she wouldn't let her daughter go out to play, and they only spoke in whispers behind closed drapes. When Kelly was supposed to return to college, she slit her wrists. She was released from hospital but was sent back in a suicidal state. Her psychiatrist told her that she sabotages herself because she believes she's not good enough to succeed. This rings true for Kelly who cannot bear to look at herself in the mirror and who at college keeps very much to herself, rarely going out with the other student nurses. Her only friend is a young Hutterite woman who has never touched drugs or alcohol, who goes to church, and (what touches Kelly the most) who has never had her boyfriend cheat on her. "It's culture shock, we play board games, but it's fun. I told her everything."

During her months in hospital Kelly tried to commit suicide three or four times, and when she had exit passes, she grabbed the opportunity to use crack. "I hate crack, but I couldn't say no," she says. In January 2002, she tried to return to school, but she couldn't handle it, and by the summer of 2003 she was working the streets.

Because she owed four months' rent and was stealing to feed Angel, she placed the child back in her grandmother's care. "I can't convey how addicting crack is. It's the first drug that takes mothers away from their children. It's true." She once saw a woman screaming in labour on the floor of a crack shack who wouldn't go to hospital until the drug dealers finally called an ambulance. The day after the birth, the woman was back on the streets. Even gang members look down on crack users as the lowest of the low; in Winnipeg there is no longer a need for pimps because the gangs control the women through their addictions. "I pride myself on not having a pimp since I was 15. Crack is totally my pimp."

While on crack, Kelly has gone 10 days straight with no food or sleep. When she's on a binge, she might service 30 to 40 men in two or three days without showering. She hallucinates, hears things, feels paranoid, pulls out clumps of hair, and burns herself on the pipes. She uses crack because she feels guilty about all the things she has done and not done. Afterward she feels even worse. "So much of me gets taken away every time I use."

The end of 2003 was a blur of suicide attempts and treatments. Finally, she went into a 14-day detox program and followed it up with a long-term residential program. She was clean for 60 days, the longest break from substance abuse since she was 11 years old. She has no clue why, but one day she left and started using again. She returned to treatment because a man took her home and to bed, saying he only wanted to hold and cuddle her.

To Kelly it felt gross, and in the morning when he began to force himself on her, she left. She thought she had blown her chances with the program, but to her amazement, the staff said, "We are not kicking you out." They guessed correctly that she was looking for an excuse to use again, and they weren't prepared to give her the ammunition. "I'm so thankful," she says.

Kelly's relations with men and ideas about sex are, to say the least, confused. She prefers sex with women but would like intimacy with men, by which she means conversation and coffee. Physical closeness is abhorrent to her. "Sex is a hard thing for me because it doesn't mean anything. When I'm working I don't move or moan." If a guy is too nice to her, it turns her off; when she's not working, she doesn't want to use condoms because they remind her of the street indignities. "Basically, guys are pigs."

"My addiction needs to be put to sleep," says Kelly, and, powered by her love for Angel and her desire to become a nurse, she is taking courageous steps to lay it to rest. She has entered a long-term women's treatment program and is learning to look in the mirror both literally and metaphorically. It's a painful process, and she's hesitant to share her workbooks with staff. She enjoys visits with Angel and carries several photos of her as a reminder of why it's important to come clean. "I'm glad I'm 26 and doing [this]," she says, confessing she was scared into reality when she heard 40- and 50-year-old women in the group praying for their 12-year-old daughters who are already smoking crack and working as prostitutes. "I don't want it to be my daughter and if I keep up what I'm doing, it will be her destiny. I don't want to be praying for her when she's 12."

Carol

At 61 Carol puts on a good face to the world, but she can't remember what it is like to be drug-free. She continues to seek out men for a roof and the frail hope of intimacy, usually receiving in return nothing but violence, degradation, and drugs.

Carol is always impeccably groomed and speaks in the modulated tones of an actor, with a good understanding of the telling pause. She loves to gossip and to drop names into the conversation—the former husband who was the brother of a famous urologist or her friend who was a minor player in the De Beers diamond family. Although it's easy to imagine her sitting behind a teapot at a garden party, she is in fact patiently waiting for her dinner at a New Westminster drop-in centre. She is an addict, has worked many years as a prostitute, and in her younger days she posed naked for a magazine cover.

Carol's mother was a female wrestler who did impersonations of Al Jolson in nightclubs. In old age, she has become a formidable dowager. Carol, who often needs cash, fondly calls her the Bank of Fort Knox. Her father, "a grand old man," was an artist, hotel maintenance manager, and womanizer.

When Carol was 14, she discovered her first boyfriend and sex. "It was lovely. I thought we would get married. He would have, but my eyes caught John," her second boyfriend. Her mother expected that "Your girlfriends at school will tell you [about birth control]," but soon it was too late for information of any kind. Carol was pregnant. Her father almost had a heart attack but put on a good face and arranged a white wedding. It was a big mistake. John turned out to be a wife-beater, bequeathing Carol a permanent legacy of ear and nose problems. He also kicked her in the stomach when she was seven months pregnant.

The couple lived with Carol's parents. One weekend when John faked a fishing expedition to be with a girlfriend, Carol's father kicked him out. Carol was pregnant again, but she had an abortion. Two years later, the divorce came through—"the nicest thing he ever did for me." In the meanwhile, Carol had taken up with Brian with whom she was infatuated. It was around this time that she started injecting heroin, perhaps because of problems with her romance. Brian once shot Carol in the stomach with a BB gun ("You'd almost think I had a death wish"), and he put her on the streets as a prostitute. "I made a lot of money for him lying on my back. He knew I was in love with him and would do anything for him. I kept him happy and kept him in cars, and then he married a nurse, and then he was murdered."

Brian's departure was painful—"one of the biggest hurts in my life"—but her mother stepped in and took Carol and her son by Brian to Israel as a restorative. (John's son had already been adopted in a private arrangement.) Being a mother didn't stop Carol from having a wild time with almost everyone she met, including the De Beers scion. She moved to a kibbutz and, when not harvesting eggplants, slept her way through all the bachelors. A photographer fell in love with her and did a photo shoot titled *Carol On The Kibbutz*, including a naked cover shot complete with flowers in strategic places. The strict kibbutzniks were not amused and planned to marry her off, but she took an aversion to their candidate. In the meanwhile, she was heartbroken to receive a letter from her father that contained clippings about Brian's murder.

On the beach in Elat, she picked up a South African actor, and within a short time they were married. Carol didn't find him the easiest person to live with because he was devoted to the stage. She would wake up in the morning hoping for a cup of coffee only to hear, "To be or not to be, that is the question."

"O, Harry, don't disturb me," she would say and roll over.

After several miscarriages, they too had a son. While Harry pursued his career, Carol volunteered in a hospital during the Six-Day War and opened a massage parlour for men. She was chagrined to discover that most of her customers expected something more than a backrub. "One client threw coins at me to get ice cream because I wouldn't participate with what he had in mind."

Harry moved back to South Africa, taking the child with him. Carol followed, but their relationship was falling apart. She developed a reputation as an alcoholic and, in an incident she doesn't dwell upon, was raped by two policemen in Johannesburg. Eventually, she left the boy with Harry and returned to Canada where she stayed with her father until she "decided to get married to Dennis the Chinaman, a drug dealer. Dad was happy because he didn't know the means of support. Dennis was a refined gentleman. He never knew who his father was and he did have a Chinese look. His mother was a Micmac."

Despite being so gentlemanly, Dennis infected Carol with hepatitis C. Living with a dealer wasn't that genteel an affair either, with the RCMP kicking their door in from time to time. They entered a methadone program together, only to get hooked on it instead. After 13 years, Dennis died of lung cancer that spread to his brain.

Carol's next affair was with a truck driver she met in a bar. He liked his booze, but Carol introduced him to drugs. "I'm the scoundrel. Now I'm just a runaround-Sue," she says, enjoying the wickedness, later admitting that she was making good money working as a prostitute from a Denman Street apartment at that time. "The tricks never worried me because I'm psychic and had the ability to control them. I always had a sense God was on my side ... and I know how to handle myself verbally and physically."

Although they share a bed, Carol doesn't have sex with her current beau and she's happy about that. Health care workers visit them both every Thursday. Having survived breast cancer and all her other mental and physical problems, including osteoporosis, she would like to make the most of the time left to her. She looks forward to the wedding of Harry's son in Florida and seeing her former spouse at it.

Depending on how trusting she feels and what's circulating in her system, Carol is somewhat secretive and contradictory about her drug habit. One story is that she kicked the methadone by using painkillers prescribed for Dennis; another is that she is still on it. She says it helps control the bi-polar disorder that has been responsible for several stays in psychiatric hospitals. She has been homeless a number of times both in Vancouver and in South Africa and describes the experience as "horrible, absolutely horrible." Generally, she says, it has been related to mental health episodes requiring hospitalization. "My life is sad ... most of the good times have been when I'm drunk. I don't know what it's like to be without any drug."

❖ ❖ ❖

Lynn

Born with an addiction, Lynn has struggled with substance abuse and violence all her life. She has, however, much cause to be proud of her sons.

When Lynn was born 48 years ago, she was already addicted to opiates. Her mother, an addict, was constantly in and out of psychiatric wards; her father was an alcoholic. All her life she has tottered two steps away from this difficult start only to fall one or even one-and-a-half steps back.

After she was born, Lynn nearly died because of the drugs in her system and spent six months in hospital. One day her grandmother arrived and, finding her in a slough of diarrhea, lifted her out of the crib and took her home. At a very young age, Lynn became mother to her own mother, raising her younger brothers from the time she was nine. By 13 she was cooking all the meals and doing the laundry, including ironing her dad's work shirts. At 15 she left for an abusive relationship. "I didn't figure it could be any worse than home." However, it was. Her man was jealous and possessive, and he hit her constantly. That didn't stop Lynn from holding down a full-time job as well as having custody of her 11-year-old brother because he was being beaten at home.

Lynn finally left, but the pattern was established, and she ricocheted from one relationship to another for the next six years by which time she was a prostitute doing speed (crystal meth), Valium, and alcohol. She weighed 70 pounds. She met a biker and became pregnant. She had been trying for a while, keeping a calendar so that she would know who the father was. When he asked her to marry him, she said yes. "The thought that went through my mind was that I'll never have to worry where to get drugs again." That said, she did quit while pregnant; because she was so focused on the child she had wanted for so long, she found it comparatively easy to do so.

Lynn became pregnant again and found herself with a three-year-old, a newborn, and a husband in jail. Sometimes the family lived in shelters; at times the children were apprehended; other times Lynn was in drug and alcohol programs and the children were put in care. Even though she's heard about worse things happening to other women's children in care, Lynn says it was a very bad experience for her two boys. "They lived with a horrible woman who forced them to call her mother. She listened to their phone calls, and I couldn't tell them what was going on. I had to lie on the phone."

Lynn still feels guilty about the time they had no-name-brand tacos for Christmas dinner. Occasionally, her sons have been very resentful of their precarious existence. Through it all, she tried to ensure the boys didn't fall prey to addictions, even though they saw her succumbing all the time. "I explained the process of addiction to them, that it doesn't make you feel good, just normal. That it's not a question of you wanting it, but it wants you."

After one rehabilitation attempt, her husband kept showing up at the door with drugs in hand, so she finally bid him goodbye and moved in with another man, but he was no better. At the same time, Lynn looked after her mother who, because of her life of drug abuse, had become an invalid. "I wanted a normal life; I just wanted to be normal and have a nice car, good job, and the kids going to school. I wanted to be downtown with working people."

After sustaining injuries in a car crash, Lynn was awarded substantial financial damages. She invested the money in a trailer park—and cocaine to keep the pain at bay. She told her boyfriend he had to behave himself, and together they tried to make a go of the business. At the end of the first season, she threw him out, and another man took his place. However, Lynn went bankrupt and had to give up the trailer park. Her mother caught pneumonia and went into hospital; the medical staff persuaded Lynn to sign the papers "to let her die ... I regret it, but they said she had no quality of life. She wasn't a good mother, but she was the only one I got." A month later her father died, and Lynn, who had just discovered one of her boyfriends had given her hepatitis C, went into another free fall of alcohol and drugs. Recognizing that something had to be done in the face of her boys' reproachful looks, she went for treatment again. This time, it was a success, and she has been officially clean ever since. Being sober and drug-free, however, did not signal the end of Lynn's troubles, not even her troubles with drugs. This time, however, it wasn't her negligence, but rather a doctor's that got her into trouble.

Lynn had a serious fall, which added to her mounting list of medical conditions: diabetes, hepatitis C, osteoarthritis, fibromyalgia, high blood pressure, chronic depression, bi-polar disorder, kidney and urinary tract infections, PTSD, and the painful legacies of the car accident. Her lower back "is screwed.... My willpower was gone. I couldn't lift nothing, I couldn't stand to make a meal. I couldn't do laundry or wash floors." In other words, she was in no condition to wonder what her doctor was prescribing. He put her on so much medication, including morphine (an opiate), that she was out of it for a year. When he lost his licence, she saw another doctor who put her into hospital to withdraw yet again.

Although Lynn was fortunate enough to obtain subsidized housing, she couldn't manage by herself, but there was no money for home care due to Ontario government spending cuts. "There are people in a lot worse shape than I am and they are cut back. I couldn't get any help." With her doctor's assistance, she convinced the authorities that a friend should be allowed to live with her to help with the housework. It seemed like a good plan, neighbourliness in action. Once the friend moved in and got her name on the lease, she became a different character, telling Lynn that she was lazy and only pretending to be in pain. Slowly but surely, she took control, stealing Lynn's money and prescription drugs, pawning her rings and using the cash to buy pot and alcohol for herself. Eventually, she threw Lynn out. Both the police and the housing authorities say their hands are tied because the woman's name is on the lease. "I have tried to get her name off the lease, but there is nothing I can do. I wish I were in my backyard enjoying my flowers and my dog."

Now Lynn is living in a shelter. Her sons visit; one is a chef, the other is training to become a chef. She has a grandson whose future looks bright. Nonetheless, she can't help but be disappointed with the way things have worked out for her. "I thought I had it made. Now what? I'm back to square one. When you get to my age, you have to wonder how many more times you can do this."

❖ ❖ ❖

Candy

In her youth, Candy was truly a wild woman, always ready to drink, do drugs, and pick a fight. Poor health and the joys of consumerism have gradually steered her toward a very different, addiction-free life.

Candy wants to meet in a mall because these days she likes to shop. Every pay day she buys something or plays a little bingo or the slots. She rents a house with a guy who is just a room-mate, nothing more or less. Now that she has a Grade 12 diploma, a home, a job, and a dog, she feels her life is complete.

Candy was born in Sudbury, Ontario. Her father was killed in a mine accident and, at six months, she went to live with an aunt and uncle, although there was never any legal adoption. Her mother was an alcoholic with eight other children. Candy still saw her and always knew about the arrangement. From the beginning she was very much a tomboy, and her mother used to say, "You should have been one of the boys."

At 14 Candy returned to Sudbury because the aunt and uncle were too restrictive for a headstrong teenager: "You can't do this, you can't do that, you are too young." They may have had some cause for concern because by 16 she was already keeping bad company and was sentenced to an adult jail for committing armed robbery with violence: "I didn't do it, but I was there."

Candy's late teens were spent in Toronto and New Brunswick experimenting with drugs such as speed, now known as crystal meth, and cocaine. She took off for Calgary where a couple of her siblings lived, including her oldest sister who had also been given up for adoption. Candy left them and lived with a man for three months, but as he was abusive she left him too. "There have been quite a few guys I've tied up with and I've wondered why after."

She moved in and out of a Calgary shelter, sometimes living in apartments, sometimes not. Wherever she was, she was always pugnacious and ready to beat people up—both men and women. She and her friend Cathy set guys up, then ditched them.

Once a friend came down from the northern Alberta oilrigs with a wad of cash. He crashed where she was staying. While he was asleep, another girl tried to rob him. Candy "beat the living piss out of her" and threw her onto the porch where a passerby wanted to know what was happening. Candy explained, and so he beat the woman to a further pulp. "Of course, I was off to jail again. I didn't give a shit, if someone gave me a dirty look, I'd beat the piss out of them."

Another time Candy noticed a guy with a pocketful of cash in a seedy hotel; she took him upstairs where she relieved him of $300 before he could even unzip his jeans. Then he passed out. "Now, I'm happy. The party's on." She drank a 26-oz bottle of vodka and took a whole bottle of "breathing (asthma) pills.... I was so sick and so scared. All I was doing was throwing up for three days. I was in pretty rough shape ... I'll never do that again."

A sympathetic shelter staff member got her into a program for abused women, but she tired of it and took off. Realizing she had let her mentor down, she couldn't figure out what to tell him, so handled it the only way she knew: she went on a bender and "drank and drank and drank." Barred from the homeless shelter for violent behaviour, she stormed into the executive director's office to plead her case, addressing him by his first name,

Roy. "This guy was bugging me," she said to justify why she had thrown a rock at another client. "Come on, Roy, you know I don't take shit from clowns, so I got back at him. Come on, Roy, you know how hard it is for women out here."

Candy left Calgary for Ontario, but only got as far as Winnipeg. She progressed from a mat at the Salvation Army to a rooming house where she descended deeply into alcohol again. She returned to Calgary and was picked up for impaired driving, among other things, while behind the wheel of a vehicle that belonged to one of her "little flings." Eventually, she responded to a girlfriend's repeated phone calls to go back to Winnipeg where she drank and used cocaine. "It was fun, but when it was over, it was over." She financed her habit by shoplifting. "I made Eaton's go broke; it's why they tore it down. I stole meat and had it sold right away four times a day. Then I was stone cold sober and took $27 worth of goods and got caught."

Slowly, Candy started to straighten out. While on pills, she fell and smashed her head—this gave her pause for thought. She was living with a man she liked and began trying to upgrade toward her Grade 12. However, after passing Grade 10, she lost her confidence and quit. She tried hairdressing, but that wasn't her thing. Neither was accounting.

Candy bought a car with a student loan, but because she doesn't have a licence a friend drove her to Ontario where she tried school again and hooked up with her family. It was the first time she had seen her mother in 13 years; her nieces and nephews were beginning to have babies of their own. Family life wasn't to her taste, so she returned to Winnipeg where she discovered an ability to fix computers, although it's not something she wants to do for a career.

She found a job that lasted for 18 months. "Now I was on the right track; money started rolling in." She quit and, because she couldn't get Employment Insurance, she obtained work in an automotive parts factory. After a booze- and cocaine-saturated weekend, she passed out on the lunchroom floor on a Monday morning. No more job.

Candy, who was bunking down at a girlfriend's house, used the time away from work to get some much needed surgery done to injuries on her left shoulder and right hand, the result of a car accident. Another friend jokingly said, "Why don't you move in here and be a nanny to my two boys?" Candy took her up on the offer and moved in. The friend lived in a Manitoba Housing complex that gave residents a chance to upgrade their education. Candy and a neighbour made a pact to go to class together. When she was tempted to give up, the neighbour hauled her through. "She stuck by me lots," said Candy, who gained seven credits in nine months.

Still living with her girlfriend, she found another job at a plastics factory making water jugs. She met a former co-worker from the auto parts factory who told her that their boss had said he would hire her back in an instant. She was back at work there within a couple of days. Realizing that she didn't "have a bedroom, never mind a life," she found her own place with another co-worker. Between them, they make $2,000 a month. Rent for their house in a rundown area is $550 including utilities. They split it and all other costs evenly. By the end of 2003, Candy had attained her dream: she graduated from Grade 12; she owned her own computer and was on the Internet. She's just about given up on men, saying, "I don't want no man in my bedroom … I don't have time for that. I do my thing." Candy has hepatitis C and damage from injecting drugs like Talwin and Ritalin when she was young. "What can I do? I did the drugs. I'm not going to die for lots of years yet. How can I die when I ain't laying down?"

◇ ◇ ◇

Lilian

Lilian's addictions blossomed in the face of a bad marriage and the death of her son. They went from bad to worse until May 2000 when she found salvation and sobriety. There are three things that are hard to avoid about Lilian: her sense of humour, her devotion to Jesus, and her former life of alcoholism.

Lilian grew up in a Northern Ontario lumber town, the middle one of seven sisters. Her father, the supervisor in a pulp mill, was responsible and caring. Her mother was another story, always bitching and hitting the girls. She thought nothing of beating her sassy daughter with a belt buckle so that she had to be taken to the vet for stitches.

When Lilian was 12 she made up two signs saying: "Please help us find our real mother. This one beats us." She and baby sister Ruby carried them around for all the neighbours to see until their father spotted them. "What are you doing?" he asked. "Protesting," came the reply.

"Protesting?"

"You know when the mill went on strike and you were nervous to go to work, this is the same thing."

Another time, when her father stopped her mother from chasing her with an axe, Lilian yelled, "That woman's chopping me up." He retorted, "Look I'm tired, I've had a hard day at work, I don't have time for this." "I haven't got time to die," retorted Lilian, who frequently refused to acknowledge her mother, saying, "She's someone you married, she's not my mother." It wasn't until after her parents died that the girls discovered what kind of a childhood their mother had had "and then all the hate and resentment lifted."

Lilian remembers other episodes when she misbehaved, like the time she cut up one of her sister's clothes. Every week her father threatened so seriously to send her to reform school that she usually had her bag packed ready to leave. Instead, they frequently ended up at the United Church where she was supposed to confess to the minister. "The reverend would be waiting for me right in the church and I would think 'There's that cross staring at me. Now I can't weasel.'" The minister was outraged by her behaviour, so Lilian pointed out to him that his position didn't stop him from smoking. When he told her that she didn't have to pick up his bad habits, she replied, "I'm a kid, it's my job."

Lilian was acquiring bad habits quite effectively without a minister to lead the way. By the time she was in her mid teens she was running with a group of bored youths who hung around the movie house on weekends. When the adults went into the show, the kids "borrowed" their cars and took off into the bush where they purchased moonshine. Even though they were drunk, they always returned the cars before the end of the film.

Lilian whipped through school fast, skipping grades as she went, finishing Grade 13 when she was only 14. She married her husband at 18 for something to do. They moved to Toronto where she became a nurse and gave birth to two children.

All hell broke loose, Lilian says, when her son died of "toxic poisoning" a few months before his first birthday. She drank like a "liquor pig" until, in the middle of a breakdown, she turned to Satanism. "You can see the Devil, whereas God's goodness—He doesn't want us to flaunt it." She was often admitted to psychiatric wards, and when she was healthy and making money, her husband was spending it on such things as flying lessons. "The first hospital it was pills, pills, pills. I was like a zombie. I was in and out, back and forth all over the map." At one point she says she participated in drug experiments with sodium pentathol, sometimes referred to as the truth serum, at the Clarke Institute. The doctor was "all shook up" when he heard her story. He told her that she had to get out of her marriage because another breakdown would leave her in a vegetative state.

In the early 1970s Lilian came out of hospital to discover the locks had been changed and the house empty. Her husband had left taking their daughter with him. Lilian still doesn't know where they are, although a few years later divorce papers came from The Pas, Manitoba. She raged at God and made a deal with Him: "You stay out of my life and I will stay out of yours and we will all be happy." Although she says she was still practising Satanism, it's clear that she had placed her faith in alcohol to deaden the pain. "I didn't drink where there was peace or serenity, I drank where the action was."

She began her days early, drinking four bottles of beer before 7 a.m. when she would go to a local hotel where liquor was served in coffee cups to deceive the police. She would drink another four bottles of beer at home and go to the liquor store when it opened at 9 a.m. to buy another case of beer "just in case." After that she made the rounds of various bars and hotels, looking for action.

Through all these years, Lilian somehow has managed to pay her rent and has never had a hangover or the shakes. "I was never sober long enough to get them." She was, however, in and out of hospital. Often she would put herself in, calling the police, saying: "My head doesn't feel right." She remembers being held in straitjackets and being tied to chairs and to her bed. Her official diagnosis, she says, includes bi-polar disorder, schizophrenia, and epilepsy. Once when she escaped, the police found her at home with a 40-ounce bottle of liquor. She invited them to help her finish it. When it was empty, one of the officers put out his hand to escort her to the cruiser. She went crazy, ripping his sleeve off and leaving him bruised and bitten.

At 2:45 a.m., 2 May 2000, God smote Lilian with sobriety.

She was at a bar when a knife fight erupted. She dashed home to get $200 stashed in her fridge to lay a bet on the outcome. She never made it back to that bar, nor indeed to any bar. Right in front of her fridge, God placed His hands on her. At first His touch was light but firm, then it began to feel like a heart attack or a stroke. "His wrath," she says wide-eyed. "I never want to go through it again if I live to be 100 ... the power and the love and the disappointment and peace all in one shot."

Lilian, who has been totally sober since that moment, says she simultaneously received redemption, anointing, forgiveness, and blessing. She tries to centre her life around God, although she confesses that she's only at the teenage stage of her spiritual journey. She speaks of Jesus in much the same way that young women speak of their first boyfriend, wanting to please Him and worrying about being abandoned. "I don't want to lose my faith. I can't afford to lose my dependency and my faith."

Sources

Alberta Alcohol and Drug Abuse Commission. 2004. *Windows of Opportunity: A Statistical Profile of Substance Abuse among Women in their Childbearing Years in Alberta.* <http://corp.aadac.com>.

Becker, Jane, and Clare Duffy. 2002. *Women Drug Users and Drugs Service Provision: Service Level Responses to Engagement and Retention.* London: British Home Office Drugs Strategy Directorate. <http://www.homeoffice.gov.uk>.

Breaking the Cycle. 2002. *Report.* Toronto. <http://www.breakingthecycle.ca>.

Currie, Janet C. 2001. *Best Practices, Treatment, and Rehabilitation for Women with Substance Abuse Problems.* Ottawa: Canada's Drug Strategy Division, Health Canada.

Flavin, Jeanne. 2002. "A Glass Half Full? Harm Reduction Among Pregnant Women Who Use Cocaine." *Journal of Drug Issues.*

Nelson-Zlupko, Lani, Eda Kauffman, and Martha Morrison Dore. 1995. "Gender Differences in Drug Addiction and Treatment: Implications for Social Work Intervention with Substance-Abusing Women." *Social Work* 40,1.

Interviews

Bradley, Nancy. Executive Director, Jean Tweed Centre, Toronto. 2004.

Cowan, Cindy. Executive Director, Nellie's, Toronto. 2004.

Neal, Lainie. Executive Director, Main Street Project, Winnipeg. 2004.

Rothenburger, Jan. Outreach Pastor, Yonge Street Mission, Toronto. 2004.

Stringer, Kathy. Coordinator of Women's and Children's Programs, St. James Community Services Society, Vancouver. 2004.

CHAPTER 5

THE HIDDEN DISABILITY

Oh, wow, it's brain damage and it's not going to get better.
—Edmonton drop-in worker on seeing
pictures of a brain affected by FASD

Fetal Alcohol Spectrum Disorder (FASD) is not a diagnosis, but an umbrella term for a collection of disorders, all of them caused by exposure to ethanol in the womb. Confusingly, the best known of these disorders is Fetal Alcohol Syndrome (FAS). A diagnosis of FAS requires brain dysfunction, growth retardation, distinctive facial features, and confirmation of the mother drinking during pregnancy. Other conditions under the FASD catch-all include Partial Fetal Alcohol Syndrome (pFAS), Alcohol Related Neurodevelopmental Disorder (ARND), and Alcohol Related Birth Defects (ARBD).

First described in 1973, FASD is the most common, non-hereditary cause of developmental delays. It is, in theory, 100 per cent preventable, but because it's impossible and undesirable to force expectant mothers not to drink, it's a bit like hoping for heaven on earth. There is no magic bullet; there is no cure; it lasts a lifetime. Experts estimate that the prevalence of FAS in North America is from 0.5-4.8 per 1,000 live births, but no one knows for sure. Rates of other alcohol-related effects are estimated to be even higher. Women who have low levels of literacy, live in poverty, or belong to minority groups are over-represented among those who have given birth to children with FASD. However, it should also be pointed out that these groups have been studied more extensively than mainstream white women and that FASD respects no social class or ethnic origin. Some people shy away from using the initials FASD, because they don't want to attach yet another label to people who are already stigmatized, especially Aboriginal peoples, although the condition cuts across all racial groups and economic strata. One worker remarked that in her experience, white children with FASD tend to be labelled as having Attention Deficit Hyperactive Disorder, but "I never met an Aboriginal child with ADHD." However, she said the term is useful in that it gives workers a starting point from which to help their clients (Bennett interview 2004).

FASD does not affect two people the same way. Its effects can range from almost imperceptible to extremely severe, depending on how much and when the mother used alcohol during pregnancy. Smoking, other substance use, a poor diet, and genetic factors can exacerbate the situation. People diagnosed with FAS have distinctive facial characteristics: flat faces with thin upper lips; wide-set eyes; and a flattened vertical groove from nose to lip. However, most individuals affected by other fetal alcohol spectrum disorders do not have these features; therefore, even though they have a disability, they appear normal to the general public, compounding their problems.

Low pre-natal and post-natal birth weight is often associated with FASD, but the biggest damage is done to the central nervous system. This can manifest itself as poor fine- and gross-motor skills; impaired memory, communication, and decision-making skills; imperfect concepts of time and place; and poor impulse control. About 25 per cent of people with FASD cannot use public transportation, almost 50 per cent are unable to cook meals, and about 80 per cent are unable to manage money and live independently. All this is a dry way of saying that these people can have tremendous difficulties coping with life. Remembering appointments, budgeting, and figuring out cause and effect are all a struggle and are skills they can never learn.

In a society that values punctuality, learning by experience, self-motivation, and making good choices, people with FASD are often victimized and told they are irresponsible. In all likelihood, they are the welfare clients who blew the rent to buy their children extravagant Christmas toys, thus upsetting all the do-gooders in their lives.

Behaviours linked to FASD can lead to a multitude of consequences including failure at school; stress in the family; difficulties holding down a job; difficulties with everyday living—banking, personal hygiene, choosing friends, etc.; difficulties finding and keeping housing; legal problems; and high risk of sexual, emotional, and financial exploitation. Repeated failures can lead to the loss of hope, self-esteem, friends, and family support. As a result of growing up in a hostile world, with no diagnosis, multiple early placements, and witnessing or experiencing sexual and physical abuse, many develop secondary disabilities such as mental health and substance abuse problems. They may enter the revolving door of the criminal justice system because they don't understand the consequences of their actions and find it hard to remember appointments with probation officers and social workers. "All that stuff about making choices just doesn't apply" (Bennett interview 2004).

A predictable, consistent, and calm environment is important for people with FASD, but they may not understand how to find housing or manage credit. Instead, they will often look for a place to stay in abandoned buildings or become long-term shelter clients. The noisy atmosphere of shelters, however, is likely to be more disorienting for them than the average person, and living rough is even worse. If they do find accommodation, keeping it is another issue. They may spend the rent or forget when it's due. Safe, stable housing is essential for their well-being; a mere roof isn't enough. On-site, around-the-clock support is required for such things as parenting, money management, cooking, medication, and housekeeping. A zero-tolerance policy, particularly for substance abuse, doesn't work for people with FASD; guidelines should be individualized, say Dinning *et al.* (2004). If this seems expensive, it's important to remember that it costs $60-$85 a day for someone in a shelter with most supports, and $90-$250 a day to keep someone in prison or a detention centre; apartments with on-site support and collective meal options come to $67 to $88 a day (Ottawa 2005).

Women with severe FASD are probably one of the most socially downtrodden groups. They are at higher risk of suffering abuse and violence from an early age and of becoming sexually exploited, which leads to self-medicating in order to survive. Working as prostitutes, they are exposed to everything from tuberculosis and AIDS to murder. When they disappear, as they have done by the score in Vancouver, Edmonton, and other cities, the rest of us fail to notice. There are very few facilities to help them. When they are inevitably picked up by the police, no one in the legal system checks whether FASD is a factor or not. Few detox and rehabilitation facilities cater to their special needs. Many of them have children but never understand why their beloved babies are apprehended; in their grief they continue to conceive babies, many of whom will also be affected by FASD.

It has been estimated that every child born with FASD will cost Canadians at least $2–$3 million over a lifetime, as well as uncounted dollars in lost potential and further uncounted dollars in pain and grief. Toronto's Breaking The Cycle (BTC) is one of the few early identification and prevention programs for pregnant and high-risk mothers in Canada. A collaboration of six partner agencies and other non-partners, BTC offers "one-stop shopping" with addictions, parenting, health, and child-development programs under one roof in an easily accessible area of the downtown core. Besides being responsive to individuals, BTC is family-centred, recognizing that women stay in treatment programs longer when their children are with them, and it addresses a multiplicity of problems—unemployment, homelessness, health, sexual and physical violence, and depression. A harm-reduction approach is taken, recognizing abstinence as the ideal outcome but accepting alternatives that reduce the damage. This approach moves away from stigma and toward developing a woman's strengths and fostering her commitment to change. In the almost 10 years that it has been open, BTC has witnessed improved child health and functioning, improved parenting skills, and substantial gains in the children's well-being. All this, of course, saves not only maternal heartbreak, but also taxpayer dollars.

In the meanwhile, what's being done for people with FASD? The answer is not much, unless prison, homeless shelters, and soup kitchens can be considered a humane response to the problem. It is unfortunate that there are few, if any, government-funded mentoring programs across Canada to assist these brain-injured people so that they have a chance at what we all want—to live safe happy lives in our own communities.

❖ ❖ ❖

Jennifer

Jennifer suffered brain damage from Fetal Alcohol Spectrum Disorder and has an IQ of less than 70. I met her with a group of caseworkers who were helping her celebrate her birthday by taking her out to a steak restaurant for dinner. My last glimpse of her was her smile of joy as she left the party to return to the streets.

The caseworker stands in the small front yard, tossing pennies at the second floor window and calling, "Jennifer, honey. Jennifer." A teenage couple joins her at the door of the dilapidated rooming house; the only new thing about it is a strong shiny lock on the front door. Eventually, someone lets the group in, and the caseworker walks past the stainless steel sink in the hall, where residents do their dishes, up the stairs and stands outside the fragile closet door that is the entrance to Jennifer's room.

The door, which is splintered from several forced entries, is slightly ajar on a flimsy chain that wouldn't provide much resistance to someone intent on breaking in. Across the hall is the communal bathroom and the none too clean toilet, dirty tissues spilling out of the garbage can. The facilities serve the rooms of four men, one with severe mental health problems, and Jennifer.

"Jennifer, honey, it's your birthday. Wake up."

For the time being, no human noise is heard except a television blaring forth. There is no movement, either. Jennifer is fast asleep and has been all day since she called her caseworker in the morning. She's somewhat deaf and has lost her hearing aid, so it is difficult to rouse her.

There is a slight movement. "It's me," says the caseworker, and, after a few more words, the heap of covers moves. Jennifer gets up, lets the other woman in and subsides back onto the mattress that fills an alcove to the left of the door. The rest of the tiny room is taken up with the TV set, a few boxes that act as shelves, a small hot plate, and a cushion. The room is so small, there is hardly anywhere to stand. The rent is $265 a month.

Still lying in bed, Jennifer lights up a cigarette and takes a few drags while her caseworker talks soothingly about the celebration steak dinner planned for that evening. "Are you still clean, honey?" she asks. The deal is that Jennifer gets to go out if she hasn't done crack that day. It appears she's clean. Jennifer says she was on the track a few nights ago when three women jumped from a car and beat her up. She's happy, though, that she gave a few good punches back. Her forehead has a long scar from a previous encounter and her left hand has another where it was slashed to the tendon.

Jennifer has FASD and an IQ of 68. Her mother also shows signs of FASD, as do her siblings to varying degrees—one of her brothers is in jail for murder and molesting a child. Because her mother was an alcoholic, Jennifer and her sister were adopted by a family on a reserve in another province when she was four. She has one word for those people: "Bitches." However, to an outsider, it is obvious that everyone involved is suffering from the deeply wrenching effects of government policies and residential schools where their Aboriginal culture was replaced by one of abuse.

The two girls became virtual slaves and, at a very young age, Jennifer was molested by the grandfather. Before she was a teenager, she had lost her virginity to an uncle. Early on, she equated sex with obtaining things she wanted. When she was 11, her male relatives paid in candy. Now that she's older, the johns pay in cash for her drugs.

When she was four, the adoptive family tied her up in a garbage bag and left her in the outhouse in a cold snap of -30°C. Jennifer complained about the beatings, but no one believed her; after all, members of the adoptive family were Child and Family Service (CFS) workers. Over the years, they explained away the bruises by saying that Jennifer had fallen off her bike. By the time she was 11, she had attempted suicide 21 times; finally, someone put all the signs together. She was taken to Winnipeg and placed in care. She embarked on a journey through several institutions, including one for troubled teens at which she was befriended by another young woman from a similar background who showed her how crack cocaine could temporarily erase the bad memories and how prostitution could provide cash for the habit. One of Jennifer's few allies, this friend soon committed suicide.

Jennifer became so troublesome that CFS called her birth mother and said, "Come and pick up your daughter and see if you can straighten her out." Jennifer was asleep when the mother she barely knew arrived to take her away. Needless to say, it wasn't long before she was back in Winnipeg and in "care" again. However, when she turned 18, CFS cut her off and, without warning or preparation, quit paying her rent. Jennifer discovered what they had done a few weeks later when the landlord changed the locks, so she couldn't get into her apartment. He kept everything, including her coat, vital for survival in Winnipeg, to compensate for the rent her worker hadn't paid. "I used to get myself into trouble so I could get a warm place for the night," Jennifer says. So she would go out to the track and ensure the police caught her. Her only choice was a night in jail or sleeping with a man called Stan who kept a gun under his bed, which made her very nervous.

Jennifer came to the FASD caseworker's attention when she was beaten up by a bad date and left hanging out of a broken window. The police couldn't induce her to go to hospital, so they called in the caseworker and a lasting bond was formed, even though Jennifer was concerned she would be rejected because she has hepatitis C. Rejection is the norm in her life. FASD makes it hard for her to recall even the simplest things and to grasp abstract concepts; therefore, almost anything she attempts is doomed to failure. The one thing that she has been able to retain is the understanding that if you don't maintain the standards set in treatment programs, you are out on your ear. With her shaky memory and low IQ, she is unable to meet those standards.

At first, she expected the FASD worker and her colleagues to give her the boot too, but over a couple of years they have helped her understand that they will stay by her whatever happens; that if she does crack, it's not good, but it's not the end of the relationship. They try to steer her toward healthier choices, and in the last few months Jennifer has been smoking pot in her search for a pain-free present. She is supplied by one of her johns who dreams of removing her from the street. The three caseworkers who have turned up for her birthday talk among themselves about how to keep her exercising at a local gym. It was they who found the lodging house where she lives, which, while not ideal, is close to the track, so it decreases her chances of being attacked to and from work.

Jennifer has been exposed to TB and needs a daily pill for eight months to ensure she doesn't develop a full-blown case. The caseworkers briefly discuss with her the best time of day to administer her medication regularly, given her erratic lifestyle. She has recently recovered from a case of gonorrhea, and the hepatitis C that has made her a pariah in her birth family because they don't understand how it is transmitted.

Today she's an excited kid. She wants a steak sandwich so badly that she is grumblingly willing to forgo the usual Tim Horton's coffee. At the restaurant she's thrilled to find that there are small gifts: a fluffy toy poodle, Winnie the Pooh water glasses, and a pink ball cap—nothing she can sell for drug money. "I stayed sober all day to get high after my party," she says proudly. In Jennifer's world, a drug-free day is a real achievement.

Gwendolin

Born to a mother who drank heavily, Gwendolin does not have an official diagnosis of FASD but often exhibits the behaviours associated with the condition. Like many other women who have suffered abuse, she also has an eating disorder.

She speaks in a flat voice devoid of emotion.

"I never had a childhood. I had to grow up fast, but to be totally honest, I'm not fully grown up. I still have immature points about me. That's what my counsellor is trying to help me with."

To say Gwendolin's childhood wasn't the greatest, as she does, is an understatement, perhaps employed to keep herself at arm's length from her own volcanic emotions. She, her sister, and half-sister were taken from their alcoholic mother at an early age because they were suffering from malnutrition. Gwendolin went from foster home to foster home being sexually abused on the way but not daring to tell anyone. She was returned to her mother when she was 11, only to be given to her mother's boyfriends for sex in return for cash to finance her mother's drug and alcohol habits. She still hasn't been able to talk to her mother about any of the abuse. What tatters of trust she had left were blown apart by a psychiatrist who, she says, sexually abused her while she was under hypnosis.

Gwendolin took off with a young man when she was 15 and immediately became pregnant although she was on the Pill. She survived by panhandling, earning $20-$30 a day and living in shelters. She stayed with her mother for a few weeks before and after the birth until she caught her mother drunk, holding the baby by his ankles, his head almost hitting the floor.

Still with the same man, she very quickly became pregnant again. "With their father it was off and on. I'm not sure if Patrick is the father of the oldest, but he is the father of my daughter. How I know is that she's exactly like him." Gwendolin claims that she always starved herself to feed the children and make sure they had clean clothes. Once, she took her son to Wasaga Beach for a few days, leaving her daughter with someone she thought was responsible. A cousin phoned social services saying that Gwendolin used plastic bags for diapers and that the older child pooped on the floor. She arrived back in Toronto to find one child gone and the authorities waiting for the other one. With no children, she lost her low-rental housing and everything else she had for them, including their cribs.

If Gwendolin could turn the clock back, she would wait until she was older to have children, but at the time she and her sisters were locked in competition to produce the first grandchild. In part she blames her mother for not raising her right and then for not helping her out, as she helped the other sisters. As the middle child, Gwendolin has always felt neglected.

After the children were gone, Gwendolin sought solace with men. First, she married one who liked to spank. Gwendolin didn't mind obliging him, but when he wanted to spank her, she called social services. This call sealed the fate of her children, she feels, because they were subsequently put up for adoption.

The first marriage lasted a year. Her second husband became violent when intoxicated, throwing coffee tables at her and, once, stabbing her in the neck. She quickly parted company with him, although she has never had a formal divorce. Her next relationship was with a young man she had known as a teenager. Leaving him, she moved to a smaller community outside Toronto where she started to get counselling to deal with her childhood sexual abuse. The man she took up with there couldn't handle the fact she was starting to change and said she was "nuts" to even think that she had been violated. His verbal abuse became so bad, she escaped to a women's shelter.

At the shelter's suggestion, she moved in with a friend on a nearby farm. Very hesitantly, she let herself be wooed by the friend's daughter, 15 years her junior. For a while, it went well. "I don't have a lot of friends who love and respect me for who I am and not for what they want. Every single frigging man has treated me like crap. The only good relationship was with Anne. Then that went sour, because of people sticking their noses in."

Gwendolin returned to Toronto where she lived with her mother until she had a scrap with one of her uncles. She left for a women's shelter, until her stepfather helped her find an apartment. Almost inevitably, she has picked up with another man. "The relationship is okay." However, her new man expects her welfare cheque to feed him too. "When he gets money, it's a different story." On top of this, he is bothered by the thought of Anne with whom Gwendolin is still in touch. "He is really jealous of her." Gwendolin knows it was probably too early to embark on another relationship, but despite everything she is still searching for love. "One day my knight in shining armour will come," she says.

In fact, he may have turned up already. About 18 years ago, Gwendolin met a man at a youth drop-in. He has since become the executive director of an evangelical street mission in Toronto. Recently, he acted as her godfather when she was baptized, giving her the money for a cross to wear around her neck. "Rick has been there for me ... as a father figure and a support. He has an open door." She knows that Rick will support her and show her it's possible to have a non-sexual friendship with a man, but in the meantime she has a lot of work to do. "I want to help myself. I want to make sure I'm healed enough to see my kids." She has hopes that as they come of age, they will come looking for her. Her son has said he's not interested, but she wonders how true this is.

After several false starts Gwendolin kicked her main addiction—alcohol—thanks to AA. Now she is trying to do something about her severe anorexia. "I don't like to eat, I'm afraid of getting fat." She knows this disease is linked to sexual abuse and to the fact her mother is overweight. She has made a decision to try to gain weight in the next six months, defying the malnutrition of a lifetime.

"Being abused as a child, I have missed a whole life and don't know who I am and if this person is going to treat me right. This is the way I have been. I don't trust a lot of people. I try and trust and eventually they turn on me." Lacking in energy, thanks to her near starvation diet, all this talking has exhausted Gwendolin. Her mother is waiting. They both like the idea of building a good relationship, they both want to love and be loved, but history intervenes.

Carmen

Carmen knows her mother drank her way through pregnancy. She has never been diagnosed with FAS or any of the related disorders, but she feels strongly that FASD has affected the way she handles situations and her addictions.

Carmen, 38, comes to the interview dressed all in black—a mini dress with a crocheted jacket over it, high heels that boost her tall frame even higher, and lots of dangling jewellery, including long earrings that swing with every toss of her long black hair. She apologizes in advance for any dashes to the bathroom—she's coming off an addiction.

In one of Carmen's earliest memories she is standing in her crib, holding her bottle and watching her mother slash her wrists all the way to the elbows. This sets the tone for the rest of her life. Her parents were part of the hidden homeless problem, drifting from family member to family member in the Prince Albert area of Saskatchewan. It was a large family, so they could keep going, staying with each relative until they were kicked out. "I still have no idea of what normal is." Children's Services put her into foster homes. "Were they normal? What's normal? We ate, we slept, we got baths daily, we were given attention and were allowed to play and had things to play with. I remember two foster homes treated us very well."

Her parents pulled their lives together enough to satisfy social workers and their children were returned to them, but appearances can be deceptive. The family was riddled with abuse and incest; at three Carmen was raped by a 14-year-old relative and then sexually abused by many different people, including female babysitters. The sins of the church sisters were being visited upon succeeding generations—both Carmen's grandmother and mother had been assaulted in residential school. Social workers thought Carmen had a speech impediment. In fact, she was speaking Cree and her mouth was full of sores because her parents punished her by washing out her mouth with "soap, mustard, and anything vile."

At seven she was sent to the US for adoption: "from the pot and into the fire." The white Pennsylvanian family who took her had its own kind of abuse. The mother beat Carmen for wetting her bed (a result of all the sexual abuse) and was so obsessed about it that she would sniff the sheets every morning. The father sexually abused her. By 12 she was escaping physically by running away and chemically by using beer and pot. "I was very angry, rebellious. I had lots of rage and pain. It still bothers me. Finally, I got smart and phoned children's services and told them what was going on. They didn't listen at first."

When she was 13, she ran away again and was picked up by a police officer whose last name was Ruby. "I'll commit suicide if you take me back," Carmen said. So he took her to hospital where she was evaluated by a psychiatrist. "Thank God, he could see the signs that I needed to be out (of that family)." She was put in a rescue mission run by another controlling personality who didn't have a clue how to handle an angry teenager. From there she moved through three foster homes. The final one was another battlefield. Carmen took to running away again and getting into trouble with her girlfriend.

One day when they were on the loose, they were playing in a farmer's field. He arrived in his car, shooed them away, drove off, and then returned. Carmen and her friend hid in the long grass of the field. The farmer drove back and forth looking for them, finally stopping when he drove over Carmen. "Nobody believes me, but I had an out-of-body experience. I came to know there is a God and that there is a heaven when we leave here." She almost did leave this world. It took four months for the hospital to fix her up. The farmer was never charged, but Carmen, even though a teenager, decided to sue. It took a year to settle, and after she paid her lawyer and the hospital, she was left with $135,000 in trust until she was 18, and lasting scars both mental and physical. "Before, I was absolutely gorgeous. After, I had scars on my left thigh and stomach. It was quite an adjustment. Because of the scars, I wouldn't wear shorts and only long sleeves because of the scar on my arms."

Carmen revolved through another 22 foster homes, seeing how far she could push before she was kicked out. When she turned 18 she got her money. She wanted to use it to enter a fashion design school in Pittsburgh. She had been accepted there but she messed up. "So many opportunities," she sighs. Someone introduced her to cocaine, and she blew all the money on three cars and drugs. When it was gone, she had neither street nor worldly smarts. She had never learned how to keep a job nor to shoulder responsibility and became homeless, supporting herself and her hard-core alcohol habit by prostitution. "The only time I was sober was when I was in jail."

Carmen has tried many, many rehabilitation programs, usually with a Christian basis. She lasted four months in something called New Life for Girls: "I tried with all my heart, but my anger and resentment came up. I got into a bad verbal argument with the teacher and was kicked out. Then I started drinking again."

A friend introduced Carmen to Gary, and, unusually, they talked first and jumped into bed later, ending up together off and on for 12 years. "So I became a homemaker and domesticated." For much of that time she was off cocaine, and she was always clean when she was pregnant. "My addictions then were shopping and bingo!" Carmen's first baby died soon after birth, but she became pregnant again very quickly, and this one, "a tough little girl," survived. Gary was in and out of the door sleeping with other women, but he came back for the births of both their surviving children.

One by one, Carmen's friends were taken over by crack. Finally, she tried a hoot, and that was it. She and Gary cooked up a way of financing the habit by taking payroll cheques from where he worked, Carmen filled them out and he cashed them. Eventually, social services were alerted, and Carmen was given a choice: take the children to Gary's parents or hand them over to the authorities. She chose the former. "My children were my world. It took everything in me to pack up their stuff and make the eight-hour drive. I couldn't tell them why I was leaving. I had to sneak out on them."

To kill the pain of losing her children, she plunged further into crack and prostitution but avoided working for pimps. "I was always tough and stood up to them, or I would sneak around and avoid them." The law caught up with her. She was sentenced to 23 months for signing the cheques and given 15 years probation. She was also given a dual diagnosis of addiction and depression. When she came out of jail, she found that, because she wasn't a US citizen, she wasn't eligible for welfare. "They said I didn't exist," which was ironic because the government had been quite happy to acknowledge her at taxation time. Without welfare, she couldn't pay her legal fines and so was in violation of her parole. She was given a way out—ratting on her dealers—but she feared for her life. Finally, her parole officer said: "Go back to Canada, we won't chase you up there because it's not a violent crime."

Carmen, pregnant again, reluctantly returned to Prince Albert, which she found racist after living among supportive and friendly African-Americans in the US. After the baby was born, she moved to Edmonton to be closer to an aunt. Welfare helped her find an apartment, but she was having trouble being a mother and staying clean, and no one heard her pleas.

> I was crying out for help. I called the Kids' Cottage, my welfare worker, and the parent aide. I couldn't take it any-more and called child welfare and gave her up. It felt like a punishment. If someone had helped me while I battled the cravings ... I had no idea what programs were here. I didn't know anything. I was fighting it all by myself. It was emotional hell. To take your child away when you are go-ing through that was the icing on the cake of failure. It's pain you can't even mention, pain you can't put into words. I never had a good female role model.... I can try. I know what not to do. None of my kids was ever neglected, and they had lots of physical affection.... I've lost so much.

Carmen hasn't seen her youngest girl in two years and her other two children in seven.

It would be easy to leave Carmen on that bitter note, but that would not be a true picture of her. She talks about life on the streets of Edmonton and the johns who she hates, calling them disgusting, cheap, pathetic creatures who come from all walks of life. They have their uses, though, as a source of not easy, but fast money. One guy asked Carmen to fuck him for $20. "Okay, I'll fuck you," she said, hopping into his car. When they got to a secluded place, she asked for the cash up front. He gave it to her, and she leapt out of the car, saying, "Consider yourself fucked." She laughs at the temerity of those who think they can have paid sex and be her saviour—it is the ultimate example of placing all the blame, dirt, and responsibility for the sex act on the woman. "There's no way I would go with a man who tried to pay me."

Besides trying to come off alcohol and cocaine again, Carmen is also coping with numerous health issues, including joint problems, asthma, PTSD, depression, an infected breast lump, and high cholesterol. She is surprised she hasn't committed suicide, been murdered, or put away in a mental hospital. "People tell me I should be a cold-hearted killer, but God didn't give me that heart."

Sources

Alberta Drug and Alcohol Abuse Commission. 2004. *Estimating the Rate of FASD and FAS in Canada.* <http://corp.aadac.com>.

Breaking the Cycle. 2002. *A Chance for New Beginnings, 1995-2000.* Evaluation Report. Toronto. <http://www.breakingthecycle.ca>.

Canadian Centre on Substance Abuse. 2004. "Introduction to FASD Overview." <http://www.ccsa.ca>.

——. 2004. "Offenders Overview." <http://www.ccsa.ca>.

Dinning, L. Bonnie, Andrea Podruski, Diana Fox, and Anne Wright. 2004. *We Cares: Practical Skills for Front-Line Workers Working with Adults Affected by Fetal Alcohol Spectrum Disorder.* Ottawa. Anne Wright and Associates. <http://www.annewright.ca>.

Ottawa. 2005. *Community Action Plan to Prevent and End Homelessness 2002-2005.* <http://www.ottawa.ca/calendar/ottawa/citycouncil/hrssc/2002/11-21/ACS2002-PEO-HOU-0009%20homelesnessactionplan.htm>.

Thio-Watts, Marlene. "Motivating Pregnant Women to Address Substance Abuse." <http://www.ccsa.ca>.

Interviews

Bennett, Brenda. Program manager/clinical case manager, FASD Community Mobilization Project/FASD Life's Journey Program. Association for Community Living, Manitoba. 2004.

Leslie, Margaret. Director, Breaking the Cycle, Toronto. 2004.

CHAPTER 6

FOR THE GOOD OF THE CHILD

> If a parent had done this, they would have been charged
> with kidnapping, forcible confinement, abuse, etc.
> —Toronto woman talking about her
> experiences with the Children's Aid Society

At 24, the young woman in the Ottawa shelter is a seasoned veteran of the child welfare system, and now she has a baby in it too. "I was given up at birth and sent to a foster home. By the time I was 16 I had been in more than 18 foster homes, and I was raped in them all. In one they put restraints around my neck." She feels that foster parents should be checked more thoroughly and that more attention should be paid to what children in care are saying. "They don't believe you, because you are 11 and you don't know what to say." Another young woman says that the authorities come down much harder on homeless mothers than middle-class ones who can sit at home smoking crack without the risk that their children will be taken away. "They think homeless people are like a bug or something and (they) have to pick it off."

Social workers tend to see the picture very differently. Invoking the mantra "for the good of the child," they have, at least in theory, moved toward sustaining families rather than removing children from them, but those who have experienced first-hand the child welfare system anywhere in Canada say not enough is being done to help birth mothers keep their children. Canada's streets are full of women who were taken from their birth mothers and put into foster care or group homes, only to receive even worse treatment. While there are many loving, wise parent figures in the system, there are others who abuse their position of trust, and that is what the birth mothers fear so much.

The word foster means to tend affectionately or to promote growth, but for many girls warmth, encouragement, and cherishing were the last things they experienced while in care; instead, they recite a litany of torture and humiliations. Women who have been raised in the system often feel that they have been denied the love their birth mother would have provided, and so they look to their own children to give them that love. Despite their every good intention, however, they don't know how to be the wise mothers they so desperately want to be because they have rarely experienced proper parenting themselves. They have no role models and no first-hand knowledge of how to parent. In addition, if they are living on social assistance, all their energies are taken up with trying to stay afloat financially; they are often forced into making decisions that compromise their maternal instincts. One common solution is to water the baby's formula because there isn't enough money to pay the utilities and buy food. They fear that, if the utilities are cut off, the reconnection fee will be prohibitive and, consequently, the home will be declared unfit and the baby will be taken away.

Many mothers report that their pleas for help are ignored or that social workers demand too much of them, setting impossibly high standards and then coming and "snatching" the baby without warning or counselling to deal with the grief. This allegation is confirmed by shelter workers across the country who also say that standards are sometimes punitively high. Women who may be addicted to drugs, perhaps living in an unclean house without food in the fridge, love their children no less than a mother with a bank account. The grief of losing a child is accentuated for the former because, from their own experiences, they know that their children are often at risk in "care" and fear for their safety. Some are also smarting with the knowledge that the foster parents will receive considerably more financial help than they did.

Because they haven't been nurtured themselves, the mothers probably don't have the negotiation skills to make a good case to the authorities to get their child back. In some provinces, they may lose their social housing in a classic Catch-22 situation: without a two-bedroom unit, they won't be allowed to have the child again; without the child, they aren't eligible for the housing.

Thus, for women, child welfare poses a cycle of problems. As children, they are removed from a bad situation and put into others that are equally bad, if not worse. At 18, having careened through several homes and institutions, they are spat out into the world with few, if any, supports or means to make a living. When they become pregnant, they vow to be better than their mothers—to love and to protect their children as fiercely as they know how—but this fails to impress the social workers who take the children, precipitating another round of pain that can only be controlled by using illegal drugs. This vicious circle particularly affects Aboriginal peoples who are still shouldering the colonial consequences of being sent to brutal residential schools, which attempted to crush their culture and language, and of the baby scoops in the 1960s and 1970s when children were put into white care sometimes as far away as the US.

A pilot study, *The Child Welfare System and Homelessness Among Canadian Youth*, conducted under the auspices of the National Homelessness Initiative, points out that there is evidence that some youth who have been through the child welfare system become homeless and that the number is increasing.

> Several profiles of the urban homes have discovered that many homeless youth and adults have a history of involvement with child welfare, including having been "in care" and are over-represented among the homes. While this group is still a relatively small proportion of youth who have been through the child welfare system, this does suggest that some, very vulnerable youth, are not getting the kind of support they need. (Serge *et al.* 2002)

While they stress this is a preliminary study and that more research needs to be undertaken, Serge *et al.* cite a US study (Roman and Wolfe 1995), which concludes that foster care can be abusive or problematic, that children have problems when entering care that are not adequately addressed, that multiple placements affect a child's ability to develop relationships, and that youth need preparation for independent living. A Canadian study (Poirier *et al.* 1999) also cited by Serge *et al.* says that 75 per cent of the youth interviewed had negative views of their substitute care and that 41 per cent reported actual mistreatment.

Whether the abuse is suffered in the birth home or in foster care, the consequences can be significant and long lasting. A history of childhood sexual abuse in women increases the risk of depression, self-harm, substance abuse, and suicidal behaviour. In fact, the risk of repeated suicide attempts is eight times greater for youths with a sexual-abuse history, and women with such a history report that they are repulsed less by death and more by life. The link between trauma and self-harm or suicide is strongest when the abuse has been long term, the perpetrator was known to the woman, and it involved force or penetration.

It is estimated by Health Canada (2004) that less than one in 10 child abuse cases is reported to the authorities. Whether the abuse happens in the birth home or in a placement, this is far too high. It is doubly tragic that children who have been removed from a birth parent should continue to be harmed—emotionally, physically, and sexually —as well as neglected.

Nikki

As a young child, Nikki was terribly abused in foster care and then in an adoption. She speaks eloquently about losing a child to the system that created so much damage in her life. Although Nikki is an addict, there appear to have been missed opportunities when supportive intervention would have helped her achieve her dream of becoming a good as well as a loving mother.

I met Nikki the morning after she had spent a night working the streets of Vancouver's Downtown Eastside. She's yawning with fatigue but can't wait to tell her story. Dressed in sweats and with her long hair falling over her face, she puts her legs up on a chair in front of her and gets comfortable. She cries often and ends our session by singing two Aboriginal songs, one honouring strong women, the other for travellers. Although we arrange to meet again, she doesn't show up. I did see her, however, several hours before our appointment—she was on the streets, dressed in a short leather skirt, her lips stretched in a smile as she approached a man.

Nikki, an Aboriginal woman now in her early 30s, was born in Terrace, BC, and was shuffled around several foster homes in her early years, although for a period she lived with her mother. While her mom injected heroin, Nikki lay in her lap. Often she became bored and tried to rouse her mother to play. "My mom died in my arms when I was six—of a heroin overdose. One day, she fixed as she usually did, and I hit her face and put water on her forehead. Most times they worked [to revive her], and this one time they didn't. The ministry told me she had died. I told them. 'Yes, I know that and she went to heaven.'"

Nikki remembers her foster homes as bleak, cruel places. One didn't give her enough to eat or drink, so she would flush the toilet several times and then drink the water; she would also sneak food from the fridge. Another time Nikki was sent to her alcoholic uncle. He took her to a cabin where he poured gasoline over her arms and then lit a match. She screamed until he put her in the back of his van and drove to the nearest bar where he stopped for a drink to fortify himself. She remembered that her mother used to put Elastoplast on cuts, so she covered her burned arms with newspaper and cried herself to sleep. When she woke up, her arms hurt badly. She began to pound the sides of the van and to scream as loudly as she could. Finally, someone called the police, who pried her out with a crowbar. Nikki was taken to hospital where she had to have skin grafts.

A white family adopted Nikki when she was seven. That was when the horrors really began. All was fine on the surface, but behind closed doors it was a different story. In public, her new father called her "Little Princess"; in private, he started to explore her body. When she was eight-and-a-half, he compelled her to have oral sex, and a year later he was having full intercourse with her. A devout family, they dressed her in handmade velvet dresses trimmed with lace to take her to church. No one in the congregation guessed that the child had been sexually abused the night before or that while she sat on the man's lap during the sermon, he continued his exploration of her little body, feeling up her skirts.

At home, she could never do anything right and was constantly punished for her perceived crimes. The man would pull her pants down, lay her across his lap so she could feel his swelling penis, and spank her—sometimes with a belt. When he stopped beating her, he continued rebuking her loudly, so that his wife wouldn't suspect anything and, at the same time, forced Nikki to give him a blowjob. "Answer me, when I talk to you, you stupid Indian." Nikki, her mouth full, was unable to respond.

This treatment was in stark contrast to the way the couple treated their natural son, the obvious favourite who never had to endure the sexual abuse, the name-calling, or the physical torture. More than half her life later, Nikki bears the scars where the man stabbed her with a fork. "I think something bad had to have happened to him to make him do what he was doing. I feel bad that he found it that necessary to hurt someone else. My belief is that the Creator will deal with [this couple] when he comes back ... It's not my right to judge. That is not how I am."

Nikki became increasingly isolated not only because friendships were discouraged but because she was not allowed to watch television or listen to the radio. Consequently, she created her own world of imaginary friends and learned to blank out reality when it became too painful; this device was useful when she took up prostitution.

Because she was born with FASD, Nikki didn't do well at school; when she was about 14, she ran away. By this time the family was living in Lacombe, Alberta, so she went to the police in nearby Red Deer where she told them about her adoptive father. The police called him in for questioning. He promptly denied everything and Nikki was sent back to the family. "He gave me one more beating, one more good fuck, and gave me $100 and told me to get out of the house. I had already learned I could get what I wanted with sex." She hitchhiked to Vancouver where almost immediately she was picked up by the police and sent to a group home in Fort St. John, BC. She ran away with a boy who used to sneak into her room for sex. They went to a party where she had her first puff of marijuana. The boy hit Nikki and another boy, Elijah, stepped in to rescue her.

Elijah sneaked her back into his parents' house where the two teenagers managed to drink and smoke all day, financing their habits by shoplifting. Inevitably, Nikki became pregnant, and they moved into their own apartment. She named the baby Leonard after her grandfather. When she returned from hospital, she found Elijah in bed with his friend's sister. She put the sheets in the laundry and coped with the situation as best she knew how—by falling into a relationship of sorts with Elijah's cousin, Bill. It's telling that she isn't even sure whether sex with Bill was forced or not. "It was a rape-style kind of thing. Sometimes it felt like rape; the way my dad would do it." When Nikki threatened to tell Elijah, Bill countered that he would say she had seduced him and that she was enjoying herself. When Bill's friends gang-raped her, Bill poured beer over her so that she wouldn't smell of sex on Elijah's return. "It was another of those times I learned to keep secrets. My life's just a bunch of secrets and now I don't like secrets; I can't stand them."

Nikki has had five children, all of whom have been apprehended by the authorities. She feels that social workers use the details of her life in order to portray her as a bad mother. "Social workers publicize my bad stuff, but they shove my betrayal under the carpet." None of the things that have happened to Nikki have hurt as much as losing her babies and that, she says, is why she does crack cocaine—to mask the grief. To buy the crack she prostitutes herself, but after a brief respite the crack aggravates her already pervasive fears and loneliness. "It's normal for me to feel scared, fear, loneliness, desperate, and terrified. I'm scared of what's beyond the unknown and I'm scared of what could be ... all night long because that's what the drug does to you."

As Nikki talks about her lost children she becomes increasingly agitated, pointing out that the social workers who accuse her of bad parenting work for the system that raised her. "If you look in the files, you will see that you [the social work system] had me from two to 18, so don't tell me that you didn't raise me. Sixteen years you had control of me, so if you want to look at how I became non-satisfactory, neglectful, self-centred, who I am now.... I feel like they [the social work system] stole my life and didn't even give me a fighting chance. They stole what little I had left. The Creator gave me five beautiful babies, and they stole all of them too."

Nikki points out that her children's foster parents are given more money to look after them than she ever received on welfare. She was given $950 for herself and her youngest child, but now his foster parents could be getting up to $650 more. Is this fair? She also feels that while under the watchful eye of social workers, she has to reach standards of mothering that are much higher than mothers not on welfare.

> They just steal them [the babies] and don't give them back. It's like I give birth for them [the government], and they just steal them. When you lose a child to the ministry, it feels as though it's dead and gone. That's how you cry when the ministry comes in. It's like they are dead, so you do whatever you can do to make the pain go away. They swoop down like vultures and leave you there, by yourself in agony. It feels like someone has taken a knife and is jabbing you, and you can't breathe, and you feel as if you are going to die. You just want to die, so you find ways to do it. Ever since I was little, I felt like a number or a statistic. As I get older I know I'm a number, a statistic.

❖ ❖ ❖

Mama

Raped in both her own mother's home and her foster parents' home, Mama is now a strong advocate of proper care and protection for children. She is dressed in not one but two oversized black hoodies that hang to her knees.

Two-thirds of Mama's 21 years have been spent on the streets of Toronto and various cities in the US. She is deliberately silent about which cities south of the border—too much information is not a good thing when there is murder, drug dealing, gun-running, and pimping involved. Born in Toronto, Mama was sent to her father's sister in New York State. Her uncle had drinking problems and beat the family, so she and her 14-year-old brother were sent to foster parents where she was raped. "They say they screen these people, but it's not enough. Anyone who has a clean home can make it look like a happy home." In the end, her brother took his revenge on the rapist, but that's another thing about which Mama doesn't want to be too explicit. "In a way I feel bad because we dealt with him, we got him back. In a way it kinda kills me. It's hard to live with abuse and revenge."

Immediately after she was raped, her brother took Mama to live on the streets. Sometimes they sheltered with a kindly black woman who had eight children of her own. Mama used to chill out with the youngest; now, he is one of her many friends who are dead. Whatever the circumstances, her brother made sure she went to school. He saw it as a way off the streets in which he was becoming deeply embroiled. "He took full responsibility. He was one of the strongest people I met in my life. He wanted to be a lawyer because he wanted to help our people stay out of jail, he wanted to help our community."

The siblings started out as stick-up kids, robbing people and "doing nice stuff." The older they were and the more illegal the activities, the more hectic life became and the more enemies Mama's brother made. Because people tried to get at him through her, he sent her back to Canada when she was 13 to look for their mother. The woman they imagined as some kind of saint turned out to be a crackhead who promptly stole $400 from Mama. "I thought my mom would be a beautiful woman. Holee!" So Mama returned south. By then, her brother was rich enough to have houses in both the US and Canada, but nothing lasts, especially on the streets.

Asked what they did to make money, Mama replies, "Hustling." Pushed, she says that it included selling drugs and guns and robbing people. "New York was fun times." It was also dangerous times. Once she was grazed by a bullet intended for her brother, who was eventually killed by someone who shot him not once but seven times. Another friend was killed by a bullet in the back of the head.

In a somewhat lighter vein, Mama recalls her "first, first boyfriend" and how he cheated on her. When she discovered that she wasn't the first person to have sexual relations with him and that the other woman "was pregnant for him," she called him over to her house and made him strip. "My boy had to walk home in boxers and socks because I ran off with all his clothes. It was so beautiful."

This illustrates Mama's penchant for being in charge one way or another. She pimped for two years, controlling four girls and learning useful managerial skills. Even her street name derives from the fact that she dragged a very drunk, much larger, comatose youth to hospital like a sack of potatoes, consolidating her position as something of a godmother on Yonge Street. Small in stature, she's large in respect, and the other kids at the drop-in centre for young people where she hangs out sense her take-charge nature, coming to her with their problems, looking for advice. "People expect me to save the day. Like this guy in jail wants me to sign the bail papers," she says partly with resignation and partly with pride.

Mama's tough exterior conceals a lot of undigested grief—grief for herself, her adored brother, her three-year-old daughter killed by "someone driving too quick in a parking lot" and for the twins she miscarried by her most recent boyfriend with whom she's just broken up. "Last week is amnesia." Understandably, she's numb, but she's not so numb she doesn't think about other girls on The Block as they call their Yonge Street territory. She worries about the newcomers, observing they want so badly to be loved that they will have sex with anyone, ending up pregnant and/or diseased. Helping others is her way of being in control these days, so she wants to complete her formal education in order to become a child care worker "to prevent foster care screw-ups; do something, you know.... Every child deserves a loving family. A child is a fragile thing. If you don't nurture a child, who knows what happens to it growing up?"

Becky

At a very young age Becky was put into a foster home that was just as violent as her birth family. Although her life hasn't been smooth, now at 39 she is fiercely proud that her four sons have never been apprehended. Currently, they live with their father.

I met Becky in a detox facility in Winnipeg; before we could finish our interviews, she left for a Native addictions treatment centre that requires participants to remain incommunicado. Afterward, she disappeared again.

It bothered Becky, and still bothers her, that her parents put her into foster care but kept her twin sister. She used to pester their mother about why she hadn't kept them both or given them both up. To her chagrin and pain, there was usually no reply. However, one day when her mother was drunk, the answer came out: "Because you were crying and wanted to go."

"She let me make decisions at six months!" says Becky, now 39 with four boys of her own.

Becky was born in The Pas, Manitoba, into a big family, which she remembers chiefly for the violence. "There was so much crap at home, drinking and fighting and mom being abusive to dad. Once she threw lighter fluid over him and was going to light it, but my brother threw himself in the way, or he (her dad) would have been torched." Her foster parents weren't any better. Her foster father "kicked the crap" out of her foster mother. From when she was about two, Becky has a vivid memory of the woman lying under the bed with "blood leaking down her face," because he had broken a broom over her head. "Honest to God, if that women's head was shaved it would be like a road map (of scars)."

Becky, who visited back and forth between the two families, was sodomized when she was four by close male relatives. She never said anything about it until she went into therapy as an adult. She lost her virginity as a teenager in what can only be described as a gangbang at a local hotel after a dance. By Grade 10 she was stealing booze from home to drink at school; after an unruly episode, she lost her temper with the principal, turned on her heels, and quit. Now she regrets her impetuosity and would dearly love to get Grade 12 and, perhaps, become a social worker. "I still don't know what I want to be when I grow up."

She met her first husband in a detox centre. He stayed the course, and when it was time for him to leave, Becky quit the program and went with him to his reserve up north where he abused her. She stuck it out for a while because it was so isolated. When she left, she asked her mother to look after her baby son while she hitchhiked to Winnipeg. There, after trying several shelters, she moved into a sleazy downtown hotel and learned how to inveigle drinks out of male friends. "I never need money to drink, but I wasn't a prostitute. I was learning how to play the game, watching people." Life was one big party. Still drinking, she returned home where she met another man. Because they didn't like her lifestyle, her parents refused to give her son back, but she knew he would be okay with them, so she didn't worry unduly.

She left that man and married for a second time. At first the marriage was "normal." Sid was a recovering addict who hadn't done alcohol or drugs for 13 years. She saw him as a safe haven, as did her parents who gave her back her "little guy," who grew up looking upon Sid as his dad. Over the years, Becky and Sid had three more boys. She was clean for all of her pregnancies and is proud of the way she looked after the four boys. "From what I knew about what love is, I gave it to them. I still don't have the meaning of that word today. There's not enough of it in the world, seeing what I have seen—all the physical abuse, the blood and the sexual abuse." However both Becky and Sid began to do drugs, cocaine in particular, and he became increasingly abusive. They slept with a shotgun under the bed in case angry dealers arrived in the middle of the night. "We didn't realize cocaine makes you very paranoid."

Eventually, they had to sell everything. Becky made sure her children were cared for, then embarked on a life of cycling in and out of mental hospitals, drinking and drugging herself into oblivion, and not eating. At times, the alcohol poisoning made her throw up so hard, she developed black eyes. "I experimented with everything. I shared needles, used morphine, took all sorts of pills, mostly downers. I didn't know you could get so much stuff into one body."

She left another abusive relationship and took a bus to Calgary where she lived with several other homeless people under a bridge spanning the Bow River. Sometimes she jokes about this time, implying that the years she spent at "501½ Bedrock City" were fun. "I'll never forget it … sometimes the cops would wake me with a horse staring in my face." However, "I get all lonesome when I think about my children … It drove me under the bridge when the children went out of my life." Her drugs and alcohol abuse continued, although she also made enduring links with a nearby drop-in centre.

The group survived by panhandling the downtown crowd on their way to work early in the morning. By 9 a.m. they had usually made enough to see them through the day. Often, Becky says, the women would talk about their children. "I was so fortunate my children never got to Child and Family Services because I hear it really sucks. People don't know how hard it is for a lot of women. My children are my life; they are still my love."

Becky finally began to ponder over what had happened to her, what she was doing and where she was going. She spent three months in a recovery program on a reserve southwest of Calgary. Returning to the city, she was beaten up and her clothes stolen. Naked, she was taken to hospital. Now she is in a Winnipeg detox centre, waiting for her current boyfriend, who is supposed to be bringing munchies to help combat the withdrawal symptoms. The other patients are drawn to Becky, and she's often at the hub of a group, exchanging jokes and stories. In private, however, her conversation is punctuated by words like abuse, pain, depression, grief, and loneliness, although she never dwells on any one feeling for long. Despite everything, her biggest sadness appears to be the loss of close contact with her boys. "I get all lonesome when I think about my children.… Some of my days, I have just a heck of a time getting through, I'd be happy to do … Every day above ground is a good one. Even if you're hurting, you've got another try."

❖ ❖ ❖

Tonia

There is another form of "care" in which many street people appear to have come to grief. Although it is not always constructive to point fingers at a particular group, it's hard to ignore the frequent stories of stepfathers who abuse young women who are, in theory, under their protection. Tonia's mother had problems and appears like many women in difficulty to have hooked up with an undesirable man. The outcome for Tonia was not good. Now 17, she has been walking alone for a very long time.

Tonia's mother started working as a prostitute at 13 and doing drugs at 16. She doesn't do either any more, but she was absent for a great deal of Tonia's childhood. "She was a young mother who partied a lot. I saw more of the babysitter than my mom." Her stepfather is a roofer for whom Tonia has little time. Apart from the fact he smells, she says that he is very, very rude and "didn't care about me and my sister because we aren't his."

Tonia was smoking by the time she was 10, and three years later she was dating much older boys, sneaking out of the house when her mother went to bed. "I would chill out with friends and do whatever. Someone in the group would say, 'Let's do a B&E (a break and enter) or go car-hopping.' It was cool, everyone else was doing it." Her mother pushed her to achieve academically, but Tonia found it hard to pay attention in school, preferring to doodle (she always did well in art) or chat. She finds that things don't stay in her head if she merely hears them, she has to see them too. In Grade 8 her best friend, who was already on probation, egged her into trouble, and in Grade 9 they were skipping classes to smoke pot or to hang out at the mall. After three years, Tonia finally did get Grade 9 and a couple of Grade 10 credits. "Schooling was not a big thing for me. I don't feel the need for it, but I know I have to get it."

As Tonia progressed deeper into her teens, her stepfather became more antagonistic, calling her and her sister names and saying things like, "Get out of the house, you little sluts." At the same time her mother made it very clear that she would choose her husband over her children. Finally, her mother and sister got into a fight, the stepfather yelling from the sidelines. In the middle of the scuffle, Tonia tried to get her sister to leave, but their mother had already phoned the police. The two girls went to live with an aunt, who was really strict. In no mood for rules, Tonia left with a boyfriend, Robin, to live in a small Ontario town where they bunked down with his friends until they were kicked out and went to live in a tent in the woods. They subsisted on canned food they stole from a store, using their welfare money for alcohol. "I used it to not think about the truth and to get out of the world."

They didn't tell anyone where they were, although their friends were suspicious when they turned up from time to time very dirty, smelling of wood smoke and wanting showers. At another point, they were paying $200 a month to sleep on a friend's couch. The friend made passes at Tonia when he was drunk. She pushed him, he fell down, and her boyfriend "jumped in and beat the snot out of him."

Tonia phoned her birth father, who found her a room in Waterloo. Robin was supposed to have his own place, but he stayed with her. Soon Tonia became pregnant. Ashamed and not wanting her father to find out, they moved back to a tent. "I wasn't handling it [the pregnancy] very well. I had no support from Robin and friends were saying, 'Get rid of it, get rid of it.' I thought about it and got rid of it. I was totally brainwashed." To this day, Tonia is very ambivalent about her abortion. One part of her says, "Whoa, you need to do a lot of stuff before you have a kid." The other part says, "I'm so stupid I killed my first baby, although it's not technically a baby, I guess." She says she had absolutely no counselling or help with the biggest decision of her life.

She hitchhiked to the hospital and back to the tent. Robin began to pester her about where she had been. When she told him she had had the abortion, his attitude changed: he said he had wanted her to have the baby. Tonia decided she had had enough of him, his friends, and the drinking. Once again, she contacted her birth father who said that if she were really serious, he would help. Tonia, her sister, and a friend all ended up living with him. He did pretty well with this influx of young women, even learning to keep the toilet seat down. Eventually the three found their own apartment, but they had a big fight. Tonia returned to a youth shelter in Toronto, then moved from it into supported housing for young people where they help residents save money to make the first and last month's payment on their own apartment when they find one.

Tonia's relationship with her mother and stepfather has improved considerably. Her sister is living in a small town, completing high school, and Tonia is acquiring job skills, distributing her resume "like crazy" and thinking about the future. She dreams of being a movie star or a model. She has already had a few gigs but balked when asked to do shots in the nude. She also wants to help other street kids. "I used to be upset, but I've been down here long enough to realize that a lot of kids have lived through a lot worse than me. Most kids from Regent's Park (a Toronto housing complex) have seen their moms shoot heroin. My mother never did drugs in front of me."

Tonia's still got a way to go before she can feel secure in the knowledge that the streets and the street life are a thing of the past. Her list of priorities is to get a job, return to school, and find stable housing. "I feel like I'm still young. There's a lot of things I can do. And there's a lot of things I cannot do and should not do. There are a lot of decisions in life that must be made, but it's very hard. If you pick the wrong ones it will affect you."

Sources

Canadian Health Network, Health Canada. 2004. *How Common Is Child Abuse in Canada?* <http://www.canadian-health-network.ca>.

Centre for Suicide Prevention. 2002. *Childhood Abuse and Suicidal Behaviours* (February). <http://www.suicideinfo.ca>.

Green, Norma. 2000. *Profile of an Aboriginal Woman Serving Time in a Federal Institution*. Ottawa: Correctional Services of Canada, Aboriginal Initiatives. <http://www.csc-scc.gc.ca/text/prgm/correctional/abissues/know/5_e.shtml>.

Poirier, Mario, *et al.* 1999. *Relations et représentations interpersonnelles de jeunes adultes itinérants: au-delà de la rupture, la contrainte des liens.* Montreal: GRIJA.

Roman, N.P., and N. Wolfe. 1995. *Web of Failure: The Relationship between Foster Care and Homelessness.* National Alliance to End Homelessness. <http://www.endhomelessness.org/pub/fostercare/webrept.htm>.

Serge, Luba, Margaret Eberle, Michael Goldberg, Susan Sullivan, and Peter Dudding. 2002. *Pilot Study: The Child Welfare System and Homelessness Among Canadian Youth.* Ottawa: National Homelessness Initiative. <http://www.cecw-cepb.ca/DocsEng/HomelessnessAndCW.pdf>.

Homelessness is about people, not statistics.

When we neglect mothers, we neglect children.

Teenagers new to Toronto's scene are called "twinkies."

Sidewalks are cold and hard for panhandlers.

*Violence is an
ever constant threat
to women.*

*Time goes by very
slowly in a shelter.*

*Sometimes the streets
are safer than home.*

More than 500 Aboriginal
women have disappeared
in violent circumstances in
the last 20 years.

Women of colour are
very vulnerable.

Even babies are affected by Canada's housing policies.

For a few women there is a happy ending.

Photo credit: Ashala Jovanovski

When applying make-up it is important not to look too garish.

Everyone has their hopes and dreams.

Age does not guarantee you a safe place to live.

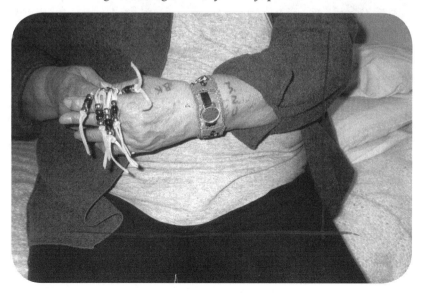

Sometimes life is like a lottery.

CHAPTER 7

PROSTITUTES ARE PEOPLE TOO

> You should see the women down here. It's awful. They are
> slaves. Either they are slaves to men or to crack. It's true,
> they are total slaves.
>
> —Recently homeless man

Lynn Allwright's body was found in a downtown Calgary park at the end of August 2004. After a family funeral in Edmonton, the Mustard Seed shelter organized a memorial service in Calgary where she had lived for the last two years. It was a collision of two worlds—the family and the street. In their different ways both mourned the petite woman.

"Her smile was her love. There were always people around her. She listened and supported. She brought people together," said a tearful street mourner. Unusually, one of the men exhorted the congregation to go to the police if they knew anything, anything at all, about Allwright's violent death.

For the family, left coping with Allwright's five children, it was a somewhat different scenario. "The hardest row to hoe is to explain to the children why she's not here," said a spokesperson. The mother's absence was something the family had been trying to explain off and on for many years. "There were five horribly neglected children. She was only a mother when it came to bearing the children. She had no idea how to nurture," said one family member, who was frequently left holding a baby. Once Allwright abandoned two of her children in a vehicle in -40°C weather while she played bingo. The sisters in her large extended family now believe it's possible that Allwright, 43, had had bi-polar disorder for most of her life and that things went wrong for her as a child. "It's a sad, sad story," said the spokesperson. "There were a lot of demons in Lynn's closets."

Allwright's life went through cycles. Although always outwardly ebullient, she often attempted suicide and disappeared, resurfacing pregnant, not knowing who the father was. In 2002 she disappeared one more time from the Edmonton scene. The family, fearing her remains would show up on

Robert Pickton's pig farm in Port Coquitlam, put out a missing person's bulletin in British Columbia. They never thought to look southward, so the phone call informing them that Allwright's body had been found in a tent in Calgary was something of a surprise.

While the details of Allwright's death have not been released, like so many other women who work as prostitutes, it was a violent and brutal ending to a short and tortured life. Just prior to her death, she had been charged with activities related to prostitution and drugs; the latter was also news to the family because they thought she was clean. The fact no one has ever been charged with her death bothers them. "Because she was a prostitute and drug user, do they just file it away?" they ask. And despite all the pain and sorrow, they still mourn the lost sister and are horrified at the manner of her passing. "She was such a tiny woman," they say. "She couldn't have defended herself from a fly she was so tiny. No one deserves to go that way."

Unfortunately, too many Canadian women do die that way. Violence is a fact of life for women working as prostitutes. They are on the streets in the first place because they are escaping violence in their homes, and it continues to be inflicted on them by pimps, johns, the public, and even law enforcers. They are frequently forced to work as prostitutes to make money for a man who, at best, offers them dubious protection, or to buy drugs, or to supplement a welfare allowance that is usually far below all standard measures of poverty.

Theirs is not the glamorous life of the "happy hooker" in Hollywood's depiction of prostitution. Besides violence, the life involves risky sex, drugs, and degradation; the women become pariahs in a society that is quick to protect the men. Women in the sex trade say that although they are frequently charged, the men—pimps and johns—get off with a mild reprimand. Even when charges are laid, the violence doesn't diminish. This is an item taken from the Bad Date List put out by the Downtown Eastside Youth Activities Society in Vancouver (2004):

LEFT CHAINED TO THE TRACKS: Two Caucasian males. First was 5'7", 190 lbs, aged 26-28 with brown hair. Second was 6 ft., 220-240 lbs with brown eyes, brown hair and goatee, very good looking. Second guy also had a piece of skin attached to the head of his penis. The first man asked the worker for a date. They went under Raymur bridge near tracks. The second man then attacked the worker from behind with fishing line around her neck and duct tape over her eyes. The two men raped the worker anally, repeatedly and viciously. They smashed the worker's eye when she tried to fight, urinated on her, and verbally abused her. Left her chained to the tracks with a tarp covering her. She was covered with bruises. The cops released her. BE VERY CAREFUL!!

In January 2004 Winnipeg's Street Connection's Weekly Rag listed some safety tips:

- Long earrings or big hoops for pierced ears may get pulled accidentally or on purpose. Wear small earrings, clip-ons, or none at all.
- If possible wear clothing that doesn't have to be removed for sex. This saves time, hides money and needle tracks. If it's a bad date situation and you have to quickly exit the vehicle or run away, you won't lose your clothes or be left naked.
- If you wear wigs, they should fit so that they can't slip over your face and temporarily blind you.
- Set a time limit for each service and tell him up-front that the service ends when he cums or he uses up the time. Be aware that he may become angry or violent if he fails to get off.
- Tell him the price, service and that *you have to pick the location, before* you get into the vehicle.
- Study the customer, the car and the door locking system while negotiating price and before getting into the vehicle.

The violence is unremitting. Project Kare, investigating homicides and high-risk missing persons in Alberta, has 40 homicides and 38 missing women on the books who fit its criteria, and the RCMP-Vancouver Police Department missing women joint task force is investigating 65 women who disappeared from Vancouver's Downtown Eastside between 1978 and 2001. Many more, particularly Aboriginal women, have disappeared from the strolls of large cities across the country. In Vancouver, according to one prostitute I spoke to in the spring of 2004, most of the women enticed to the Pickton pig farm had lost their looks and/or had a serious addiction and/or life-threatening health problems; in other words, they were the most desperate. They were offered free crack and, after a few hits, would be sufficiently trusting to go anywhere, even though word had been out on the streets for years that killers were at work. Some of the women who turned up at the notorious Port Coquitlam pig farm were identifiable only by their DNA.

Would legalized prostitution make the work safer for women, either in a controlled red-light area or bawdy houses? "Ending the criminalization of the sex work is an essential step toward reducing the harms experienced by sex workers," says *Voices for Dignity: A Call to End the Harms Caused by Canada's Sex Trade Laws* (Pivot Legal Society 2004). This detailed analysis reports how the present law more than discriminates against street workers—it actually does them harm, herding them into dark areas, out of sight, out of mind, where they are at greater risk of falling prey to predators. Women interviewed in the report also say that because of the way the law currently stands, they are forced to jump into cars without having the chance to assess the potential for violence and that they have to conduct their business outside rather than indoors. Every prostitute can relate at least one and usually several incidents of very close calls with death at the hands of men, including police officers. A small number report good relations with specific officers, but for the most part they do not view the police as their protectors but rather as their persecutors and people to be feared.

Voices for Dignity goes beyond legal matters to show how violence, poverty, lack of housing, addictions, and health issues create a tangle of problems for homeless women. It pinpoints an "urgent need" for changes to improve the lives of sex workers and to make it easier for them to leave the streets. In addition to other barriers, the fact they have blank resumes and few work skills makes a job search even more difficult. Other avenues of revenue open to an unskilled woman, such as panhandling and busking, are as likely to get them into trouble with the law. However, the very fact that it's not necessary to have to show a social insurance number, photo identification (such as a driver's licence), or immigration status card makes prostitution a viable option for trans women, who say that the sex trade actually validates their womanhood. They don't face discrimination in prostitution as they do in other jobs because there are men, not all of them obnoxious, who seek them out. "It's upgrading, not degrading," they say.

Legalizing prostitution, however, might have its drawbacks, pushing the most frail and the most vulnerable even further into the shadows where it will be harder to keep an eye on them. At what age, for example, should prostitution be legal? Our society is unlikely to condone sex with 13-year-olds, but there will always be johns who desire children. What about women who have HIV/AIDS or hepatitis C? They would not be welcome in a government-regulated bawdy house, and yet they still must find some way to supplement their meagre welfare cheques or to pay for drugs. Working in a society where some prostitutes are legal would inevitably push child prostitution deeper underground and older, sicker women further out onto the margins of society, making them much more vulnerable and harder to protect. And the market for them is not going to mysteriously go away because the legal and health risks involved add *frisson* to the experience for some men; this is not about love, or even sex, but about power and control.

Detective Constables Raymond Payette and Oscar Ramos who set up Vancouver's DISC (Deter Identify Sex-trade Consumers) program tell about a stockbroker they found haggling over a $25 sex act with a prostitute. He was negotiating from his brand new Jaguar while she stood on Howe Street. "Your socks are worth more than you're offering that woman," said Payette. "They cost me $63," answered the man.

❖ ❖ ❖

Diane

Diane isn't afraid to say exactly what she thinks, a trait that doesn't endear her to those who experience the rough edge of her tongue. She has been charged many times, but the men never.

A cop just gave me a ticket for jaywalking. I was rushing home and he stopped me and said I hadn't used the crosswalk, so I told him to get out of the way unless he wanted milk all over him as I had to go home and feed my baby. He said, "None of that lip or I will take you down to the station."

Diane pushes back her long blonde hair and pauses to let her audience at a New Westminster drop-in centre take in what she's saying. Her full breasts weigh heavily under her blouse, she smiles what would have been a gorgeous smile had her front teeth been in shape. Diane is not humble and probably in most people's estimation not very deserving, even though she is poor. She has been in trouble with the police many times, sometimes because of a decided gender bias in the way the law is upheld and other times because of her lack of meekness, in part prompted by her sense of justice, which doesn't always match that of officialdom.

He kept me for half an hour while he ran the C-PIC on me, so I said to him, "Go back to Tim Horton's, you faggot." Then he gave me the ticket for $119.

"How are you going to pay that on welfare?"

I'm going to pay $2 every week and, if they don't like that, $1 a week.

Diane's record is a long and serious one. She has been charged two or three times with prostitution-related offences, 48 times with assault, several times for uttering death threats, 38 times for failing to appear in court, and once with accessory to murder. Those are the bald facts. Below them, though, is another reality. The 48 assaults and the death threats were directed at johns or partners who had turned violent. The 38 failures to appear in court were usually because she was on the run and in hiding from those violent partners. The accessory to murder charge was laid when Diane encouraged her partner to turn himself in for killing a man and she became entangled with the investigation. As Diane says, right next to female prostitutes who inevitably get into trouble there are men selling crack and cocaine who are ignored by the police.

Diane, now 39, has fond memories of growing up on a farm in Ontario. She was very much a daddy's girl and at 13 was devastated when he died. Shortly after that she took off for Toronto where she was raped by a group of men. She met Joe who made her work as a stripper and prostitute. If she didn't obey him, he beat her and on one occasion stabbed her. Finally, she threatened a john because she didn't want to sell her body anymore. Joe told her she had to do it, and Diane protested with force. The result was she ended up in "hell," in other words, the Kingston Penitentiary for Women, which, she says, makes other institutions look like Mickey Mouse facilities. "It was the scariest penitentiary I have ever been to."

In prison, Diane had to fight not to become a "sugar kid," a woman forced into sex acts. In fact, she saved one girl who was destined to become a slave to a couple of the rougher inmates. They pretended to be a couple, although they were just friends, and her protegé ended up marrying one of Diane's nine brothers.

After release, Diane moved around Ontario, linking up with different men all of whom seemed to have two things in common: a predilection for drugs and violence and the ability to father daughters. One of them beat her head against railroad tracks and then wouldn't let her get stitches. Another made her get down on her hands and knees and bark like a dog for his amusement. "I had to ask permission to go to the washroom and to eat. Then I met Peter. I got to hate him with a passion." It's hard to figure out what distinguished him from the others: he was a bodybuilder who used her baby bonus to feed his drug habit, and he tried to drown one of his own daughters. For this, one of Diane's brothers beat him up with a hockey stick.

By this time, Diane's mother was looking after her oldest child, and her second, Sally, was in foster care. Sally was born blind, Diane believes, because of the beatings during that pregnancy. Tired of it all, Diane packed up the two younger girls living with her and moved west. Peter promptly charged her with kidnapping, so she returned to him for another couple of years.

She returned to British Columbia where she "bought" the second Peter in her life at a bar. A tow-truck driver, this Peter had been in jail for murder, but Diane thought he seemed like a nice guy. When his girlfriend offered to "sell" him for a pair of jeans, Diane willingly paid the price. However, the second Peter put Diane back on the streets, beating her if she returned home without the money he expected. About seven years ago when a friend tried to intervene, Peter kissed him on the cheek, said, "I love you, brother," and slit his throat. The friend survived, but the incident petrified Diane. She was too scared to flee; she had never heard of women's shelters.

One day after she had finished her shift at a bar, Peter came home, covered in blood, and told her he had slashed a man 39 times with a machete. He wanted to go to his mother's to get rid of the stained clothes, but Diane prevailed on him to see if there was anything he could do for his victim and to call the ambulance. In minutes, the cops had them surrounded. Eventually, Peter was sentenced to 18 years in prison. Diane was held for about a week while the police tried to squeeze information out of her because they suspected Peter of committing three other murders. She had nothing more to give them, despite their threats. "What happened to him can happen to you," they said.

Diane met her present partner, Red, six years ago. Red, 54, works two jobs, in construction and in a warehouse, and is a member of a biker gang. He has only once struck Diane and that was when he discovered she had turned a trick to buy cocaine. To her surprise, he put her over his knee and spanked her. "I love him very, very much. He treats me beautifully. I could never ask for a better man."

In February 2004 Diane and Red had a daughter, Kelly. Without her knowledge, Diane was tested for drugs during her pregnancy. Twice traces of cocaine were found, although there was none in Kelly when she was born. Diane, who said she had only used coke twice during the nine months, was totally distraught when the baby was taken away from her.

Even Kelly's arrival into the world was surrounded by violence. Seven months pregnant, Diane walked into her welfare office to see if she could pick up a few things in preparation for the baby. She stopped to chat with three other women when a man came up to them and, handing out cigarettes, asked them their names. Five minutes later, Diane was arrested in her doctor's office by half-a-dozen police officers including the man who had given her a cigarette. Her crime? The usual: failing to appear in court. The police shackled her ankles and bound her hands with handcuffs attached to a belt. Diane could only shuffle along, stooped forward over her belly. She was taken to holding cells in Vancouver. The next morning, the police removed her jacket and shoes, making it even more difficult for her to walk. As she was climbing into the paddy wagon, she slipped and hit her back on the door. "They told me to shut my face. They didn't even ask if I was okay. He said, 'Shut your fucking mouth. If you've got a complaint, get hold of the sergeant.'" Within 24 hours, Diane's waters broke, and Kelly was born, weighing less than four pounds. Diane breastfed a baby for the first time in her life and was totally enchanted. However, hospital staff told her that she had hepatitis C and forbade her to nurse again. Recently, that diagnosis has changed and Diane was told she may not have hepatitis C after all and that she may be able to feed Kelly on visits to the foster family. She has kept the milk flowing at some inconvenience and cost.

Diane has to be tested for drugs once a week, but she is voluntarily going every two days. So far, the results have been negative. "They can't even find Aspirin." The stress is getting to her, though, and she's smoking up to a pack a day as she waits to hear about custody and the results of new hepatitis C tests.

She describes her welfare worker as "a bitch from hell" who goes strictly by the books. This looks like the construction of mysterious reasons to keep her and Red away from their daughter. The worker wants her to enter a residential detox and drug assessment program, but that would mean giving up her apartment. Diane is trapped in a situation we have seen before: she can't have Kelly without drug treatment, but without an apartment the worker says she is automatically disqualified from having her baby. "I think they [the workers] are there more for the money than the child. It seems like they are selling babies and don't give anyone a break."

Diane receives $450 a month from social assistance. After she pays her rent for her one-bedroom basement suite, she has $55 left to feed and clothe herself. Without food banks and drop-ins she would starve. It's no wonder, she says, that some women resort to prostitution. She doesn't like asking Red for money, partly because she's worried what he might spend it on and partly out of pride.

If social workers make life difficult for Diane, the police also show her a very biased interpretation of justice. Although, by her account, nearly all her troubles were instigated by males, the men have never been charged or even cautioned. The worst that happened was that a john was told to move along. Although Diane had good reasons for failing to appear in court, no one ever took the time to discover that she feared for her life—and charges were never brought against the men who were threatening to kill her. "I don't think it's fair. We [i.e., prostitutes] take chances with our lives and for what?"

Diane dreams of being able to gather up her five daughters and her grandchildren by her oldest child and take them all to a farm where they can go horseback riding and work the land. "I want my daughters to have a better life than I have." In the meantime, she is doing her valiant best to turn her life around. As well as the drug tests, she goes to anger management and life skills courses at the Elizabeth Fry Society. She volunteers at a drop-in centre and her time with Kelly has increased substantially. Propelled by the power of motherhood, Diane is doing her bit to change, but it's a big question mark whether society is moving to meet her. However, besides having determination, love, and a candid tongue, she is also optimistic for the first time in years. "I never thought there would be a hope in hell for me. Now there's hope."

(Diane did eventually satisfy the authorities and is now very happy being a mother to Kelly.)

Sylvia

A life of violence has taken its toll on Sylvia. One of the things she deeply regrets is that she worked as a prostitute because it was the only way she could provide for her children.

Sylvia wheels in to the interview on her motorized scooter. She describes herself as a "tea granny": she has three daughters, nine grandchildren, one great-grandchild, two stepdaughters, and three stepsons. As she chats, her husband Vance looks in solicitously from time to time, offering her cold drinks and tea.

A former alcoholic, drug addict, and prostitute, Sylvia has led a life that is hard to imagine. As a child she was tossed out of school for fits of temper; she has been raped at least twice, once when four-and-a-half months pregnant; she was beaten up by her mother; stabbed in one incident 172 times; knocked over by a car; and there was an episode when one of her lovers did something so awful, she can hardly mention it.

Sylvia is 53. She looks more like 73.

Sylvia was born and raised in Toronto's Cabbagetown and has an Irish surname that suggests long roots in the area. Despite her angry episodes, she doesn't think her upbringing was particularly notable, although she was inconsolable when her father died. Her mother often beat her, once attacking her with a broom when Sylvia, a young teenager, was eight-and-a-half months pregnant. She left home shortly thereafter at the age of 14.

When Sylvia announced she was pregnant, her mother and grandmother advised her to have an abortion, although it was then illegal; she retorted, "I've made my bed and I'll lay on it." The father took off shortly afterward, but Sylvia soon married a French Canadian, and they had two more daughters. It was while she was with him that she turned to prostitution to help put food on the table for the little girls. "I did what I had to do and would never do it again."

Her husband left for another woman but always kept in touch. The last time Sylvia saw him was in 1973 when they bumped into each other on the street. He asked whether she would look after his two children by the other relationship. She agreed. He was to get back to her about the arrangements, but two days later the children, aged six months and three-and-a-half years, were found with his body in their apartment. "He tried to commit suicide so many times and I saved him. I guess I wasn't there to do it."

By this time, Sylvia's own children were revolving in and out of care. Although she fought for them "up and down, up and down," they were removed because of her alcoholism. She says repeatedly, "I never abused the children; I never abused the children." Sylvia's own mother certainly didn't teach her constructive parenting skills, and there was a lot happening in her life sucking up her attention. It's not entirely clear what happened when, but there was an on-again, off-again relationship with the father of her oldest daughter and a great deal of violence from different men. Once when she was staying with her oldest sister, Sylvia was raped as she walked along the street. It was dark and she was hit from behind, then stabbed as well as violated.

A boyfriend slashed her forehead with a knife and pushed her downstairs, causing her to lose a baby. Some years later, she was raped again. This time she was pregnant and she lost that baby, too. As a result she had to have a hysterectomy; the blood transfusions she needed during that operation were tainted with hepatitis C. For a while she lived with a very angry man who sent her to hospital six times with various injuries. On another occasion, when she was working as a crossing guard, a hit-and-run driver knocked her down, breaking both legs. She was in a wheelchair for ten weeks, she says, because the doctors were unable to put casts on them.

Sylvia has arthritis, high blood pressure, heart problems, emphysema, and hepatitis C. For a while she was on experimental drugs, but they made her so depressed that she is back on her former treatment of three shots a week. However, once she was diagnosed with hepatitis C, she gave up drinking; 11 years ago she started dating Vance, and eight years ago they were married. This has proved to be a solid and happy relationship. For many years Sylvia had been attending an evangelical mission, but comparatively recently she was born again—something that makes her very proud. Although she's barely literate, she derives a lot of comfort from trying to read her Bible, sounding out the words as she goes, and from her family.

> My faith is starting to mean a lot. It brings me closer to the Lord. I am really, really bothered by what I had to do [prostitute herself to earn money to feed her children]. I worry about disease and bad drugs ... When I was younger I had no brains, now I'm older, I'm more wiser. The only thing keeping me around are my nine grandchildren and one great-grandchild. They are the only thing really keeping me alive. I have good children and my children in the Lord [her foster children]. My life has turned around since I met Vance.

❖ ❖ ❖

Karen

Karen has panhandled and worked as a prostitute. While business people in many cities discuss ways of tightening up bylaws to rid the streets of beggars, Karen says if people were more generous, she wouldn't have to sell her body.

Karen was badly treated from an early age, raped as a child and then sexually abused by her stepfather and in her foster home. "No one defended me." She went into a youth centre, but although was glad to get out of there, she was not so happy to end up on the streets where she has lived since she was 18. "It's hard. It's sickening, you get abused physically and verbally; all the swearing and the yelling. Women get more abused than men. They get beaten, raped and hurt. Anything. They get put on the streets as a hooker. I think women need more help."

Karen has five children, all of whom she has lost permanently to the system. "I'm angry and sad about that, but I know it's my fault because I have a solvent abuse problem." Karen, who is allowed to see two of her children, hasn't been to visit them for a couple of years. "A condition of seeing them is that I'm clean, and I wouldn't go there sniffed up. I'm not that crazy. But my kids are doing good, really good. My worker told me."

Karen herself isn't doing well. She doesn't like panhandling because it doesn't make much money and because "damn cheap rich women" tell her to get a job. In fact, she has a life-threatening illness, which she is too ashamed to name, that prevents her from working. She's not prevented, however, from making better money as a prostitute, which she continues to do. If women supported other women—in this case by responding to her requests for spare change—she might not feel it necessary to sell her body to men. The shame of admitting this almost brings the interview to a close. The pain is expressed in monosyllabic answers that sound insolent but act as a dam to hold back the memories, particularly of her children.

She speaks for many women when she says all she wants is to "hopefully one day to get off the sniff and to have a home to have my kids in."

❖ ❖ ❖

Melissa

> Besides prostitution, panhandling is one of the few ways women without education and job experience can make money. Melissa has never worked as a prostitute, but she panhandles daily to pay her extortionate electricity bill. The sidewalk is hard and cold, passersby can be rude, and she risks being picked up by the police.

Every evening the rush hour crowd disembarking from Vancouver's Sky Train at one of its busiest stations walks by Melissa with her little sign asking for donations. Most of the people hurrying home to their evening meal don't even notice the worried-looking teen. Some have come to know her well and others are downright rude.

It's certainly not as easy as one might imagine being a panhandler. The sidewalk is a hard unyielding seat. If Melissa doesn't bring in the money, she has no food and no heat either. The 19-year-old, her boyfriend, and two other people live in one room of a three-room apartment that used to be a marijuana grow operation. The previous tenants left without paying their hydro bill, and so the owner won't turn on the electricity until someone— indeed, anyone but her—has paid it. In some ways this suits Melissa and her friends quite well because they aren't being charged any rent. They do, however, pay one of their neighbours $20 a day for a power cord, and they run everything they can off it, mainly a heater. This comes to $600 a month. By comparison, a family of two adults, two teens, and two younger children, who live close by, received a bill from BC Hydro for $268.32 for the period 10 January to 10 March the same year. They run two fridges, a computer, a washer and dryer, two air purifiers, and a blender as well as electric lights and sundry other appliances like hair dryers. Melissa and her friends have no light and no hot water. They cook soups and noodles on a propane stove. In the winter, the water pipes blew causing a flood. "This place is crazy. But it's a roof over our heads and it's free."

The apartment over a shop is not in a salubrious area of Vancouver; it is dirty and infested with rats and mice. Melissa wouldn't be surprised if there were bugs as well. The owner would like to rent out the other two rooms, but Melissa says they are full of junk, and so far there have been no takers. On top of their other bills, Melissa and her boyfriend have somehow become responsible for the owner's rotweiler that costs a considerable amount to feed. The owner got rid of the dog when it attacked her. Since it's been with Melissa, it has calmed down, causing her to theorize that the landlady abused it. The boyfriend is an out-of-work roofer who also can't get employment because his address is so unfixed. Melissa says he's good to her and looks out for her. She finds the streets quite scary with all the reports of "perverts killing girls and kidnapping them."

So, how does a 19-year-old end up begging? It's a short story.

Melissa was born in Oshawa, Ontario. When she was four, two things happened: her father left and she and her mother moved to Vancouver. With ADHD, she didn't do well at school and was picked on by the other children. "I didn't have many friends and the teachers were so-so." She knows that she needs to study at her own, slower pace in a place where she can focus.

Her mother was a severe diabetic and Melissa did her best to look after her. Then when she was around 13, despite her pleas, she was taken into care because her mother became too ill for a teenager to care for. Shortly afterward, her mother died. "It's still hard."

Melissa's remaining relatives blamed her for her mother's death, saying she became so stressed by her daughter that she took a fatal dose of insulin. Understandably, Melissa was unwilling to turn to them when she did need help four years later. In the meantime, she continued to live in group homes, which she didn't like because the staff played favourites. At 17, she entered into an independent living arrangement sponsored by the government. In her case, she was expected to find her own place and to budget without any help. When she turned 19, with very little warning, she was cut off from funding because she wasn't in school and didn't have a stable address.

Melissa is now without any form of assistance, although she hopes to get onto welfare shortly after five months of surviving by panhandling. She usually brings in about $10 an hour. On days when the Vancouver Canucks hockey team wins a game, the crowds are more generous. Although many passersby suggest she find a job, it's a little difficult to see how she can get one without access to a phone, a real address, bus fare, and a way to clean herself up. She only has Grade 11 education and no specific training. She hopes that welfare will enable her to finish Grade 12 at an alternative high school geared to students like her.

Sometimes a man will ask if she will suck his dick for $20. In response she tells him to go to Hastings Street on the Downtown Eastside. The police, she says, are "idiots," moving her on at least twice a week. They tell her she shouldn't be within 50 feet of a bank, when the law states within 10 metres. She is probably too close, but she never pesters anyone and has made friends with the locals.

Melissa has four dreams for her future: "to be living in a nice place, to finish school, to be working, and having some kids. I can't say I want to be a millionaire because I know I won't be." She would like to be a veterinarian because she has always liked animals, but she thinks it's more realistic to aim to be an accountant because she has an ability with numbers. "My brain is a phone book."

It's been a good day. It's sunny, and the crowd is in an amiable mood after the Canucks defeated the Calgary Flames the night before in a drawn-out game. By early afternoon, Melissa has enough to pay for food and heat, besides having been given a few apples and some other goodies. Stiffly she rises to her feet, shoulders the daypack stuffed with a blanket and her gains, and walks up the street to catch up with her boyfriend, another day done.

But it's not. When Melissa arrives home, the guy who extorts $20 a day for the use of the extension cord and electricity is demanding a further $20 or he will cut them off. It's blatant blackmail, but he's not going to step down. Despondent, Melissa persuades a friendly bus driver to give her a free ride back to her spot, puts out her cup, and starts to beg again as the evening draws in.

Sources

Downtown Eastside Youth Activities Society. 2004. Bad Date List. Vancouver, 16 February. <http://www.deyas.org>.

Pivot Legal Society Sex Work Subcommittee. 2004. *Voices for Dignity, A Call to End the Harms Caused by Canada's Sex Trade Laws*. <http://www.pivotlegal.org>.

Project Kare. 2006. <http://www.kare.ca>.

Street Connections, The Weekly Rag. 2004. Winnipeg. 26 January.

Vancouver Police Department Vice Unit. 2004. *Deter Identify Sex-Trade Consumers*. Press kit. Vancouver: Police Department.

Interviews

Malchow, Paul. Detective, Calgary Police Service. 2004.

Payette, Raymond and Oscar Ramos. Detective Constables, Vancouver Police Department. 2004.

Ward, John. RCMP Staff Sergeant, Vancouver. 2006.

CHAPTER 8

WHEN FIRST NATIONS
COME LAST

We are refugees in our own country.
—Aboriginal woman in Calgary

From the mid nineteenth century onward, British Crown and then Canadian government policy was to convert Aboriginal peoples (including Inuit and Métis) into Canadians by sending them to Christian boarding schools where they were divorced from their families and culture and punished for speaking their own language. Many lived in terrible conditions and were physically and sexually abused by people supposedly imbuing them with the love of God. As a result, the children grew up traumatized and without parental role models. Moreover, the education they received—basic reading, writing and arithmetic; cooking and cleaning—did not equip them to go far in white society. Whether it was intended or not, sending children to residential schools had the effect of breaking down Aboriginal culture and family ties. These were further disrupted by a second policy: from 1870 to the mid 1980s under the federal Indian Act, women who married a man who was not Aboriginal or who was from another community lost their Indian status and the right to live in their home communities. Tens of thousands of women were uprooted and cut off from their families, leaving them very vulnerable.

In the 1950s and 1960s as the residential schools were phased out, a new wave of child seizures, known as the Baby Scoop, occurred. Provincial child care programs apprehended Aboriginal children and placed them in white foster and adoptive homes, sometimes as far away as the southern US states. Often the placements were less than satisfactory, rupturing families and the culture even further, and the issues that put the children at risk were never addressed.

These policies have been disastrous for Aboriginal peoples in Canada. Not only do they have to deal with widespread racism on a daily basis, but, according to Rodolfo Stavenhagen, a UN special investigator:

> Poverty, infant mortality, unemployment, morbidity, suicide, criminal detention, children on welfare, women victims of abuse, child prostitution, are all much higher among aboriginal people than in any other sector of Canadian society. Economic, social and human indicators of well-being, quality of life and development are completely lower among aboriginal people than other Canadians. (Stavenhagen 2005)

He concludes his report by warning that housing shortages, health issues, and suicide rates are reaching crisis proportions. He also points out that Canada's high ranking on the UN's human development scale would fall dramatically—from a position in the top 10 to 48th out of 174 countries—if the country were judged solely on the economic and social well-being of its First Nations people.

Canadian statistics back up Stavenhagen's findings and construct a tragic social portrait:

+ Indigenous women aged 25 to 44 with status under the Indian Act are five times more likely to die as the result of violence than all other women. This figure is very likely on the low side because many police forces across the country don't always record the ethnicity of crime victims or missing persons (Amnesty International 2004).
+ Life expectancy for female Registered Indians is 76.2 years compared to 82.6 for the general female population (IAAW 2003).
+ Aboriginal women are three times more likely to commit suicide than non-Aboriginal women (IAAW 2003).
+ Hospital admissions for alcohol-related accidents are three times higher among Aboriginal women than they are for the general Canadian population (IAAW 2003).
+ Aboriginal women have over five times the rate of diabetes compared to women in the general population (IAAW 2003).
+ Aboriginal women represent 1–2 per cent of the Canadian population, but 24 per cent of women sentenced to federal penitentiaries are Aboriginal. The average Aboriginal woman offender is generally 27 years old with a Grade 9 education and limited employment skills. She is single and has two or three children (Green 2003; Pate 2002).
+ The Prostitution Alternatives Counselling and Education Society study of prostitution in Vancouver showed that 30 per cent of sex workers in that city were Aboriginal, although they comprise less

than 2 per cent of the population. They are probably also over-represented in other Canadian cities (Amnesty International 2004; PACE 2001).

+ The average income of Aboriginal women is $13,000 compared to $19,495 for non-Aboriginal women and $18,200 for Aboriginal men (Morris 2002).

+ So concerned is Amnesty International about systemic racism against native women that it released a report, *Stolen Sisters: Discrimination and Violence Against Indigenous Women in Canada* (2004), stating a number of concerns, particularly the over-policing and under-protection of Aboriginal women.

+ The Native Women's Association of Canada says that in the last 20 years probably more than 500 women have been murdered or have gone missing in violent circumstances (Amnesty International 2004).

Stolen Sisters (Amnesty International 2004) concludes that Aboriginal women have been pushed into dangerous situations of extreme poverty, homelessness, and prostitution that make it easy for men, both Aboriginal and non-Aboriginal, to be extremely violent toward them. These acts may be motivated by racism and by the knowledge that Canadians, including the police, are indifferent to their fate.

The brutal mantle of colonialization—and all that it entails in terms of wrecking a society—lies heavily on the shoulders of Canada's Aboriginal people. Until the white supremacist culture is changed, there will always be a problem, says Donna McPhee (interview 2004), who is of both Cree and Blackfoot ancestry and who was formerly on both the Calgary Homeless Foundation's Aboriginal Standing Committee and the Calgary Coalition for Social Justice. Furthermore, she says, with every wave of immigrants Aboriginal peoples get knocked to the bottom of the heap. "I usually think, 'Oh, good, more allies,' but in reality it doesn't work like that. Canada doesn't include the Aboriginal community." For instance, she cites the case of cultural difference involving taxi drivers, who are usually male immigrants, and Aboriginal customers. Because tipping is not part of Aboriginal culture, an Aboriginal person proffering a $10 bill for a $9.90 fare expects 10 cents back, and so there is often "a little disagreement." The police are called, and, inevitably, the officer will take the driver's side. "Do you want to be hauled off [to jail] for a dime? It all depends what's happening that day, how strong you are, and if you want to exercise your rights for a dime" (McPhee interview 2004).

Even on the street Aboriginals are "tromped over" because they are perceived as having benefits that others don't—a free education, cheap cigarettes, and so on: "It's systemic racism." McPhee's sister, who has never touched alcohol, has severe diabetes. Inevitably when she seeks medical help she is accused of being drunk and, when she denies it, she's accused of lying. Now the family makes sure that someone always accompanies her to the doctor or to the emergency department so that she receives proper treatment. Similar assumptions were made when McPhee, who was recently hit by a car, was denied painkillers at a Calgary walk-in clinic because they said she was an addict. In reality, it's the rare Aspirin that passes her lips.

Profoundly depressing as all this is, some Aboriginal women see hope as a new generation with better parenting skills starts to have babies and as more young people move into professional jobs. McPhee points to a photograph of her great-niece with her newborn daughter. "I'm worried for the little baby, but she's my hope; she has to be."

❖ ❖ ❖

Beatrice

In her late 50s and an Elder, Beatrice was taken to residential school as a young girl. Infected by her anger and hatred for white society, one of her sons became violent and has been imprisoned.

Beatrice speaks softly but powerfully, and the entire room is spellbound as she tells the story of how her father hid her so that she wouldn't have to go to residential school. Her family retreated deeper and deeper into the bush of northern Saskatchewan, staving off the inevitable for two years. Finally, the authorities caught up with them and wrested the seven-year-old from her parents and everything that was familiar.

Beatrice considers her father, who has moved on to the Spirit World, a hero for defying the government. She believes that those extra two years with her family, learning the traditions and speaking her language, gave her more resiliency than most Aboriginal girls her age and enabled her to move on from being a victim to a woman who can speak eloquently on behalf of others. She shudders as she recalls her first night away from her parents, lying between frigid sheets that felt dramatically different from the warm furs she was used to sleeping in. Everything she held dear—her family, her culture, her language—was held up not just to ridicule but also to deep racist judgements. She was told her family was heathen and that her parents would rot in everlasting hell. Love and warmth were replaced by anger and hate. The teachers believed they were instilling civilization and true religion; in fact, Beatrice, and many others, were learning to loathe themselves and their culture. This was nothing short of a systematic dismantling of Aboriginal families and society.

Years later, one of Beatrice's adult sons was charged in Regina with a very serious crime and was likely to be incarcerated for many years, if not for life. As a mother, Beatrice knew she had to do something. She made her way from Vancouver where she was then living to Saskatchewan, and she convinced her son's lawyer to let her speak before the sentencing. Almost overcome by nerves and shaking violently, she stood up and appealed to the judge. "It's not his fault," she said, telling the court that her son was an indirect product of the residential school system. "That's where I learned to hate, where I learned anger." Because of that experience, she believes she failed as a mother. Blame the system, she said, not her boy, and certainly not all the other young natives who come up in court. The judge thanked Beatrice for increasing his understanding before handing her son what she considers to be a very fair sentence. Having served his time, the young man continues to do well.

❖ ❖ ❖

Carol M.

An Aboriginal mother, Carol M. has felt the "ripple effect" of residential schools. With seven children she also faces discrimination in the rental market. She has defied the odds to become a champion for oppressed women, working in a Vancouver women's drop-in centre.

Carol M. is a statuesque woman with a quiet determined demeanour that inspires confidence. She describes herself as a "ripple of the residential schools" and is living proof not only that the wounds extend down the generations but that it is possible to reshape those effects into something positive. Her extended family encompasses all the women of Vancouver's Downtown Eastside. She seems to know everyone by name, and many stop to talk with her as she walks to the bus to make her way home to an Aboriginal housing project in the suburbs. She shows no sense of urgency, although the journey takes more than an hour if she misses her connections.

Carol M.'s life hasn't always been so well ordered. She has hit the bottom of the bottle, but even when things were very rough indeed, she always tried to move one step forward through education and counselling. She was raised in a white home and assumed many of her foster parents' values, including a commitment to work in which she has sometimes buried her problems. "I have always worked since I was 16, when I got my first job. I'm a workaholic, working night, day and weekend jobs. I never let anyone close [to me] because I didn't trust."

Carol M. didn't discriminate in her lack of trust. She wasn't close to white people nor to her birth family, and she was reluctant to reconnect with them. She calls herself the typical "apple"—looking like an Aboriginal but white at the core. Her birth mother, who was filled with self-hatred because of her residential school experiences, took it out on Carol M. and her sister by beating and berating them.

Eventually, Carol M. was persuaded to visit her birth family only to be told that she didn't belong and that somehow she counted for less than other family members. "I didn't fit in anywhere." She went to a family dinner where there was a lot of drinking, and, without thinking, she joined in until she passed out. She woke up to find her uncle having sex with her. "He plopped off, out of me. It was so gross." Without a word to anyone, she left for Vancouver, wanting to kill herself.

Rather than commit suicide, she anaesthetized herself with work. She was repulsed by the condition of urban Aboriginals in Vancouver. "When I first came, I was embarrassed. I had never seen poverty so bad. They were discards. Me and my snotty-nose attitude! I didn't want to lower my nose. Oh God, what a person I was. Then I ended up with one of them." She became too busy working and looking after six children to notice that the father had a severe addiction. He was also very abusive but "loneliness got the better of me." So she stayed with him.

Figuring out she couldn't wallow in sorrow for the rest of her life, she went back to school and finished her Grade 12 in five months; because she liked the sound of the keyboard clicking away, she took a computer course, "had a few kids," did more courses in everything from pottery to tenants' rights, and undertook some family community counselling. It was the first time she was able to stop the robot inside her and pry open the little box where she kept all her secrets. "It stabbed my heart; my feelings and my guts were everywhere. Someone actually listened."

Her sister took her to the Downtown Eastside to do some volunteer work. "I was all dressed up in my little heels and fancy little nylons. It was so funny." Gradually, she metamorphosed from a volunteer into a staff member, holding down increasing amounts of responsibility, but she found that the clients' pain triggered her own problems. She didn't know how to look after herself, so she took to the time-honoured consolation of alcohol. "It was so stupid, I thought no one would know."

A woman at an evangelical Christian mission pulled Carol M. out of the hole. "Religion is religion. You don't have to take everything. I like the possibility that there is someone up there who loves me." She has since connected with native spirituality, blending it with a belief in angels. The woman from the mission, who "never gave up on me," reserved a place for her and her children at a camp on Vancouver Island. Up until the very last minute Carol M. wasn't sure she would go. She slept for three days and woke to the sounds of children singing around the campfire. "It was the first time I felt part of something. I felt really welcome."

A turning point had been reached. She returned home much stronger. When her partner's violence put her in hospital, she put a stop to his physical abuse and name-calling. "Useless mother; lesbian," were among his favourite epithets. "I decided I can't take this and the kids can't see this. It was the hardest, hardest, hardest thing I ever did. It hurt, it hurt, it hurt. But when you make choices for yourself and for the kids it really counts." Hard though it was, she was instantly rewarded. Carol M. began to experience some healing and understanding. "I became more alive, like the wind."

She had an affair with another man, the father of her last child. Realizing that he, too, was abusive "rather than losing the kids and my sanity," she decided to go to Toronto. Heavily pregnant and with six kids in tow, Carol M. clambered on the bus, trusting that all would be well. And it was. People helped her for the three days she travelled across the country. On arrival, she applied for native housing in Scarborough where people also rallied around. "Total strangers, everybody was bringing stuff—mattresses, pots and pans. It was so great there."

After a year, the Vancouver centre offered her a job, and she decided to return to the West Coast, only to find that with so many children she was virtually homeless and had to beg a male friend for a room in his house. "One room! ... You should have seen the places I looked at." The hovels that were available in her price bracket had no running water or cockroaches in the cupboards. There were also the excuses to turn her away. "It's humiliating, you feel like a beggar, standing there with the children, their big eyes looking up at them [the landlords]."

Eventually, Carol M.'s friend moved and left his house to her, although she had to produce a damage deposit and the first month's rent, almost a prohibitive sum. She and her children lived there for three years until the pipes burst and the taps wouldn't turn off, the most visible symbol of its decay. She applied for native housing in Surrey, BC. Once again she had to find the damage deposit and the first month's rent, not to mention babysitters for the youngest child, bus passes, and school lunch money. "Oh, my God, I'm working so hard, where's it getting me?"

On consideration, Carol M. realizes she has come a long way. She has quit drinking. Any man will have to be almost perfect before she considers a relationship with him. She has passed a host of courses and almost has first-year university credits in criminology. Financially, she's on a bit of a roller coaster, but she makes sure there is good food and plenty of it for the kids.

As for the future, she's sick of band-aid social work. She wants to effect real changes so that more women, especially Aboriginal women, can move forward. This, she realizes, means pressuring the government for such things as transitional housing and better health care. She sees the shortcomings of present programs and the many hurdles governments set in the way of women on low, or no, income. "I do not see anything in place where people get something positive out of it. If we all pressured the government for a little bit of change, think what we might achieve. It surprises me that no one makes an effort. I can think of a million things to do, if we all linked hands."

As Carol M. interweaves the story of her life with her thoughts about the system and her job, which focuses on preventing disenfranchised women from falling irretrievably between the cracks, she talks with knowledge and passion about the problems Aboriginal women have finding suitable housing, especially if they have children. "The system shuffles people around so much. Where do they go?" Racism and prejudice are still rampant. No landlord will look at a woman who looks sick, is on social assistance, is Aboriginal, and/or has teenagers or small children. It's hard to find beds for women leaving abusive relationships and women with mental health problems. "The things you have to do.... It's a fine line you are walking so you don't jeopardize your name."

Carol M. is waking up to her own considerable strengths and to the noise women make when they speak with one voice. She's ready to rattle chains. "I really believe in feminism. There is no way that word has men in it (unlike women). I love that word. It's a statement of what I believe as a woman. The world will get to know Carol M."

Beth

Almost 40, Beth's addiction still drives her life; it's hard to come clean when there is nowhere safe to live.

Beth has lived on the streets of Winnipeg since she was nine when she ran away from home in northern Manitoba because her parents fought and her father beat the kids when he was drunk. She lived under bushes and under stairs in old apartment buildings; often she wasn't shod or clothed properly. By 10 she was drinking and making her living through prostitution. She recalls it was very "scary" and that there was one john who, when she was only 12, beat her if she wouldn't have sex with him. No one noticed her, and when they did, they put her into foster homes and youth centres from which she always ran away. She has been in and out of jail since she was 17 and started sniffing solvent when she was 18. "I never grew up. It didn't feel good. I've never been around people my own age, always older people; older men, never younger men, because they [the old men] had money. They sort of used me and I used them—for a bed."

Beth has five children who live with her grandparents in Ontario. She writes to them all, and sometimes they reply. Her eldest, a boy, is almost 19 and works with his uncle on a farm. He has a girlfriend but tells Beth they are too young for kids. "He's a smart boy."

Three years ago, she gave up prostitution because she didn't want to catch AIDS, and she hasn't been in jail for a couple of years. About that time she met Ed and fell in love, perhaps for the first time in her life. Although Ed is more than twice her age and uses a wheelchair, he has awakened something in her. "He gave my life back to me. He treated me good and made me happy. He's never hurt me; he's never hit me. Nothing. He's very gentle, talks lots and talks sense and jokes around a lot. I was sort of lost, but God showed me the way. I'm trying to turn my life around because I love Ed, and I want to be what he wants. I wish I were a strong person and not so weak." Beth first noticed Ed because he is kind to everyone, not a quality she has encountered very often. He has seizures and has to take Dilantin, so he doesn't drink, but he's happy to go to Alcoholics Anonymous and church with her. However, Ed is in hospital, and Beth doesn't know why. She's pregnant, but she's so depressed, she took a bunch of pills and she's not sure what effect they have had on the foetus. "It's better if God takes the baby." When she visits Ed in hospital, she has a hard time leaving him. She is puzzled why he's been committed and is on a locked ward when she thought he was being treated for a bad leg. If they don't let him out soon, he will appeal to the patient ombudsman, while she seeks help at the Manitoba Métis Federation.

Before Ed, Beth was in a relationship with another man who appears to have been very abusive. "He made me do things I didn't want to do. I felt like a slave." She is too embarrassed to elaborate, although she is quite candid about other things, like being raped by a police officer. Surprisingly after this experience, she can walk past a community police station and remark, "The guys in there are really nice." She says that shelters, in which she has often stayed, are frightening places because there is always the potential of being physically and sexually abused, especially when you are sleeping beside a man. She also finds it difficult to connect with male staff. "It's better to ask a woman when you have girlie problems. It's good to have women as counsellors because some of the women have been through almost the same thing and straightened out."

Beth's sniff addiction is hard to give up. She is always renouncing it and then starting again, even though it gives her headaches, and she deplores the way it makes people wobbly on their feet and how their noses run and their mouths drool. While she waits for Ed to get out of hospital, she tries to hold her life together, making preparations with her worker to move into a cheap hotel that is described by another social worker as one of the most rundown in Winnipeg. Beth, who has seen the room, says it will be the best place she has ever lived in. When she's paid her rent, she will have $114 a month left from her welfare cheque to clothe and feed herself. She knows where to find food and shelter, tramping around the city to get breakfast there, lunch here, counselling at a third place, and a bed at a fourth. She knows which alleys to avoid because they can be dangerous and likes to take shortcuts through the University of Winnipeg campus because she can briefly pretend to be a student.

Although she's had offers, she's not tempted to cheat on Ed while he's in hospital. "I don't want to and I would feel guilty. I don't want to hurt Ed like that. He's hurt enough being in that place." She has to take a bus to see him and it's not always easy to find the cash on her meagre budget. "I want Ed to be out. I feel lost without him."

Peggy

Born to an alcoholic mother and raised in foster homes, Peggy, 28, was introduced to solvent at 12. She has tried many forms of alcohol, including mouthwash and hairspray, but gave up drinking a couple of years ago.

My mom was an alcoholic and didn't want me. She's sober now. She doesn't smoke or drink beer, she just eats and sleeps. She's a nurse; she cleans up rooms, changes beds—that kind of nurse.

Peggy went to her first foster home when she was about two years old. She lived in so many she can't recall them all, although one family does stick in her mind. They gave her her own room, guitar lessons, a bike, and the opportunity to ride horses. This "cool" couple still keep some stuff for her. Most of the other homes were very strict and Peggy didn't like the rules nor the punishments for breaking those rules.

A cousin introduced her to solvents when she was 12. She has tried to quit, but has only lasted a week before putting a rag soaked with paint thinner to her mouth. She went into a detox program for alcohol two years ago and says she hasn't drunk anything since. Sniffing "doesn't get me high or anything. It just gives me bad breath and stinks me up." She has also drunk hairspray and mouthwash. "Man, did it get you drunk fast. I didn't think it would get you drunk or anything, but four shots and I couldn't walk." She has also tried crack cocaine. She did six flaps and ended up in hospital.

When Peggy needs money, she panhandles on Winnipeg's Portage Avenue, making about $10 an hour from men who hand her toonies. Occasionally, if her boyfriend is not around, she sells her body but only to men she knows, phoning them first. If her boyfriend finds out, he usually beats her and takes the money. Her boyfriend, she says, is generous and buys her stuff, but he also has a very short temper. "I don't like being alone. That's why I stay [with him]."

Currently, Peggy is pregnant by one of her regular customers. Her boyfriend doesn't know, and she's hoping to have an abortion. She's not entirely clear how many times she's been pregnant. She miscarried once because she was "drinking, not eating and doing solvent and getting into fights." Another was a tubal pregnancy and had to be terminated. She gave up two babies for adoption. Another died in Peggy's arms immediately before she was supposed to take her home from the hospital. "I felt her take her last breath and she squeezed my finger. I just burst into tears."

When Peggy looks to the future, her only wish is to get all her children back. But right now she's living in the present and desperately trying to stop shivering before going into the winter cold. She raises her face to a shelter worker and gives him a glowing smile as he hands her a towel and a bar of soap for a shower. She's found a way to warm up for a few minutes, and so she's happy.

❖ ❖ ❖

Theresa

Both Theresa and her husband were scarred by the residential school experience, which resulted in violence, addictions, pros-

titution, and the dissolution of their family. After a hard life on the streets of Winnipeg, she has found a safe place to live and has her addictions under control.

A few years ago Theresa, a matronly woman in her late 60s, was raped by a man who was so determined to harm her that he smashed through three doors to reach her. Today she sits in the safety of her room at the long-term stay shelter, surrounded by pictures of her children and grandchildren, and symbols of her native spirituality. She talks about her fear of venturing out again, and she shudders when she recalls that night and that man. She feels safe at the shelter, but just as she plucks up courage to live alone, the newspaper reports another break-in or an assault, and all her fears return. "I pray and talk to the Creator. That's my comfort and how I survive. I've always prayed, even when young."

Theresa grew up on a reserve in Ontario. Her mother spent most of her time cleaning and cooking and caring for her children. She died at 46. Theresa's relationship with her father was always problematic, though she has difficulty explaining what exactly was wrong. He never abused her, but his feelings toward her were certainly not ones with which she is comfortable. "I wonder which way he cared for me. I'm confused that way and it affected me a lot in my married life." She is sure that if she hadn't left to marry he would have forced her into a sexual relationship. On the positive side she's proud he was the first Aboriginal person to finish high school in Kenora. Both Theresa's parents were heavy drinkers.

Theresa and her sister, aged seven and five respectively, were sent to residential schools, where all the children were treated badly by the nuns who picked on the younger girls, making them cry. The windows were so high the children couldn't see out, and 200 students were crammed into one playroom. The toilets were filthy making it difficult for Theresa to use them. "I used to be homesick, and I used to think of my mother every night and my brother and sister and pray, okay, I hope she [her mother] comes so that I can see her. My little sister used to cry." The girls caught chickenpox, and their parents, unhappy with the quality of care, moved them to another school, which was much better even though the nuns hit them, grabbing them by the ears and neck. One day she and another student were told to clean the priest's rooms. As she worked, Theresa could hear her friend giggling, so she went to have a look. "The priest had her over his knees, face down, and he had his hands between her legs. He gave us 25 cents each and said 'Don't show this to sister.' I asked the other girl why she was giggling and she said, 'He was tickling me.' I said, 'That's not nice.'"

Both Theresa's grandmothers had taught her the traditional ways, but the nuns told her that she was indulging in devil worship; they denounced dance ceremonies especially. As punishment for various sins, the nuns held her back. Consequently, she repeated Grade 5 several times with progressively younger children.

At 15, Theresa left school to get married. At 16, she had her first child, and she had another one every two years for a total of seven by her husband and one more with another man. She has 30 grandchildren and a dozen or so great-grandchildren.

Theresa's husband, a trapper, was sexually abused by Roman Catholic brothers and physically abused and thrown out of the house by his stepfather. The young couple made an agreement not to drink if they had children, and for a while they kept that promise. Theresa worked hard, cutting wood and hauling water. "It was a good feeling sitting outside the log cabin playing checkers, the kids all cuddled up, and all of a sudden you would hear the wolves. I am grateful that I gave that to my children because they will carry that. I was comfortable out in the bush. Everything around us was sacred— the animals, the trees, the ground we walked on—everything like that." Her mother-in-law taught her more of the traditional ways and such skills as preparing medicines from animal fat and plants and making moccasins and pemmican. However, not everything was idyllic. Theresa's husband began to have affairs, leaving her alone with the children, sometimes for several days at a time. When she asked him what he was up to, he would reply that he had a meeting. Mostly she let it go, nursing her pain in silence, but inside she was increasingly angry. Once she threw a jar at his head, and he didn't come home again for four days.

When Theresa was about 35, she began to use alcohol and to pop pills to take her mind off her troubles. She developed tuberculosis. While she was in hospital in Thunder Bay, her husband had an affair that produced a child. Theresa started drinking with a man, provoking her husband's jealousy. "But you've got a woman," she protested. "That's different," he said. "I'm a man and I can." Finally, her husband made her move out. She took the children with her, but they returned to their father. She started to have her own affair with a man who physically abused her. He tied her to the bedpost, ripped off all her clothes, and hit her with a chain until she blacked out. When she said she was leaving, he threatened to take their baby boy, so she returned, and the cycle of violence started again. Scared to death, she tried to figure out what to do. Violence overtook her. "I don't know what got into me. I had had enough of the beatings and I was full of anger, so I took a stick to him and broke his legs." Finally the little boy's paternal grandfather intervened and pleaded with her to leave before someone died. Theresa left the boy with him and went to Winnipeg in search of safety. Instead she found the dangers of street life laced with alcohol and pills. "Another family left behind."

Theresa stayed with her sister until she was kicked out. She made money the only way she could—by prostitution. She cycled through highs and lows, shelters, programs, and men, in a state of disbelief that she was doing all the things she had sworn she never would. "I don't know how many times I had a close call to getting hurt. I did all kinds of things that are not nice. I did those things to get money." Once a customer pushed her out of his car while it was moving. Another regular john always carried a hammer: "I could kill you right now," he said, finding his fulfillment in scare tactics. Another picked her up in a bar and drove her to the country. While he was fumbling around, she made a break and ran to the highway. As he caught up with her, a police car arrived, and her assailant disappeared. Theresa slept in abandoned cars or under road ramps with a group of people. One of them started yelling in the middle of the night. The others told him to shut up and went back to sleep. In the morning, they discovered he had been stabbed to death.

Now that Theresa has been off the pills and alcohol for a year, she worries about her children as she sees her life being replicated in theirs, and she grieves for her oldest son who took off for the West Coast 20 years ago, never to be heard from again. She tries talking to her family, but her hard-gained wisdom falls on deaf ears. These days she concentrates on her beadwork and sewing. When she's tempted to dwell on the bad things, she turns to the Creator from whom she derives great comfort. "I'm pretty sure that before I'm too old I'll find something that will keep me happy."

Sources

Amnesty International. 2004. *Stolen Sisters: Discrimination and Violence Against Indigenous Women in Canada.* October. <http://web.amnesty.org/library/index/engamr200012004>.

Canadian Health Network. 2006. *What Were Residential Schools?* <http://www.canadian-health-network.ca>.

Green, Norma. 2003. *Profile of an Aboriginal Woman Serving Time in a Federal Institution.* Correctional Service of Canada Aboriginal Initiatives Branch. <http://www/csc/scc/gc/ca/text/prgrm/correctional/abissues/know/5_e.shtml>.

Institute for the Advancement of Aboriginal Women (IAAW). 2003. *Resources for Aboriginal Women in Alberta.* Edmonton. <http://www.iaaw.ca>.

Morris, Marika. 2002. *Factsheet: Women in Poverty.* Canadian Research Institute for the Advancement of Women. <http://www.criaw-icref.ca>.

Pate, Kim. 2003. "Prisons: The Latest Solution to Homelessness, Poverty, and Mental Illness." Speech given by the executive director of the Canadian Association of Elizabeth Fry Societies. Calgary, 18 September.

——. 2002. "Women and Girls in Prison: Canada's Alternative to Equality and Justice." Speech given by executive director of the Canadian Association of Elizabeth Fry Societies. Winnipeg, 24 October.

Prostitution Alternatives Counselling and Education Society (PACE). 2001. Vancouver. <http://www.missingpeople.net/pace_report_on_violence_against_ sex_ trade_workers-june_2001.htm>.

Stavenhagen, Rodolfo. 2005. Mission to Canada. United Nations: Commission on Human Rights. <http://www.ohchr.org/english/bodies/chr/docs/61chr/ E.CN.4.2005.88.Add.3.pdf>.

Weber, Lisa D. 2002-04. *Can You Hear Us?: A Report on Human Rights Discrimination Against Aboriginal Women in Canada.* Edmonton: Institute for the Advancement of Aboriginal Women.

Interviews

Blind, Reta. Downtown Eastside Women's Centre, Vancouver. 2004.

McPhee, Donna. Formerly on the Aboriginal Standing Committee of the Calgary Homelessness Foundation. 2004.

CHAPTER 9

WHAT DO YOU MEAN
YOUR NAME IS TERRY?

It's a population that people don't do a lot of research on.
—Calgary chartered psychologist

It was 9 a.m. on a sunny late spring day. At some point during the night, two women had spread out sleeping bags to cover the ground in a bus shelter at the busy Toronto intersection of Parliament and Dundas. This is an area that boasts extreme wealth and extreme poverty, where very upwardly mobile people rub uneasy shoulders with addicts, immigrants, and prostitutes. The women were fast asleep, curled up in each other's arms, oblivious to the passing crowds peering through the glass into their makeshift bedroom. Why, one asks, is this very public place apparently safer for these two women than nearby shelters? In Calgary, another homeless woman tells how staff and clients alike felt very uncomfortable when an openly lesbian couple lived together in the shelter. "The two women were out and open ... everyone was relieved when they left ... the things said and talked about were rather nasty."

Although the gay, lesbian, bisexual, and trans (GLBT) community in Canada totals only about 10 per cent of the general population, some care providers and homeless women say they may total as many as 40 per cent of the people on the streets of our cities. One lesbian interviewed at an Edmonton drop-in centre for women and trans individuals involved in street prostitution estimated that 75 per cent of the straight street population in that city has also "encountered same-sex partners at some particular point." There is, though, a dearth of research, especially Canadian data, on the GLBT homeless community, even though it faces some very distinct problems. These figures are almost anyone's guess and probably vary somewhat from city to city depending on how homophobic and transphobic it is.

The GLBT community embraces a very diverse group of people who, according to the Canadian Rainbow Health Coalition (2004), have in common "a physical and/or emotional attraction for people of the same gender or a gender identity that varies from their genetic one." It is important to draw a distinction between a person's sex and their gender. For most of us the two go hand in hand. For members of the trans community, their bodies may indicate they are of the male sex but their heart and soul tells them that their gender is female, or vice versa. In this short space, it is impossible to go into the wide range of sexual orientations and gender identities; the acronym GLBT embraces that diversity to its fullest, including Aboriginal two-spirit people.

Without more information on these women, many of whom for safety reasons have not come out, it is difficult to provide suitable assistance for them. But we do know that they all face not only the same problems as heterosexual women but even further discrimination in housing, custody and access, and employment, plus gay bashing to boot. The problems are compounded further if they are Aboriginal or from other racial minorities, are seniors, or have disabilities. "They carry the burden of that minority. It's another cross to bear," says Kathy Stringer, Coordinator of Women's and Children's Programs, St. James Community Services Society (interview 2004).

Britain's Stonewall Housing (2004) says that their sexual orientation can cause young lesbians and gay men to be homeless. Sometimes they are thrown out by their families, or they decide that it's prudent to leave before a catastrophe, or because their life is made miserable by frightened or angry parents. They may also become homeless because of family breakdown, disruptive parental behaviour, violence, abuse, bullying, and religious and cultural expectations. In all likelihood, their homelessness is caused by a combination of factors, some related to sexuality and some not.

While Canada leads the way in legislating gay marriage, there is a much bigger, darker underbelly to the world inhabited by GLBT women. Research shows that it is clouded by alcohol abuse, smoking, illicit drug abuse, depression, low self-esteem, feelings of isolation, risk of parental rejection, peer abuse, school dropout, unemployment, physical violence, unsafe sexual behaviour, and high suicide rates. For example, the Canadian Rainbow Health Coalition's document, *Health and Wellness in the Gay, Lesbian, Bisexual, Transgendered, and Two-Spirit Communities* (2004) points out that young lesbian women smoke at 14 times the rate of their non-lesbian peers. It is still difficult for GLBT women to find appropriate counselling; therefore, it is harder for them to maintain self-esteem, acquire social skills, and cement family and interpersonal ties—all are important in preventing suicide. Once these women become homeless, their problems are magnified, and they have fewer chances to deal with them, especially as there is a lack of role models and mentors in society in general and on the streets in particular. Being GLBT can add to the difficulties experienced while being homeless in several ways.

First, the struggle to come to terms with their orientation without access to proper support can lead to depression and the use of alcohol and drugs. Often their experiences with professionals have been far from happy—teachers who have failed to stop bullying, doctors who have tried to argue them out of their orientation, and so on. One Edmonton homeless lesbian tells of being sent away from hospital with a dab of antiseptic ointment for a life-threatening infection. Fortunately, someone lobbied for her, and she was placed on intravenous antibiotics at another hospital. Another woman talks about the "innuendoes, swearing, and whispering" that she has encountered.

Second, because of our society's rampant homophobia and transphobia, many homeless lesbian and bisexual women do not use shelters, preferring to sleep rough, couch-surf, live in dangerous situations, or form a liaison with a man (known as a "mark") for protection and camouflage. Many don't come out, finding it safer to masquerade as straight women. "I would talk about my 'husband' to fit in," says one who has used the shelter system in Vancouver, Toronto, and Calgary. The trans-identified, while a small minority, have a particularly hard time in shelters as they are judged on their externals only. Unless they conform to someone else's expectations of what a man, or a woman, should look like, they may be directed to inappropriate toilets, showers, and sleeping areas, which make them vulnerable to all sorts of violence.

If they use shelters or other services that are not sensitive to their problems, GLBT women may leave without having their needs met, returning to dangerous or abusive situations. If they stay and suffer homophobic or transphobic abuse—physical, verbal, or any other form—their problems, like low self-esteem and drug usage, can escalate. "To be or not to be" is the question for many. Michael, who grew up in Saskatchewan as Mary, left home in 1950. His family didn't see him again for 53 years; he turned up wandering on the streets in Calgary, confused and suffering from dementia. The family was shocked that he was living as a male and that he had been a fixture at drop-in centres. For some there's no denying their orientation, but others are reluctant to reveal it, so they live a lie. "What damage is done by denying who they are for years and years?" asks Stringer (2004). "You have to be who you are."

Some women are confused by their sexuality and their feelings. Often coming from very conservative backgrounds, they feel they should be with a man but will confidentially admit that they are more comfortable with a woman. "I felt used when I was with men because I wasn't aroused. With women I have a lot of affection, caring, and foreplay, and I found it very beautiful; that's what threw me to women," says a lesbian who works as a prostitute.

Women who have been sexually abused may also have more acceptance of moving across the barrier from loving men to women, says Jane Oxenbury (interview 2004), a Calgary chartered psychologist who works with this population and credits them with a broader view of sexuality than the mainstream. Put slightly differently, one formerly homeless lesbian says, "There are so many crappy men out there, so many assholes that it's only natural that they [women] would lean toward another woman. Women, when they are stressed out, seek other women for support. In every woman the potential is there and after a horrible relationship with a guy, they say, 'Yuck, I'm signing off on that.'"

Like other homeless women, but probably to an even greater degree, the GLBT group does not take advantage of preventive health services for fear of being misunderstood or rejected. Lesbians may find it hard to get a routine Pap smear to detect cancer of the cervix because some doctors consider them a low-risk group. However, studies (The Centre 2002; Frankowski 2002) show the rates of cervical cancer are about equal in lesbian and heterosexual women and suggest that lesbians may be at an even greater risk for breast cancer due to higher body weights, greater alcohol consumption, and either not having children or having them later in life.

If the medical situation is bad for lesbians and bi-sexuals, it's dire for trans people. Some, wanting to discard their female body, may be driven to injecting their own anabolic steroids. Those moving the other way will dose themselves with estrogen and silicone obtained on the street or perform surgeries on themselves because of barriers in the health system. Others have died of bladder infections rather than consult a contemptuous doctor. They also face a host of other problems (Pyne speech 2004):

- Many are illegal immigrants fleeing violence in their country of origin.
- They have very high addiction rates.
- They are often in abusive relationships.
- They are targets of hate violence and police violence.
- Up to three-quarters of the street-active community is HIV positive.
- Many are homeless with all the attendant problems of no fixed address.

- Many have low-self esteem.
- If they have ID, it may not be under their current name or appearance.
- Sex-change operations are costly, even if they are still available in their province.
- Employment is hard to obtain—"What do you mean your name is Terry?"

Many women's shelters are reluctant or refuse point blank to take trans people, even though both trans women and men say that women's shelters are the safest places for them.

In 2003 Toronto, which probably has the highest concentration of trans people in the country, led the way in North America by adopting standards that all shelters must be accessible to trans people and that shelters must support them by providing services in the gender that they identify as the best for their safety. Toronto is also home to The 519, an organization that ministers to the needs of trans people. One of its initiatives is the Trans Communities' Shelter Access Project, a team of trans women and men funded to develop and provide workshops and policy assistance to shelters, hostels, and detox centres to make their services more accessible. Jake Pyne, the shelter access project co-ordinator, says that the keys to making shelters safer are training and education of staff and residents (Pyne interview 2004).

Often a shelter will say it lacks the appropriate physical layout, but the problem goes deeper than ensuring a trans person can go to the toilet or a shower without feeling humiliated or beaten up. Some shelters lay down arbitrary rules—for instance, that trans women must wear dresses, forgetting that few heterosexual women on the street wear them, or that they have to be on hormones, or that they have to have had surgeries that are rarely covered by health care and that can cost $20,000 to $50,000. If trans women are accepted, they are often segregated in one room. Because so many shelters are dangerous for trans people, they are more likely to become stuck on the streets because they are denied assistance with issues like employment, ID, and housing. "It's a class system," says Pyne. "Whose issues get addressed? Whose comfort gets addressed?"

Shelters usually cite potential violence and the legitimate fear of abused women being around "someone with a penis" when denying entrance to trans women. Pyne says, though, that the shelters fail to look at the perpetrators of fights. If straight women are uncomfortable, they will often start a quarrel in the knowledge they won't be the ones barred, that the trans will be the first to get the boot, no questions asked. "A lot of transgendered women are at the end of their rope. They are harassed in bathrooms and on the bus. Then they just lose it and get kicked out. They learn to defend themselves and it's labelled 'male aggressive behaviour' when they need it to survive." Discrimination against trans women is on a par with racism, ignorance about mental illness, and homophobia. Most shelters have policies and procedures to guide them in these areas that can be applied to transphobia (Pyne interview 2004).

As for abuse survivors' fears that a re-run of their violent pasts will be triggered by the presence of someone they perceive as male, Pyne and his team say that there is a difference between causing and triggering a trauma and that triggers can be managed over time. If a crisis is blown open, it can be used as an opportunity to get appropriate support and counselling. Newcomers should be prepared at intake for the presence of trans women, who are in all likelihood survivors of abuse themselves. "Workshops with residents go surprisingly well," says Pyne. "Unlike community workers, they are not afraid of saying the wrong thing and tend to speak their minds and get the information they need because they ask for it."

Stringer, of Vancouver's St. James Community Services Society, which successfully integrates lesbians, bi-sexuals, and trans women, says it's instructive to look at who does best in our patriarchal society and who is the most marginalized. "But we are all the same—that's the message. These are not weirdos. All of them are people, no matter what" (Stringer interview, 2004).

Ginger

> *Because Ginger Austin, 47, has suffered so much to be accepted as a woman, she wanted her real name used in the hopes that it would give credibility to her story, which is dedicated to Liz Choquette, the counsellor who gave her confirmation of her womanhood.*

Ginger knows what it's like to be Cinderella. Every Thursday she used to go to a club for cross-dressers, drag queens, and trans people. She listened to the singing, made new friends, and most of all basked in the acceptance. For a few brief hours she enjoyed being herself. No one thought she was strange, even though nature had played a mean trick by giving her a woman's heart in a man's body. At midnight, the fantasy ended, and Ginger was out on the mean streets of Vancouver where straights and gays alike thought that she was fair game for a good beating. For her own safety, before leaving the club she removed her wig, her make-up, her dress, and her high-heels and reverted to neutral sweats and a more masculine demeanour.

Ginger lives in a converted hotel, a home for a number of "hard-to-house" people on Vancouver's Downtown Eastside. It's supposed to be safe, but she's been attacked eight times in two years. For the interview she's wearing sweat pants and sandals, but her small closet contains several dresses and a few high-heeled shoes. In the bathroom a couple of lacy bras are hanging up to dry. Although Ginger's body continues to betray her, among other things sprouting hairs in unseemly places, she is at her core very much a woman. When she was looking after her youngest son, the baby development worker asked how she could be so nurturing. "Because I'm living as a woman," she replied.

When Ginger was 18 months old, her parents handed her over to Ontario Children's Aid. As a country-raised child, she was spanked not because she wanted to play doctor with the girls but because she wouldn't play Ken to the neighbouring girl's Barbie. "I wanted to be Barbie's girlfriend. I never wanted to be Ken." At 15, she had already lived in four foster homes and two group homes. The first family she can remember was extremely cold and at times violent. One of their natural sons started to molest her at the age of four or five. By the time Ginger was seven, the seducer had it down to a fine art, rewarding her with candy. Things most kids take for granted, like properly fitting shoes, were denied Ginger, so her feet were shoved into second-hand ones, squashing them for life. Oddly, this became an asset when she wanted to wear high heels.

"All through this time, I was always wanting to wake up as a girl." She started to experiment with make-up and wearing her foster sister's underwear. Once, she was caught by the father who dragged her through the house, humiliating her in front of another foster brother whom Ginger adored. "Look at the clown," yelled the father. To this day, Ginger cannot bear any insinuation that her make-up looks garish. After several spankings, she soon realized that she had to hide her true nature. In order to try and gain the family's affection, she valiantly did all the farm chores, but when she finally won his approval and the father said, "You can call me father," she didn't want the privilege any more. "There's no way in hell that I'm accepting him as anything but a man married to a woman [and both] are full-time babysitters."

As she worked her way through foster homes, Ginger's awareness of the need to live a lie was reinforced. In her teen years, she was given more privacy and more opportunities, and she took to wearing women's underwear on a permanent basis.

If I didn't look in the mirror, I was starting to feel more feminine and that side of my personality was starting to develop, but I still had to play a role. As a child, the hardest part was school—knowing I couldn't let the boys know and watching groups of girls that all I wanted was to be friends with. Luckily, I was good at sports, so the guys liked me.

Ginger made excuses—any excuse—to use the changing rooms after the boys had left. Once, when she thought she was alone, a coach caught her in her panties. She started to cry. The coach tried to comfort her, saying, "It's okay; just make sure the boys don't find out."

By the time she was 12 or 13, Ginger was not only struggling with all the changes occurring to her body that were making it pronouncedly masculine, but she also developed a desire to meet her birth parents. Children's Aid tried to dissuade her, saying that they had never loved her. To prove their point, they revealed that the parents had kept Ginger's sister. "It made me want to be the person I was inside even more. I thought, if I had been a girl, my mother might never have given me up. I really started disliking myself as a male." Finally, Ginger was allowed to visit her father. It was a disaster. The man she had put on a pedestal raped her when she asked for help with her homework and shattered all her dreams by revealing that her mother was a prostitute. From this point Ginger didn't want to have anything to do with anyone. Mad at the mother she had never met, she started to molest girls on the street.

Confused, Ginger, 15, ran away to Toronto where she survived by panhandling and offering herself as a boy to gay men, her lingerie not withstanding. She detested being treated as a boy, but it meant survival. Finally, her luck turned and she met Harold, who as a lawyer and psychologist was a total contrast to her birth father. "He took me off the streets, taught me how to shop, and never touched me once." Children's Aid wanted Ginger back, but Harold told them that he would sue them for all the abuse that had happened to her in their care. He called their bluff and won. "I was so proud he stuck up for me. They said to me, 'You have made your bed,' and I replied, 'At least I made it a little better than you did.'" Ginger was aware of Harold's feelings, but as a teen she was unable to recognize his platonic affection as love. Now, she says it's thanks to him that she knows there is "more to love than the mechanics."

At 17, Ginger realized that she had to forge her own identity and left Harold to move to Edmonton where she secretly indulged her dreams of dressing up, sometimes checking into a Calgary hotel to maintain her anonymity. She also went shopping regularly for women's clothes.

> I would tell the [sales] clerk they were for my sister, but I was very scared inside. There was a lot of anxiety going into the women's department to the point where I would be sweating, and I would get in and out as fast as possible. I felt if anyone found out I would be embarrassed, ridiculed. If anyone saw me dressed up—a fear, a panic, a shame; I was terrified that I would not be liked at all, not wanted by anybody.

When her money and her time in the hotel started to run out, Ginger was thrown into despair because she knew her spell as a woman was running out too. She cried all night, not wanting to become a man again and realizing she would have to start the whole cycle of earning enough money for a precious few more days of wearing her dresses and frothy underwear. She tried to commit suicide several times, and it did not console her in the least that, when she went for help, she was told she was a cross-dresser. In her heart of hearts she knew that wasn't the case, even though for a while she had a wife. The marriage broke down when the wife accused Ginger of adultery. "The reasons why I left for a night or two were because I was going to a hotel. Adultery? I don't think so." The judge laughed when he heard her version of the story and believed it rather than her wife's allegations. When it was all over, broken-hearted and betrayed because she discovered her wife was a prostitute too, Ginger took some money from the restaurant where she was employed and fled to Vancouver. After one more suicide attempt, she was referred to a psychotherapist, Liz Choquette, whom she saw for nine years. "She gave me compassion and understanding without reservation. It took a while to convince me that I'm a good person because I truly thought that part of me was evil. She finally convinced me, and I started believing I was okay."

Ginger met others who helped her emerge as a "trannie," including a lesbian friend and staff at a drop-in centre where she learned how to apply make-up, how to dress appropriately, and how to live safely. She makes sure she sits near the front of a bus; she never walks across parking lots by herself; and, until it was stolen, she carried a cellphone.

Ginger bumped into Tracy at a residence for people with mental health problems, and they formed a bond. They have two little boys. The oldest, Paul, is now in his mid teens and was adopted by a family that Ginger selected over two others because the mother was unable to have babies and because she works with handicapped children. Ginger fought tooth and nail to keep Shane, the younger of the two, who is now about seven. Tracy wasn't able to help because her schizophrenia deteriorated drastically after Shane's birth.

Ginger believes the cards were stacked against her keeping Shane, even though she jumped through every hoop, going to numerous parenting programs that awarded her "rave reviews ... I know what not to do with another human being ... You do not press your beliefs, you guide them. Always stand behind them so they have some guidance and so they won't get hurt. Never stop them from enjoying themselves."

Eventually, it became obvious that Ginger was pitted against a system bigger than she was, so she kept her promise to make sure that Shane wasn't adopted by arranging for Tracy's aunt and uncle to have custody of him. "It was hard, but I kept my promise. I love both my children and not a day goes by that I don't think about Shane and Paul."

Although Paul is in a closed adoption, Ginger hopes that one day he will look her up and says she's willing to put her sex change on hold until she can explain it to him. "He's going to be looking for a father and a father image and that's what he's going to see. Hopefully we will develop a friendship, a best buddy thing. I won't take away from the adoptive parents." Since the BC government has cancelled all such surgery, she doesn't actually have an option at this point. However, she has been on hormones to start the sex-change process. She took medication to block her male hormones and was prescribed estrogen. She purchased progesterone on the street for eight months because her doctor was reluctant to give it to her. She reacted adversely to the treatment, so has been off it for a while. As a result, her chest hair has started to grow back, and she developed an infected nipple from a nick caused while shaving. On top of that, she has serious health problems, including a debilitating form of arthritis and two crushed discs in her back that prevent her from going more than a few blocks without a walker.

For her own safety, Ginger doesn't go out in public wearing a dress or make-up. She is more than happy, though, to display the real woman when it's safe. She dabs away at her face: "How does it look? Do I need more foundation? More lipstick?" She crosses her legs elegantly and drapes her arms over her breast. "This is a reflection. Dressing like this is a reflection of who I am inside."

❖ ❖ ❖

Bree

Like many women on the streets, Bree's tough exterior conceals a gentle, thoughtful, albeit pained interior life. In more supportive circumstances she might have grown up as a role model for girl athletes, but her attributes are used very differently on the streets.

At 30, Bree is still struggling with the fact that she was blamed for everything and that her geeky half-brother could do no wrong. Even the fact that she was born a girl was problematic for her father, who wanted a male to perpetuate his not uncommon Scottish surname. "What it boiled down to, I was a mistake. I was supposed to be a boy. Everything about me makes my family angry." Her mother even called the police because Bree, aged two, had taken some valuables and buried them in the backyard.

Her father was a miner, and the family was always on the move for his work. As Bree says, "Where there was a hole, there was us." From a little girl's point of view the constant motion was very disruptive. Bree's father, an alcoholic, and her mother, a "dry drunk," were both equally inept at parenting. "They put the fun in dysfunctional." Because of all the fighting and yelling, she was often on the loose at an early age. "It was easier to be out of the home. You can't scream at someone you can't see." In the meantime at home and school, her older brother was the ideal child. He was only grounded twice, made the honour role with no effort, and captained the debate and chess teams. Living in his shadow, Bree felt like a second-class citizen.

Bree says she herself doesn't remember much from her early childhood, just the stories she was told. The stories are obviously the family's version of history, not hers. She re-tells them with humour, but she is relieved when the official version is challenged. One day when she was about four, she was sent to nursery school as usual, but when she came home, she found her mother had left, abandoning both children. The situation deteriorated even further because she ceased to exist for her dad. "Tell your sister to go to bed," he would say to Bree's brother, his stepson. "I was invisible, I was nothing. It didn't matter what I did and the less attention I got, the more I acted out."

When she was five, the children were apprehended by social services and sent to their mother in Barrhead, Alberta. By then Bree hated the woman who to all intents and appearances had abandoned her. Her mother, who worked in bars, moved around Alberta looking for jobs. "There are not many small towns in this province that I don't know real well." Her mother also had a succession of new partners, several of them drug dealers, all of whom had to be addressed as "Dad." The two children learned to fend for themselves. By eight Bree was already drinking heavily. "I just didn't care; it took me away from everything."

When Bree was 10, her mother remarried a disciplinarian who looked, appropriately, like Hitler. By this time, Bree had had a good half-dozen "fathers," and her first bid for independence was to refuse to call him Dad, which didn't go down well. The more he tried to control her, the more it became her "mission to break every rule he set down." The following year she was sent back to her birth father in British Columbia. Father and 11-year-old daughter became drinking buddies when he wasn't beating her. Bree also smoked pot, dropped acid, and experimented with mushrooms. On the side she did break-and-enters, although she didn't lack cash because her father often gave her $50 to go away for the day. "Too much time and money, and no supervision."

School might have been Bree's salvation, but it wasn't, and the fact that teachers ignored her bruises and believed her preposterous explanations still rankles. "Great school systems we have that protect children." She once turned up with a face so swollen she could see her own cheek. She told the teacher she had tumbled downstairs. "Okay," said her teacher. Bree concluded that no one cared. The school also failed to pick up on the fact that she was dyslexic and could neither read nor write. She continued to advance grade after grade because she was good at sports—basketball, swimming, volleyball—and to play on the teams, you had to pass. Bree didn't just play, she excelled. Failing her was not an option.

"Kids are dumb," says Bree, who gives the impression of being anything but. One day when her father threw her against the wall, she rose up taunting him, "Is that the best you've got?" He promptly picked her up again and hurled her right through the wall. It was after this episode that her mother found out what was going on. In three months, Bree was back with her in Devon, Alberta. Her mother wanted to turn Bree into a best friend, but too much had happened and, besides, she hadn't really wanted to come back to a situation where she was inevitably compared to her brother who was successfully blaming Bree for all his petty misdemeanours. Looking back, Bree says it was "the 13th degree of hell."

At school she was isolated. Her predilection for heavy metal and picking fights, the drinking, the drugs, and her criminal record all set her apart in a classroom of "spoiled, rich kids.... I had that ever famous attitude problem—a chip on my shoulder. I used to tell them I've earned my chip, leave me alone." She started school in Devon at the end of the spring break. By the end of the year she had been suspended five times, a pattern set long ago in kindergarten where she was kicked out because she didn't play well with other children.

By the next year she was in foster care. For the first time ever, Bree felt she was in a place where someone actually cared and, once she got over this novelty, she settled down. As she grew older, she wanted a little more independence, and the rules rankled. Another girl jumped off the roof, and Bree was yanked out of the house at 3 a.m. In the next two years she was placed in about 60 homes; some gave up on her almost before she had crossed the threshold. A lot of the time she was on the lam doing break-ins and various drugs, including cocaine and alcohol. When she was 16 there was a warrant out for her arrest, and she was pregnant, the result of a rape.

Bree was given a choice: "Sit on my ass in a corrections centre for nine months, or go home." She went home, quit the drugs and alcohol, and waited for the baby. It was an easy delivery, but shortly afterward she started to bleed, had a reaction to the blood transfusion, and nearly died. Her heart stopped and her lungs shut down for over three minutes. While the baby boy was released in two days, Bree fought for her life for a month. When she was well, the doctors told her that she wouldn't be able to have another baby. "I figured out if he was my only child, I better give it a shot, so I kept him for a month and then walked out. Shades of my mother."

Questions produce a slightly different version. Although there was lots of attention for the baby, there was very little support for Bree, still a child herself and recovering from the dual traumas of rape and near death. "Suck it up," said her mother, unaware of the rape. "You did an adult thing, now take the adult consequences."

At one level Bree berates herself for leaving, but at another she knows she did the right thing. From time to time she receives news of her boy. She knows, for instance, that he's well loved and that at 13 he's athletic and intelligent. It's the little details for which she thirsts. "The fact I don't know his favourite colour drives me nuts.... I love that child very dearly, but it [love] doesn't provide food, shelter, or clothing. He has a good life. I admitted I couldn't do it, and I couldn't do to him what was done to me. Love had everything to do with my decision."

When Bree gave her baby up, nothing seemed to matter. She lived on the streets, couch-surfing, and selling and doing drugs. "If you needed something, I could find it." She's ashamed to admit it, but she became a pimp, running six girls. "It gave me such a rush. It was a power trip—them giving me their money and me telling them to do what I told them to do. I was finally in control, and it didn't matter what I did because I didn't have to answer to anybody." Although she feels a bit guilty about pimping, Bree is very proud of the women who worked for her. A couple of them have become "amazing" mothers and one has a management degree. Although two are dead, she sees a lot of hope in the lives of the survivors because "it's not easy to quit the streets when society slams doors."

All the cash from the dealing and pimping gave Bree even greater access to drugs and alcohol, but nothing filled the void in her heart. She and a couple of the girls were arrested on prostitution-related charges. She says she was the first female pimp arrested in Canada and the second-youngest woman to be convicted on pimping charges. "And I thought *I* was horrible at 18."

Bree entered what she calls the U of C (the university of crime), the Fort Saskatchewan Correctional Centre. It was a period of growth in several senses. Before her sentence began, another woman told her that jail would change her, but it was up to Bree to decide if it was for good or for bad. Although Bree "blew her off," the words stuck. For once she felt secure enough to do some thinking, and, during her second year, she decided she didn't want to spend her life in jail and took some programs including anger management and life skills. She left jail believing she had the world by the ears, but she hadn't taken into account that the world had moved on and she had remained relatively stationary, her only job experience pimping and selling drugs. She had also increased her criminal network.

Bree discovered that a woman with no lawful skills, no references, and no resume has no chance in the job market. She returned to her old activities. In particular she was known for finding what people wanted: drugs, guns, televisions, whatever. "I knew somebody who had it." Bree had grown in other ways. She entered jail at five foot six inches and 160 pounds and left five inches taller and 90 pounds heavier. This upped the violence in her life: "When you are that big, people are always picking fights; I spent every waking hour being angry."

Drifting in and out of lesbian relationships, she discovered the "wonderful" drug, crack. "It was my pal, my companion, my best friend, my lover, my enemy, my everything. And the more I smoked, the worse I felt when I came down." For four years Bree was so obsessed that she didn't speak to her family; when two close friends died, however, she went into treatment. She came out clean but aimless and began dating a prostitute who was a crack addict. In 18 months she was using again.

The pair made a good living, Bree selling pot, making $300 to $400 a day, and her lover working the streets. It kept them "happy little crack heads." They broke up two months ago, and now Bree is living at an Edmonton shelter concentrating on dealing with her addictions, not easy for someone whose only coping mechanisms are getting high and lashing out.

Despite her lack of education, Bree thought a lot about a society that is so cruel to women and then blames them for what has happened. "It amazes me the violence toward women. It truly does. I have a lot of respect for women, especially women who work the street. If you are homeless, a prostitute, or a drug dealer, you are just a number, not a person."

Bree recalls when she first went on heavy-duty medication for long-term mental health issues, she walked around like a zombie for the first three months until her body adjusted. She went to social services looking for financial assistance because she was unable to hold down a job, legal or otherwise. "You're young and fit," said the counsellor. "It's not our problem, you should be able to find work." A lesser woman would have given up. Not Bree. She went back time and again until she found a sympathetic worker. "I refuse to give up. I refuse to let anyone break me and I refuse to be just a number. There's too much time passing the buck instead of spending the buck."

When Bree finds her pace and her place, she would like to go to university and take a law degree and/or one in forensic sciences. In fact, she would love to spend the rest of her life as a student to make up for all those years she didn't learn anything. Today she's concentrating on her recovery, well aware it won't be an overnight miracle. But she puts in a final plea for dignity. "We are somebody's daughters. People seem to forget that a lot of us didn't have a choice—it's the only life we know."

❖ ❖ ❖

Crystal

Smartly dressed, although she spent the night in a back alley with a concealed switchblade for protection, Crystal, 42, has had to work all her life for recognition as a woman.

Crystal grew up in a conservative family in St. Catharine's, Ontario. Both her parents worked for General Motors. In their time off, her mother liked to keep a clean, orderly house while her father, who was a bit of a jock, played golf and other sports. Her two younger brothers have gone separate ways: one also works at GM and has a steady family life, while the other at 36 likes to party as though he were 16.

Childhood was not a good time for Crystal. She used to lie in bed agonizing about her inappropriate male body parts, and at school she was bullied and taunted for being girlish. "I couldn't handle the torment." Early puberty was the worst time because, to her great grief, her male features developed rapidly. She was also sexually assaulted by a family friend. She has blocked out what happened in the rape, but it has left its scar in the form of PTSD. In Grade 9 things began to look up. She started to sell drugs—marijuana and LSD—to other students and using them herself so that she "was in an altered state most of the time." She became a social butterfly, thanks to the drugs. She even had a couple of girlfriends, enjoying the relationships more for the intimacy than the sex. "I had something to talk about. I like a relationship to be full, whether it's with a man or a woman; it doesn't matter that much."

During this period, fashion was on Crystal's side. She dressed in hippie shirts, bell-bottoms, and platform shoes and grew her hair below her waist. With her high cheekbones and other physical attributes she was often mistaken for a young woman and was sometimes even redirected from the men's to the women's toilet. Alone, she posed in front of the mirror, accentuating her womanly qualities. In everyday life she had to force herself to act like a man.

One day she and a group of friends took a car trip to the US where they went to a triple-x rated theatre and bookstore. There Crystal discovered a magazine entitled *Shemale*. It cost $30, so she stole it, stuffing it under her jacket, and smuggling it into Canada. It was a revelation. "I had it for a long time. It was pretty good with lots of pictures and it showed me I wasn't alone. Before that I didn't know anyone like me."

Although they never discussed anything, Crystal now feels her parents had some idea of her predicament because they wanted her to go to the Clarke Institute in Toronto, a psychiatric facility. When she did go, she didn't feel totally comfortable because she felt their definitions of what constitutes male and female were too hidebound. For example, she says, the psychiatrists weren't impressed with her femininity because she's interested in hockey and enjoys cycling.

Crystal began to make secret trips to Toronto in quest of her true self. She stopped at a hamburger joint en route, entered the washroom as a man, and emerged as a woman. On one of her first forays, she cruised around until she found the trans stroll and picked up one of the prostitutes to whom she said, "This may sound strange, but I don't want sex. I want to ask you questions because I'm like you." They spent three hours together. Crystal drove home knowing a lot more, most of it bad news, about how rough life is for trans women: landlords don't like them, and everyone else considers them fair game.

In 1984 Crystal decided to move to Toronto where she had a job in sales. She couldn't handle the situation, so returned to the Niagara area, vowing never to leave. Back home she was successful both in legal and illegal business. She had several lines of work including interior design, landscaping, importing clothes from Guatemala, and dealing cocaine, making substantial sums of money. She also embarked on a relationship with a woman that lasted seven years. "She knew everything. She was all over the place. She was upset my underwear was better than hers. She is bigger than me and used to try and squeeze into my outfits, then she would be upset and say, 'It doesn't look good on me.'"

On the whole, this woman was very accepting of Crystal, taking pictures of her in bikinis and generally supporting her until 1995 when the businesses started to fail and Crystal was sent to jail briefly for unspecified crimes. While inside, she made the decision to end her life's lie. She came out as a woman and told everyone. For the most part, people said, "It's about time, too." All except her grandmother, who quarrelled, not so much about what she had done, but with her fashion sense: "Your skirts are too short. You can't go down the streets looking like that."

Crystal was clean, sober, and pumping large quantities of female hormones, supplied by her general practitioner as directed by Crystal who had educated herself on the subject. Friends rallied around. One buddy of 30 years said, "If someone becomes a problem, I'll handle it." Another friend in Toronto offered her a place to stay.

As Crystal gains confidence, she goes back on her narrative, each time edging a little nearer to the truth. For example, at first she says she merely uses crack to stay awake at night so she won't be attacked on the streets. It gradually transpires that it's a major factor in her life. It's not entirely clear what happened when, but for sure Crystal has been living and working on the streets of Toronto for a while, when she's not in jail.

Loss, violence, and death are recurring themes in her stories. Recently, for instance, she stashed all her things in a dumpster that was emptied by a garbage truck before she could rescue them. Friends too have disappeared in as abrupt a fashion. Crystal heard about Paula's death almost by accident. They had been very close, but Paula's boyfriend had warned her off, saying he would break her neck if she continued to hang around. At a soup kitchen one day, someone said to Crystal, "Did you hear what happened to Paula? She got murdered." "You must be joking." "No, it's here in the (Toronto) Sun." Shaking and crying, Crystal ran out of the soup kitchen and embarked on a two-week bender. "I can remember distinctly asking, 'Why her, why not me because I'm on the street?' I still find it difficult because I get choked up inside."

Crystal is still out "working on the street corner," although she doesn't want to be there much longer. She reckons it's not as demeaning as panhandling, "but you are still selling yourself for money so there is a certain amount of degradation." Trans prostitutes are at a high risk of being beaten up by their customers, but Crystal says she has a knack of being able to smooth over a bad situation. Several times men have been surprised by her male endowments, but for the most part they know what to expect. Many will ask, "Are you fully functional [as a male]?" which is, for many johns, a desirable quality in trans women. Crystal, who although full of estrogen, has never been operated on, turns them down. She says her penis is "just there" now. "The only thing it's good for is that I can pee against a tree when I want to."

Sex and love are something of a conundrum for Crystal.

> I feel dirty, guilty, shameful after working on the corner. I can't have a relationship after I have been bobbing up and down sucking on someone's penis. Then my boyfriend wants it. Why do something I get paid for, for nothing? Love isn't going to put money in my pocket or get me dope. It's demeaning working out there. I want someone who connects emotionally and mentally. I don't care for the sex act. I don't see any real gratification in it. I have become cold, but that started before. It may be from being abused, too. It affects a lot of aspects of life. It spills over into everything. When it comes to trust, I'm always leery. It's why I gravitated to no-strings, for money, quick dah-di-dah-and-it's-done-with sex. I would rather smoke a good joint or drink a good glass of wine.

Right now there is a guy in Crystal's life who, she thinks, may really like her. She's a bit ambivalent about him and his values, simultaneously wanting something more normal and rejecting it. "He's got to accept I'm in the trade." She both appreciates and worries about the fact that he doesn't like watching her destroying herself and that he will buy her meals but won't pay for sex. "Being frugal with his money is being smart. He knows how to budget. The other girls say, 'Go for everything you can.'" That's not Crystal's way though.

Beneath her banter and carefree talk, Crystal suffers from deep depression as well as PTSD and has attempted suicide many times because of the discrepancy between her mind and her body. There are services for trans women, but they can be hard to find. Many women's shelters won't accept them, and in men's and mixed shelters they are very vulnerable. "Something will happen one way or another. You will be beat up or raped. The threats are always there." She feels safer in jail.

Ideally, Crystal would like to get an apartment a couple of subway stops from her street corner so that she's away from the scene, but there's the question of affordability. She's on a disability pension and not sure that anyone would rent to a drug user and a prostitute. "They mostly don't rent on these counts, not because I am transgendered. They see me buying off a crack dealer or at the corner. That's where my problems come in the most."

However, Crystal doesn't want the world to think that all trans women are into the drug scene or prostitution.

> Some are because society hasn't given them a chance. My ex, Danielle, is now working [in a legitimate job] and I'm happy for her. What people see on the street isn't an accurate barometer of what it's all about. We aren't circus freaks, we are just like everybody else. It's not good to laugh at a person because there is a lot of despair as it is; that's where the drugs and alcohol come in.

❖❖❖

Kylie

A street kid in Toronto, Kylie was taken home by a counsellor who had an affair with her. Now 40, she is moving away from the street, but sometimes the so-called good life seems like an unobtainable mirage. The interview is in a trendy, middle-class coffee shop, where she fits in with no sign of her tumultuous life and the tight-rope she walks.

When she was 19, Kylie woke up one day and realized that she had recently turned a trick for $10 so that she could get a cup of coffee for breakfast. "There must be more to life than this," she thought. "What can I do?" What she did was to start moving away from the streets, but it wasn't easy to leave the one place where she felt safe and accepted. "I'm still on that journey. Nothing in my life is long-term. It appears I'm stable and settling down, but I don't know how true that is. At any point my life could fall apart ... Stability is all an illusion. It's a joke."

I first met Kylie a year after she acquired a low-paying job with a social services agency in Calgary. A year later, she is working at another agency for higher pay, but she is still struggling financially and in other ways to make it in society. Services are so few and far between for people that at times she wonders if it's worth it; life is so much easier on the streets. "How do you stay off the streets? I'm working but barely covering the bills. I have a roof over my head, yes, but now I'm more in debt than when I was on the street what with rent, utilities, and food. When I was on the street I contributed whatever money I had. It makes you wonder."

Sexually abused by her father, Kylie is unwilling to dwell too much on her childhood. Her parents split up when she was 12, and she and her mother moved to Toronto. She ran away from home at 15 and took to the streets. "It's not an environment I would want to inflict on anybody." She met up with a group of young people who became "family" to each other, scrounging food and sharing squats and other resources. She made money "the obvious way"—through drug dealing and prostitution. Once she even took a nannying job, but it didn't last long; she was called back to her friends.

The one stable person in Kylie's life was her maternal grandmother, whose door was always open for a night or two and a home-cooked meal. As a token of respect, Kylie never did drugs at her grandmother's except once, when the grandmother invited Kylie's mother along for Christmas. In retrospect, Kylie is more sympathetic toward her mother, realizing that she came from a culture of "see no evil," believing, or hoping, that if you didn't see it, it didn't exist. Ironically, some of her mother's problems of trying to make it in the world as a single mother with few or no job skills are now Kylie's problems.

Kylie tried to go back to school to upgrade her qualifications, but she wasn't successful until she turned 18 and entered an alternative high school where she finished Grade 12. After her revelation in the coffee shop, she went to a shelter where she met a counsellor who took her under her wing and gave her unconditional support. Like her grandmother, but in a different way, this woman also had an open door, so that even when Kylie relapsed she knew she was welcome back as soon as she was ready to work on her issues.

> You need to know you can make the mistakes and run away, but you need to know you can go back. It's extremely important to have someone willing to have faith in you and willing to work with you unconditionally; who will walk along the beach with you or go to the coffee shop. I always had to know that I could get up and go, that I could relapse and fall down and then say, 'I want to come back.' It was very, very important. It makes a huge difference what happens to the rest of your life. If the counsellor had said no....

An open door policy has to be there. The right counsellor
is so important. A bad counsellor upsets you for life.

As Kylie was coming to the realization she had to get away from the
streets to kick the drugs, another counsellor, Yvette, invited her home to
live with her family. Kylie and Yvette ended up in a relationship that was
conducted under the noses of the counsellor's husband and children. On the
plus side, Kylie was introduced to museums, galleries, travel, trendy clothes,
and other niceties of middle-class life. On the debit side, there was a lot of
secrecy, control, and manipulation, and she always came second, especially
at times like Christmas. Yvette cautioned her not to tell anyone about the
relationship because "no one would really understand the true meaning" of
what was going on. "I was extremely torn. I was living in a traditional home-
setting on the surface, but I was very lonely beneath it. It was a house of
horrors, very like my old home life."

If Yvette had a double life, so did Kylie who explored her sexuality to
the full by having affairs with two men; she got pregnant twice and had
two daughters, Faith and Robin. She moved out of Yvette's house into an
apartment with five other women, but still she was engaged in a dance with
Yvette and with Dave, a rebel and a free spirit, who was Robin's father and
who had another woman on the side. "He came and went in my life and as
I started to open up, he accepted it all. He was also an abuser and part of a
biker gang. He drifted in and out and when I got pregnant with Faith, he
was always upset that I had Faith first. He always had a hold on me." Kylie
wonders how she ever survived being tugged by two such people as Dave
and Yvette. Gradually, she started to stand up to them both, if not for herself,
then for the girls' sake.

Kylie changed her identity and moved to a Catholic worker community
far enough away that Yvette couldn't drop in. She began to parent herself and
her children simultaneously. In his absence, she realized how abusive Dave
was. Then it became apparent that he had sexually abused their daughter.
History was repeating itself; her worst nightmare was transpiring, and there
wasn't even enough evidence to convict him.

Kylie fled to British Columbia. Dave had always vowed he would wrest
Robin from her, and, sure enough, he tracked her down through the courts
because her address was on a number of documents. Terrified, Kylie went
even deeper underground, moving to the US and marrying a man for legal
and moral support, even though she describes him "as just a piece of paper."

When Kylie's hepatitis C took a turn for the worse, she returned to
Canada for treatment and to try and instill some stability into her daughters'

lives. Faith was rapidly approaching her teens and was fed up with traipsing around. She had a yearning to go to school, live in the suburbs, and be "normal" like other teenagers. Kylie found the medical treatment brutal and in the end took herself off it, but her health has held sufficiently for her to move out of the shelter system and to find a series of jobs in social service agencies, all the while home-schooling Robin who hasn't always fitted in to a conventional school. In short, she has tried to find herself a productive niche in a city that she says is exceptionally harsh on lesbians.

Although she felt safe in Toronto and Vancouver, in Calgary Kylie keeps her orientation under wraps unless she is very sure of her company. "The things said and talked about are nasty." She is facing another round of treatment, similar to cancer chemotherapy, for her hepatitis C. Even though treatment is supposed to have improved, she isn't convinced that she will go through with it. The chance to have some more good years with her daughters is a big incentive, although she is unwilling to inflict a permanently sick mother on them. "It comes to the point when you have given your kids all the tools you can give them and it's up to them to work with them or not work with them."

Without much of an education and a slender resume, Kylie has found it difficult to put a foot in the employment door. But each time she goes out looking for work, her lengthening track record speaks for itself. Even so she would like to see more long-term help for women. She says there are plenty of temporary fixes; however, they are not sufficient to see a person off the streets permanently. She would like more supports for women leaving abusive relationships, better shelters, longer stays for women to find their feet, and continuing supports once they move into their own home. "One month [shelter stay] is not enough." Too often, shelters are run so that volunteers can feel good about themselves rather than putting the clients' needs first. For example, shelters without some kind of child care are not very helpful to mothers who have to find accommodation and jobs.

Kylie says she was unusually lucky because people were willing to go out on a limb and to break the rules to help her move on. "Staff who are willing to fight for your rights and do what it takes to support you are few and far between."

Sources

Canadian Rainbow Health Coalition/Coalition Santé Arc-en-ciel Canada. 2004. *Health and Wellness in the Gay, Lesbian, Bisexual, Transgendered, and Two-Spirit Communities, A Background Document.* April. <http://www.rainbowhealth.ca>.

Frankowski, Barbara L. 2002. "Sexual Orientation of Adolescent Girls." *Current Women's Health Reports* 2.

Mottet, L., and J. Ohle. 2003. *A Guide to Making Homeless Shelters Safe for Transgendered People*. New York: National Coalition for the Homeless and the National Gay and Lesbian Task Force Policy.

Pyne, Jake. 2004. Speech given to Mayor's Task Force on Homelessness (Gender and Sexual Minorities Sub-committee). Philadelphia. March.

Rothblum, Esther D. 1990. "Depression Among Lesbians: An Invisible and Unresearched Phenomenon." *Journal of Gay and Lesbian Psychotherapy* 1(3).

Stonewall Housing. 2004. *Meeting the Needs of Homeless Lesbian and Gay Youth, A Guide for Housing and Homelessness Agencies*. <http://www.casweb/stonewallhousing>.

The Centre. 2002. *Lesbian Health Matters, Health Information for Lesbians and their Service Providers*. Vancouver.

Trans Programming at The 519. 2006. The Trans Inclusion Project: Supporting TransSurvivors of Abuse and Violence. January. <http://www.the519.org/programs/trans/trans_inclusion_project/index.shtml>.

Interviews

Hohendorff, Shawna. Program Coordinator, Kindred House, Edmonton. 2004.

Oxenbury, Jane. Psychologist. Calgary. 2004.

Pyne, Jake. Project Coordinator, The 519 Trans Shelter Access, Toronto. 2004.

Stringer, Kathy. Coordinator of Women's and Children's Programs, St. James Community Services Society, Vancouver. 2004.

CHAPTER 10

THE AMBULANCE IS WAITING
AT THE BOTTOM OF THE CLIFF

> Being poor in Canada is treated as a crime. It implies ac-
> countability (explaining your actions, and your poverty);
> it implies apology (for being poor); it implies punishment
> (welfare is a punitive distrusting system); it implies the
> loss of rights and privileges (such as privacy); it implies
> fines and incarceration (prostitution, panhandling, loiter-
> ing, basking); it brings condemnation of character and
> morality; it brings surveillance and rehabilitation (parent
> training; job hunt reports; house checks). The poor are
> kept hidden and invisible, through gentrification, arrest
> sweeps, detox sweeps, hotel closures, psychiatric commit-
> ments, segregation, and imprisonment.
>
> —Moore and Bunjun (2005)

The slight woman with long brown hair and a backpack with two teddy bears poking out desperately wanted a shower before going to a job interview, but she didn't want any of the boisterous men in the shelter to know. As she was about to enter the cubicle reserved for women, a young man pushed past her and entered one of the men's. "I can't do it, he's in there. The guys will know I'm in here," she said to the elderly female volunteer monitoring the showers that day. The agitated young woman turned on her heels and fled. Later a male staff member responded, "Oh, she probably has issues," but no woman in her right mind would have felt comfortable in that particular shower stall with its flimsy door.

We set up a lot of systems that purport to help the homeless but which, in fact, only dig the hole deeper and in some cases throw soil down on top of the hapless woman, making it almost impossible for her to clamber out. The system is set up in several ways that prevent women from getting the help they need.

1. Many mixed shelters were established mainly by men for men, so they do not serve women's needs as well as they might. In fact, many women are reluctant to use them for a number of reasons, although safety is often at the top of their list. A woman in a Calgary shelter woke up in the middle of the night to find a man urinating on her. Disgusted and wondering what else he could get away with, she now prefers to sleep rough. A woman who has been raped or sexually abused may well be reluctant to share co-ed shower facilities even if she has nowhere else to wash. We know that women are turned away daily from domestic abuse shelters on the grounds that there are no beds available, but these women will not go to homeless shelters, perceiving dangers there. Large numbers of women are making do by sleeping on friends' floors or in cars or by going back to their abuser.

Women in mixed shelters, however vigilant the staff, say they are hit upon by the men or that they are unable to concentrate on what they need to do because they are distracted by the male residents. Most say they feel very threatened with men around, especially if they have children with them, and add that male staff tend to dismiss their concerns, if they even see them. It may be a matter of perception: if your life has been comparatively free of violence, especially if you are a male, behaviour that appears to be innocuous may look totally different to someone who has been raped and sexually abused. It is important to remember that unless a woman feels safe, she cannot begin to work on her issues.

Women's sense of privacy is also violated in mixed shelters. It is difficult, for example, for a woman to ask for sanitary supplies and medication for conditions like HIV, which she considers to be private, from male staff— sometimes her only choice. Although most shelters have rules about staff not having relationships with clients, life being life, the inevitable happens in facilities where males are looking after the needs of women as well as men. One women's shelter (which did not want to be identified here), considering hiring male staff, asked the existing staff for their thoughts and took a vote on the issue. It was resoundingly defeated 19 to 1. One of the staff said:

> HORRIFIED and FRUSTRATED is how I feel about the possibility. HORRIFED at the safety issues this entails with male staff considering the extent that women residents and staff have experienced sexual/physical/verbal abuse in their past and present lives *mostly* from male relatives/partners/co-workers and strangers. We have a particularly large population of sex-trade workers as resi-

dents, and our shelters are one of the only places they can feel a modicum of safety. Access to child residents is also a great concern for all the safety issues mentioned above.

Another commented,

> The question would be: If a male did an intake, would the female be willing to express her crisis freely? Would the male worker be able to listen to a client talk about rape, child sexual abuse? I asked one client if she would be able to talk in front of a male worker—answer was no—because a male is not emotionally able to understand severe pain—only offer strong arms. It would also result in a lot of flirting, bickering over who is going to get the male workers' attention.

The shelter decided against hiring men, saying, "We need to consider the lives and experiences of the women who use our services, the social context of male violence against women and children, and the reality that women are objectified, exploited, raped and abused. And this is why they are seeking a safe women-only space."

Often, programs at mixed shelters do not take into account women's special needs. While traumatized women fresh off the streets need to rest, rehydrate, eat, and get medical attention, these programs throw them immediately into a goal-oriented course that they cannot sustain. They are frequently intimidated, or effectively silenced, in mixed recovery groups. A Vancouver woman summed up the shelter system, describing it as divisive: "They are all meant to degrade you, to break down your self-esteem," she said, calling to task shelters of all kinds for setting short time limits like a week or a month on a woman's stay when it takes so much longer to reverse a multitude of issues. "They [the clients] are asked to suppress the trauma and move on," added a shelter worker.

2. Many women on the street have a dual diagnosis of substance abuse and at least one mental health problem, but very few mental health counsellors will take clients who also have an active addiction.

3. Services are usually scattered in different offices and buildings in different parts of a city. Women, often with children in tow, are expected to find them and pull them all together, although they may have no phone, bus money,

home, and/or food. It can be an enormous problem to find the 25 cents needed to make a phone call—if one can find a working pay phone. The problem is exacerbated if the only thing at the end of the line is a recorded message. Without a phone number to give for a return call, the money is wasted. Thus, should a woman want to turn her life around and move away from the streets, the system does not make it easy. As the British agency, Turning Point, wrote in its report *Turning 40* (2004):

> Imagine trying to get your car fixed after it breaks down and finding that you have to take it to a different garage to fix each part. One to change the brake cables, another to fix the windscreen, a third to change the tires and so on. Even worse, each garage is in a different area and none of them share information so you repeatedly have to explain the problem and fill out separate forms at each visit. It sounds bizarre, but people with serious health or personal problems frequently suffer similar experiences when trying to get help.

In Canada we have very few places with "one-stop shopping," as it were. We expect people to make heroic efforts to connect the dots to understaffed, underfunded, overused services. Most clients do not fit into the categories neatly defined by social service agencies, whether they be government institutions or the not-for-profit sector. It is quite common for people to be bounced around, becoming increasingly entangled in red tape and seemingly pointless forms until it just seems easier to sink back into the old ways. Also, as we have seen repeatedly, they find themselves in Catch-22 predicaments that make it all but impossible to move ahead without cheating. In many jurisdictions, a woman cannot rent a place without putting down a damage deposit, or the first and last month's rent, but she cannot get a social services cheque until she has an address. A woman might acquire subsidized housing for herself and her children, but because welfare is not enough to cover all contingencies, they don't eat very well and sometimes not at all. The children are apprehended, and she loses her home and is unable to get the children back because she doesn't have appropriate accommodation. But now she can't get housing because she doesn't have the children.

Then there is the stinginess of welfare across the country. In 2002, for instance, a single mother with one child in Ontario received $957 a month before deductions and likely spent around $675 on rent and $200 on groceries. This left her with $82 to pay electricity, telephone, heat, school needs, clothing, soap, haircuts, repairs, sanitary napkins (many women go without), and anything else that comes up, like medical expenses not covered by health care. A woman in such a situation cannot buy in bulk because she has no car to transport her purchases and no cash to do so in the first place. She finds it difficult to explain to her daughter why she puts water in the milk and why the daughter cannot go to a birthday party (they can't afford a gift), why she can't go on a school outing, and why her clothes are weird (they come from a clothing bank).

A National Council of Welfare report (2005) called the welfare situation "dismal" and pointed out that when adjusted for inflation, many welfare incomes were lower in 2005 than they were in 1986. In most provinces, they peaked around 1994 with one-third of households losing $3,000 or more by 2005. Four provinces—Ontario, Manitoba, Saskatchewan, and British Columbia—recorded the lowest levels between 2000 and 2005. In Alberta the income of a single person on welfare ("Supports for Independence," as the province calls it, unaware of the irony) has dropped by 50 per cent in real dollars since 1986. In that same province, the richest in the country, a single parent receives only $12,326 a year. There are 1.7 million Canadians, or 5 per cent of the population on welfare; it should be remembered that half a million of those people are children.

The fact that welfare does not cover the most basic of expenses plays out in punitive and cruel ways. As Kim Pate, executive director of the Canadian Association of Elizabeth Fry Societies, has pointed out, Kimberly Rogers, who died in August 2001, "was essentially sentenced to death for welfare fraud.... Although everyone knows that it is impossible to live on welfare without some supplemental income/support, to be caught doing so means an almost certainty of criminal prosecution" (Pate 2002). The 40-year-old, eight-month pregnant woman died while confined to her house in Sudbury, Ontario, during a heat wave. Rogers had tried to get an education while on welfare and had received student loans as well. She was caught and charged with receiving $13,300 in welfare payments. She pleaded guilty and was convicted of fraud, sentenced to a six-month conditional sentence, and ordered to repay the amount in full to the province. Although aware that she was unable to seek employment because of her pregnancy and because one of her sentencing conditions was that she could not leave the house, the provincial government cut her off welfare because she was not looking for a job. Even if she had remained on welfare, after she had paid her rent and made the mandatory repayments to the government she would have had $18 a month to feed and clothe herself.

What happened to Rogers should be seen in the big picture of the increasing criminalization of the poor and the most marginalized in society, particularly Aboriginal women, women of colour, the elderly, and the disabled. When it comes to the working poor, women are not much better off. Many are employed—or perhaps one should say exploited—in the restaurant, home care, domestic, garment, and farm industries that are beyond the protection of unions and are outside labour, health, and environmental standards. They are sometimes pushed further and further underground into the sex and drug trades in order to earn enough to feed themselves and their families. Elizabeth Fry Society statistics show that 80 per cent of criminal activity by women is poverty related and that the average level of education attained by these women is Grade 7 (Pate 2002). Clearly, there is something very wrong with this picture.

As Lord Victor Adebowale, the chief executive of Britain's Turning Point (2004), said, "Too often for people with complex needs we're providing services that are like an ambulance at the bottom of a cliff, rather than trying to stop them falling in the first place. This is incredibly costly to the individual, to their community and the taxpayer."

Chris

Chris yearns for her own place but at the same time fears that she has become too institutionalized to find it.

Somewhere in the City of Toronto is a storage locker filled with household items that Chris has purchased over time. She hasn't had a house, an apartment, or even a room to call her own in years. Currently, the former actor is living in a women's shelter; before that she stayed with friends very much on sufferance. "How did I lose my aim on what I'm doing and what is my aim right now? I can't figure out what I should be doing."

One minute the faded 63-year-old woman is joyfully discussing the pleasures of playing Antigone on stage and the next she is sadly talking about the difficulties of living in a shelter and how habituated she has become to institutional life. "This has become my life again. The hostel is a way of life, you forget what your priorities are. When I first came in here, I was looking for an apartment."

Like a Greek chorus, her constant refrain is, "If only I could get stable, I could do that again." But like so many women, she finds it hard to stabilize when she doesn't have a place of her own, and, because she is on a disability pension, most places are out of her financial reach. She also finds that the longer she stays in a shelter, the less energy she has and her bouts of illness are more frequent, making it increasingly difficult to address her issues. Even something as simple as a private phone call to her doctor requires her to find the 25 cents and a pay phone in the vicinity.

It wasn't always like this for Chris who grew up in a middle-class family on the West Coast. After Grade 12 she went to the National Theatre School in Montreal. As a student she also lived in poverty, but then it was by choice and didn't seem to matter. She became a successful actor, based in Toronto, working on stage and in film and making television and radio commercials. Money was never a problem, and in fact she did well financially.

The first sign of trouble occurred when she joined a popular meditation organization. After a few years, she had a breakdown, claiming that the change in diet, prescribed by her guru, affected her metabolism and that the constant retreats isolated her from her friends. "I pulled out of it. It didn't seem to be doing my head any good." It had, however, changed her outlook on life in that she had become more interested in personal development than her career. She hitchhiked to Mississippi with eight cents in her pocket. There she met a man who repaired air conditioners, and they became engaged. Chris smiles, realizing that most people will think that there is a huge discrepancy between household mechanics and the arts. "He was not your typical Mississippian, in spite of what he did; it was really the same thing I did. I was always interested in the truth of the character below the words. He loved the mystery of looking at a big furnace and figuring out the problem. We were both trying to get to the root of something."

Chris hints that it wasn't always an easy ride in the US and that from time to time she had trouble with the police. She went back and forth for years, visiting her fiancé, then returning to act in Canada. When she came back for good, she started couch-surfing, living with friends who were less than companionable and at least one man who meant nothing to her. ("It wasn't a choice," she says.) When their patience and hospitality faded, she turned to shelters.

On a pension because of "emotional problems," two years ago Chris was diagnosed with fibromyalgia that makes her feel weak, tired, and achy. She has severe arthritis in one knee, the result of a car accident, so finds it hard to walk any distance and is susceptible to all the colds, flu, and other maladies that blow through shelters. Once she came out in blotches all over her body. She was worried that she had picked up lice. Eventually, it was discovered that she was obtaining super-strength cleaner from street nurses to do her laundry and had come out in hives in reaction to it. "I was afraid I would give bugs to the 30 other women and children here. But the doctor said, 'The reason you have them is because you are living with 30 other women and children.' I was washing too often with that stuff."

Recently Chris heard of a job that would bring her $100 for one day of work. She had to go to three places just to apply, as well as make the journey on the day she was required. It was almost more than she could cope with; even the thought of all that to-ing and fro-ing made her feel weary. She wondered if it were worth the cost of the bus fares. "I'm not feeling well again. There is so much to do. Do I go here, or there, or do I just go to bed?"

She talks about how difficult it is to live in a shelter, how small things, like using the kitchen Ajax for the bathtub, can really upset people. How making breakfast can be an exercise in frustration, taking up to an hour, because no one leaves the pans, or even the salt, in the same place from one day to the next. Then there are the fights and the jealousies. Her pregnant roommate, for example, is having a rough time with her boyfriend and takes it all out on Chris, who points out that most women in the shelter have disasters in their lives and, cut off from children and other loved ones, tend to be emotionally volatile. Most of all, Chris hates the apathy and lethargy that have stalked up on her and would like a break from communal living so that she can figure out what her priorities are and start working on them. She dreams about being on her own and the small liberties it brings. "When she can't sleep, my girlfriend reads all night. I wonder what that would be like."

Chris figures that many of her problems have come about precisely because she is living in a shelter, or with someone else, and that adapting to those lifestyles has vanquished her self-confidence. She would like to be able to make even small decisions again, like choosing when to eat or not to eat, or whether to open the door to a stranger. "If I got out on my own, just me and myself, I would find out all those things again. I would really like to know that kind of freedom and independence."

It's unlikely, though, that Chris will get a place of her own soon, despite the stuff in storage. She has been told that there are 41,000 people ahead of her on the list for subsidized housing in Toronto. From her vantage point, it looks as though she's always being bumped back by other people's emergencies. She talks about a depressed woman who had been on the housing list for 10 years. Suddenly she was informed that she had a place. Her mood changed completely, and she went out to buy candles, something she could never have done before. "Very dysfunctional and depressed people change when they get housing."

Chris is not sure why she bought all the stuff in storage but says it could be because she deeply yearns for her own place. However, after all this time of being looked after and told what to do—for even her friends bossed her around when she stayed with them—the prospect of being alone is frightening. "When was the last time I had dreams? I'm so mixed up. I wish I could get away from everybody for a while and figure what my dreams are."

❖ ❖ ❖

Cathy

Many factors contributed to Cathy's homelessness, but the last straw was loaded on by a hospital emergency department and the police.

When Cathy's former boyfriend called long distance to tell her that her cat had died because a pack of dogs had chased it up a power pole and it was electrocuted, she told him to fuck off. "It feels weird to speak like that again," she says, a little abashed by her language. These days Cathy is sober and clean; she has an apartment and has embraced Christianity with all her heart. None of her former boyfriends compares to Jesus. "I'm very happy. My outlook is a lot better. They can try and beat me down, but they are not going to succeed because Jesus carries me all the way." Many people contributed to Cathy feeling beaten down. She has couched-surfed, slept in parks, been picked up by the police, and hospitalized for psychiatric problems. Today, though, she volunteers at an evangelical mission in Vancouver and helps teach Alpha courses, which she describes as "Christianity 101."

Cathy was born in Winnipeg, but her family moved to Victoria when she was six. She was baptized four years later but rejected everything to do with Christianity when her father died, an event that shook up the family. Her sister moved out to live with her boyfriend's parents, and for a short time Cathy was put into foster care while her grieving mother regained her equilibrium.

Cathy started working at 14, getting by in school with Bs and Cs, even though she worked late most nights. By 18 she was managing a root-beer franchise, but she was also drinking heavily and smoking pot every spare moment. "I always had money, food and clothing, and a social life. I partied hard when I was working. I partied hard, but I kept the two separate." After dating a man for three years, she made the scary move of finding her own apartment. However, she had a good job in a restaurant that also had a catering arm. "I had a lot of fun; I enjoyed meeting people and helping and teaching people." Her boyfriend treated her well, but their paths began to diverge. He was rapidly moving up the social scale, increasingly interested in making money. He asked Cathy to sign a pre-nuptial agreement. She refused on the grounds that if she married, it was for life. So they broke up.

A year later she met David. They both drank and got into cocaine, their behaviour becoming increasingly erratic. One day, the landlord informed them that the house was about to be sold. David wanted to live in Sooke [about 40 kilometres southwest of Victoria, BC] with a friend, who told Cathy that if she worked in town, she was not to expect any rides from him or David. "My jaw just dropped, and I told David that he needed to decide who was more important—me, or his alcoholic friend. And, he didn't like the fact I got so angry, so we started fighting and it went on for a week. He really looked up to this guy. He was 10 years older and they had become buddy buddies." Cathy told the man to get out. The next day at work, she fell, breaking her arm and twisting her ankle. She called David and his friend from the hospital, but neither of them responded to her frantic messages to pick her up. However, she cadged a ride home with a work colleague. Several hours later, David arrived drunk and yelling, "Why did you call me?" She held up her arm, saying, "It could be because I broke my arm." A bunch of inebriated friends followed David into the house, so she told them all to leave. When David returned the next morning, they had a long discussion, agreed the relationship wasn't working, and broke up.

Two days later Cathy left to stay with friends and found solace in two 26-ounce bottles of liquor and in cocaine. When she came to, she moved in with the foster family she had stayed with after her father died. "Apparently I did some strange things. I ripped off the shower curtains and wrote things on the mirror." It was sufficiently bad that her foster mother took her to hospital where she was given a drug to which she had a highly allergic reaction. She lapsed into a coma for seven days and woke up in the psychiatric ward. When she was able to get out of bed, she went downstairs for a cigarette and who should she meet but David complete with her dog, a stuffed rabbit, and a bouquet of flowers. He wanted her to go to Sooke with him. Sorry, no, she said.

While in hospital, she went to detox and met Gary who was also trying to make a comeback. Within six months they were living together. She cut back on her drug use—"all we did was pot and alcohol." Her first fight with Gary didn't go well as he had been doing coke, was drinking, and had invited a former girlfriend around. That night—November 29, 1997—Cathy made a big decision: she decided to stop drinking and has been sober ever since. Two weeks later she started a computer accounting course, getting straight As and finishing a month early. Neither Gary nor Cathy could find work so, after eight months, they decided to go to his home in northern Saskatchewan. She found a job in the local library; he returned to alcohol, drugs, and women. It was a very bad time for Cathy.

> We were homeless because every time his family got fed up with us, they would toss us out. We went from relative to relative, but we had no home. It was terrible because all my life I had been self-sufficient and very proud of the fact I could take care of myself. I watched him totally come apart and not really care that his fiancée was suffering. At one point we were sleeping underneath the staircase. We sold off all our possessions, all my stuff. He was basically transient. There was an oak table I had had for 12 to 15 years, and he sold it for $200. It deflated my self-worth. I had worked so hard to get where I was and now things were falling apart and I had no control.

Cathy thought of returning home but couldn't face the humiliation. She satisfied her pride by throwing her engagement ring at Gary. She worked hard to try and raise the money to leave with dignity. Gary appeared with a second engagement ring and dropping to his hands and knees begged her to stay. "Learn to trust me," he pleaded. "I'll never forsake you and I will never give up on us, no matter what." They were standing in the cemetery in front of the family plot, so Cathy said, "Do you swear on your father's grave?" "Yes," said Gary.

Less than a month later, Cathy left the house where they were staying to go to work. She looked up the hill and saw Gary staggering behind his girlfriend. Shocked, angry, and frustrated that Gary would let her down so badly she went to a shelter in La Ronge. The shelter sent her to hospital because she was yelling and scaring the children. She contacted relatives in Vancouver who invited her to stay, but she started to act strangely again. Her cousin called emergency services which took her to a suburban hospital where she was seen by a doctor and a social worker. "They told me they had no facilities for me and they would not transfer me, so I was out on the street. I had 75 cents."

Cathy flipped one of her quarters to see if she should phone her cousin or get a bus. It indicated she should phone, but the line was busy, so she got on a bus and asked the driver to drop her where she could get food and shelter. He let her off at a shelter. Although it was a round-the-clock operation, the shelter didn't allow people to sleep. If they nodded off, they were woken up. "The pit of my stomach was turning. Why am I here, what happened?"

The shelter was very frightening. Everyone kept to themselves, except once an hour when staff brought out goodies, and then fights erupted. "I was not used to that. It was a total 180-degree turn for me. I felt so vulnerable as a woman." Eventually the shelter called the police because they said Cathy was unruly. She says it was because she asked for her bag three times before showering because she couldn't make up her mind what to wear.

> Someone knocked on the door of the shower. It was a male police officer. He said, "Apparently you are causing trouble, so we are here to take you out." He asked me which bags were mine, grabbed them and said, "Come with us." He threw the bags and me on the back seat and proceeded to drive me to the Sky Train. When I asked what was going on, he marched me up the stairs and said, "Get off at Main Street and don't come back. Here's a ticket."

Cathy, who had no idea where she was going, followed instructions, getting off at Main Street on the fringe of Vancouver's Downtown Eastside. From there she didn't know what she was supposed to do, but seeing a park, she lay down under a tree. Some guys getting drunk kept a watch on her while she slept. When she woke, she asked the way to social services and was directed to a church, but it was closed, so she walked to another park in the heart of the Eastside. The first night was very disturbed because a movie shoot was in full fling. A young prostitute offered to let her sleep in her apartment, but when Cathy arrived, she withdrew the offer because she had just picked up a trick. Cathy returned to the park. At times the sprinklers came on, soaking her. She had to change her clothes in the open as the public washrooms were locked. Once she heard some voices saying, "Wow, that's a cool gun, what should we do with it?" She was terrified they would try it out. "Dear God, please don't let them shoot at me," she prayed. "He heard me as I'm still here."

Other nights she slept in doorways. She found a drop-in centre where they let her stay for three nights. Even though her backpack was stolen with her glasses and all her ID, she applied to stay there longer but was refused because the director was away. Not knowing what to do, she went outside where a man gave her a cup of coffee and said he would sneak her in. Halfway through lunch, someone tapped her on the shoulder. It was a female police officer, asking her name. "Today it's Mary Poppins because my

ID was stolen." In seconds, she was handcuffed and carted off in a paddy wagon. The police dropped her off at a women's centre that managed to find her a room at the YWCA, but social services wouldn't give her money for food. She managed to find free meals twice, the only times she ate that week. The second week, a family also at the Y helped her out.

At the end of two weeks, Cathy tried to contact her worker. Social services said they had no idea who it was. Desperate, she got the desk clerk to phone for an ambulance. "I'll have a holiday in hospital." The holiday turned out to be 10 weeks in the psychiatric ward. At the end of it, she heard from Gary who had squeezed her address out of her mother. He begged and begged Cathy to return, but she stood her ground, and with the help of social services found herself an apartment complete with mice coming out of the bed and rust in the water.

She started to look for something better and found two men who wanted a third person to help with the rent. All they had for her was a couch, but it was better than the mice. After three months she began dating one of the men, and they moved in together as a couple. The next welfare day, he confessed that he had already spent his entire cheque on cocaine. He had hepatitis C and was using cocaine to cope. Cathy forgave him, and he promised not to mess up again. But the next month, the scenario repeated itself, plus he tried to stab her with a pair of scissors before taking off. A few days later, he returned early in the morning and stabbed Cathy as she slept, then tossed her round the room, demanding money, even though she had only $40. Eventually he left, but when she went to the store, he was lying in wait. She called the police who asked her if she wanted to go to hospital, where she stayed for about two months.

Cathy was diagnosed with schizoaffective disorder and lupus. She was also very scared of re-entering the world. "Again, I had no resources and no knowledge of where I would be living." However, she found a room in a first-stage mental-health housing complex and gradually began to calm down. Her social worker obtained a small lump sum from Victim Services for the stabbing.

One day, the front-door clerk said to Cathy, "You don't need to keep cooking here. Just go a few blocks up Cordova Street." Taking his advice, she found the Union Gospel Mission. A few weeks later she began the Alpha program and after several sessions found Christ.

The last few years have been good. Cathy was re-baptized and "became a free and beautiful child of God"; she moved into a small, subsidized apartment close to UGM, again in a supportive situation; and she is now on a Canada disability pension. She goes to see her mother every couple of months and is able to put a few dollars in the bank by dint of careful budgeting. She often eats at the mission because a wholesome diet is important since she has been diagnosed with diabetes. Most of her clothes are second-hand.

There is a yawning gap between the woman who was kicked out of shelters for causing disturbances, who used drugs and slept on park benches, and the placid, matronly woman who is speaking today after serving supper at a women's drop-in centre as she does several times a week. "I feel very happy; I have a lot better outlook on life." When she is asked for advice by other women, she tells them: "Try and stick it out; try not to give up hope. Try any avenue you can to get back on your feet."

Cathy also has words for those who criticize people down on their luck: "Just because people are homeless doesn't mean they don't have a heart. Everybody has a story, and they all need love."

❖ ❖ ❖

Cynthia

In the shelter system Cynthia is seen as a trouble-maker because, after a lifetime of abuse, she is beginning to speak her mind. She has a clear analysis of how mixed shelters frequently fail women.

Cynthia takes up two seats on the bus because she doesn't have enough bags in which to pack her clothes, so she's wearing them all, even though the weather is mild and sunny. A smile hardly cracks her face, not even when someone she knows boards the bus a few stops closer to downtown. Normally, Cynthia, 50, lives in a shelter, but for the last few nights she and some friends pooled their money to stay in a hotel on the outskirts of Calgary. It's been a break from crying children, snoring men, never feeling safe, and never having any privacy. "I haven't been able to wear my nightgown since I don't know when," says Cynthia, whose stocky appearance belies her fragile health. She suffers from an array of conditions—osteoporosis, diabetes, fibromyalgia, depression, and high blood pressure. It's not easy for her to carry much luggage around town, although she has a lot of metaphorical baggage in tow. "My life wasn't glorious from the beginning," she says sadly.

Cynthia's mother was an alcoholic and wanted to give her up for adoption, but her grandparents talked her into keeping the child. The children were left without food in the house for days at a time. Her stepfather sexually molested Cynthia and used to put her in a corner with her hands behind her back, calling her a slut. "I hate corners and I hate people who put kids in corners."

Nothing was ever discussed in her family and to this day, she doesn't know if any of her five siblings were abused too. "It was hush, hush." At 13 she tried to commit suicide and as a result went to live with her grandparents. They never knew the cause of her despair, and she thinks they would have run over her with the car had they known. At the same time, without them she wouldn't have survived. "There was no place to run when I was younger, there was no place to help out, but I loved my grandparents. They spoiled me quite a bit and I called them Mom and Dad." To this day, Cynthia still longs for the loving mother she never had. She has always been hard on herself and in adulthood has had a number of abusive relationships as she searched for that elusive warmth and companionship.

At 19, she moved out of her grandparents' home to marry a man who, after six months of courtship, turned into an ogre the moment they married. "I couldn't look out of the windows, or he would hit me on the side of the head." He also broke her bones and tried to choke her. When she became pregnant, she had the wit to return to her grandparents' Montreal home, surviving on welfare. Although she was constantly nagged by the older couple, she says, "We lived good until my son was five." Then she became pregnant again. She never told the father, a wrestler, that he had a son. Finally, after one too many arguments with her grandparents, she decided it was time to become independent.

Even with two little boys, Cynthia put herself through college so that she could teach developmentally delayed children. "I had to work really hard to put myself through school. Really hard. It was a lot of stress to make something out of yourself." Then, although still legally married to "Number One," she met the love of her life. He was in the Armed Forces and they moved around a lot, but Cynthia continued to teach and they had a child together, this time a baby girl. Cynthia describes the relationship as a team effort. "We fought off and on, like every other couple, but there was no abuse ... He was a really good man to me."

Ten years ago Cynthia's husband had a stroke and three months later died of a fast-developing brain cancer. Cynthia broke down completely, sold everything, and lived on what she had for two years before she started to collect a Department of Veterans Affairs (DVA) pension. By now living in Calgary, she was in a very vulnerable state when she met the next man—she didn't like the way she looked and she felt worthless, believing she was the cause of all the abuse. Mostly, she was lonely. She could see all around her seemingly happy couples who helped each other through bad times. Number Four was to all intents and appearances a kind, caring, soft-spoken man. She succumbed to his charm, only to find that he was an abusive gambler. She kicks herself for not seeing his true nature. "There are no signs like they say there is. With some men you don't see them."

"He told me many times how I wasn't worth anything and not a good person. He said I took too much stuff for pain [for the fibromyalgia]. I would clam up and wouldn't say nothing." While he was happy to gamble away her pension, he complained bitterly if she ever wanted cash for over-the-counter painkillers or cigarettes. He also warned that if she left, he would come after her. "Just because you're a woman, it doesn't mean I won't hit you," he said. He broke her ribs and her foot. She didn't call the police because she didn't want him to be sentenced and then "out (of jail) in two or three months even more angry."

And so, Cynthia left. But at what cost?

Instead of knowing where the enemy is, Cynthia feels hunted and is scared to walk by herself on the streets, lest her former partner find her; she's had reports that he's out looking. She has lost a home and the status and friends that go with it. She has also lost her dignity in the shelter system. "I feel like my life just stopped."

Cynthia tried to find refuge in domestic violence shelters but as a single, older woman she was given low priority compared to younger women with children, and she was turned away. Ironically, a homeless shelter continued contributing to her negative feelings. When she arrived, she was exhausted, in pain, and needed to rest. She was placed in a residential program with personalized goals. However, there were days when she wasn't up to doing anything. Then staff jumped on her case. "I felt they were abusive, no better than my boyfriend. My counsellor screamed if I didn't do what she wanted." Cynthia theorizes that the shelter system is all about control and that if clients aren't under their counsellors' thumbs, then they withdraw their help. "When you are on the street, you are always controlled whatever you are doing."

Cynthia moved on to another shelter where participants are housed in different church basements every night. The quality, she says, depends on the church. At one she overheard guests referred to as "You people." At another the volunteers stayed in the kitchen, and at a third volunteers, trying to show interest, appeared to be overly nosy. At most churches, men aren't segregated from the women and children, which is very threatening and frightening to women who have had bad experiences; some churches don't have showers; and above all, there is no privacy. Not all volunteers are bad, though. "A lady the other night said, 'I feel so bad for you, but I don't know how to make it better.' She made us feel we counted; there aren't many like that."

Some have suggested that with $960 a month in a DVA pension, Cynthia should just find a place of her own and quit complaining. She explains it's not that easy. By the time she has paid for her medications (about $300 a month), she doesn't have enough money left for a damage deposit, and, as a pensioner, she's not eligible for any of the security deposit programs.

The kind of housing for which she might be eligible leaves her cold. Cynthia wants somewhere that feels safe when she walks in at night and where she can have grandchildren to stay and not worry about them. She is very aware that some people think she is too fussy, but because she's poor she doesn't think she should be grateful for sub-standard favours. If she has let herself be pushed around over the years, she's beginning to take a stand.

She says homeless women, especially the single ones, are shortchanged compared to the men. "Men have more rights, more places and can get counsellors. We have to fight for everything. You get to complain and complain."

Women need more support; better, safer places to stay; more help with damage deposits, so they can find appropriate housing; and better counsellors who help people rather than push them toward the streets. Cynthia decries the quick-fix solutions both for abused and homeless women. "There are women out there trying to commit suicide because their life has gone down the drains completely. What's their next move? It's hard to keep yourself together."

Being alone is hard for Cynthia, and yet she doesn't have many other options. "I'm kinda stuck. God only knows how long before I can get out."

Sources

Moore, Shelley, and Benita Bunjun. 2005. Women's Studies 300: Introduction to Gender Relations. Vancouver: University of British Columbia.

Morris, Marika. 2002 (3rd ed. 2005). *Women and Poverty Fact Sheet*. Canadian Research Institute for the Advancement of Women. <http:// www.criaw-icref. ca/indexFrame_e.htm>.

National Council of Welfare. 2005. *Welfare Incomes 2005*. <http://www.ncwcnbes. net/htmdocument/principales/onlinepub_e.htm>.

Pate, Kim. 2002. "Women and Girls in Prison: Canada's Alternative to Equality and Justice." Speech given by executive director of the Canadian Association of Elizabeth Fry Societies, LEAF breakfast, Winnipeg, October.

THE AMBULANCE IS WAITING AT THE BOTTOM OF THE CLIFF

Social Issues Committee. 2000. *The Right Thing to Do*. Calgary: YWCA, 31 May.

Turning Point. 2004. *Turning 40: Four Decades of Turning Lives Around and a Vision for the Future of Social Care*. October. <http://www.turning-point.co.uk>.

United Way of Calgary and Area. 2000. *Living on the Edge, When Paying for a Prescription Means Going Without Food*. Calgary: United Way.

Women and Welfare Project. 2005. *Lobbying for Change to the BC Employment and Assistance Regulations*. Vancouver: Vancouver Status of Women, Feminist Working Group, March.

Interviews

Robertson, Angela. Executive Director, Sistering, Toronto. 2004.

Shymka, Trudi. Coordinator of Women's and Children's Programs, St. Elizabeth Home, Vancouver. 2004.

Stringer, Kathy. Coordinator of Women's and Children's Programs, St. James Community Services Society, Vancouver. 2004.

LOVE THY NEIGHBOUR

Never Again
—Tattoo on the right buttock
of a formerly homeless woman

By taking a turkey to the home of the grateful Cratchit family, Ebenezer Scrooge experiences a personal redemption in Charles Dickens' *A Christmas Carol*, and almost magically Tiny Tim is able to walk again after partaking of the festive bird. This is the feel-good message about charity that most readers derive from this story. They conveniently forget that it was the Boxing Day follow-through that really made the difference to the Cratchits—Scrooge gave Bob Cratchit a pay raise and took on Tiny Tim as his personal cause. In other words, he made changes that enabled the family to stand on its own feet and to live with dignity. The story helps perpetrate two other falsehoods: good works can only happen at Christmas, and there are both the deserving and the undeserving poor. After all, the Cratchit family was not as desperate as some. Tiny Tim, crutch in hand, didn't go begging, Martha wasn't prostituting herself, nor were the brothers stealing. In fact, one of the points of Dickens' romanticized portrayal was that the Cratchits' value system was far superior to Scrooge's. Today, though, it's a different matter. Instead of glamourizing the poor, we have come to demonize them; and, instead of taking assistance to them, we expect them to gather it where they may.

On the face of it, the solution to the multi-headed hydra of women's homelessness and poverty is simple: create more housing; ensure all women have an adequate income to live with dignity; put social safety nets into place that are easy to access; end violence; and, finally, ensure all children are loved wisely. This is easy to say, but it is much more difficult to make come true. However, we shouldn't give up trying.

As we have discovered, there is no right to safe housing in Canadian law, so perhaps that's one place to start. Enshrining the right to safe housing in law would draw attention to the problem and make the public more aware that blaming someone for not having a home is not constructive when there are insufficient homes to go round. Blame only ensures that the poor don't have legs to stand on, let alone socks to pull up. We need a comprehensive approach that would include the construction of more social housing, refurbishing present rental properties, and supplying more supervised housing for people with various problems like mental health issues and addictions. We also need to look at the issue through a gender lens to see what works for women, many of whom have children. This means they will need a safe place where their children can play; that is close to buses, schools, stores, and other amenities; and to prevent constant moves, the lease should be in the women's names.

A fact sheet put out by the Winnipeg Prairie Women's Health Centre of Excellence points out that recent studies have found among other things that:

+ safety is the number one concern for women when looking for housing;
+ landlords sexually harass women;
+ health and safety standards are frequently not addressed in low-income apartments;
+ women have not had the opportunity, nor do they have the tools, to do basic maintenance and repairs;
+ 44 per cent of women living in private-market housing had moved in the past two years, with ensuing family disruptions;
+ none of the women in co-op housing, which is cheaper to subsidize than social housing, had moved in the last two years. (McCracken and Watson 2004)

Besides more co-op housing, their recommendations include "extensive consultations" with women as well as the development of stable, longer-term, low-cost housing to reduce multiple displacements; addressing allegations of harassment; bringing housing up to basic standards; and providing training in gender-based analysis for policy-makers.

According to the report, co-op housing has several benefits for women. The first is affordability, although sometimes the initial deposit can be hard to find. Once in residence, women say it is easier to budget because, since utilities are included in the monthly payments, there are no unexpected surprises, and, if their financial situation changes, they are able to talk to the manager about making arrangements until they are back on their feet. Secondly, the women feel safe and have more money for food, clothes, and medication, so their general well-being improves. Thirdly, the co-ops give the women not only a sense of community but also a voice in the organization, thus boosting their confidence. Finally, mixed income co-ops reduce the stigma of poverty that often afflicts those living in subsidized housing.

One of the report's researchers, Molly McCracken, has criticized social assistance policy manuals that are written in very technical terms so that people almost need an interpreter to understand their rights. This observation illustrates the problem with almost all government services: they are not set up to assist those who need help but to create employment for civil servants—at least that's the perspective from the bottom up. It cannot be emphasized too strongly how difficult it is for a woman on the edge to trail from one office to another trying to round up necessary documents. If someone forgets to give her the correct piece of paper, she can be financially burdened for weeks. And, when she finally does get her papers in order, welfare is often never enough to cover even the most basic requirements such as food and a telephone.

Women have taken the brunt of governmental cutbacks across the country. When the British Columbia government chopped the core funding of $1.7 million for 37 women's centres in 2004, the BC Government and Service Employees' Union (2004) calculated that this was less than the amount Premier Gordon Campbell had forgiven in unpaid fines and penalties against fish farms in the province. The women's centres had provided a wide range of services from counselling to food and clothing programs to legal aid workshops, job entry programs, and advocacy. This is an eloquent, although comparatively small example of how our priorities have become skewed.

Social service cutbacks, Employment Insurance reductions, and low minimum wages, set against a background of inflation, the rising costs of sending a child to school, depleted health care resources, and violence against women, coalesce into a picture of the systemic denial of a secure healthy life to certain segments of the population. As one woman on social assistance said to me in an interview, "Poverty puts me in harm's way." To change this scenario, we need increased financial supports with more flexibility built into them so that women can become truly independent. For example, as women move into the full-time work force, welfare should look at ways of continuing to pay certain health care bills that are too heavy to shoulder on minimal wages.

Poverty has far-reaching ramifications. We know, for example, that it is one of the biggest factors in determining women's health and that children who go to school hungry and not dressed like the other kids don't fare as well academically and are more likely to become ill. Ethnic origin, class, language, disabilities, and sexual orientation can also raise the barriers even higher for women needing health care. It is important to hear from women themselves about what would make health care more accessible to them and to involve them in planning a broad range of services including physical, mental, social, and spiritual aspects. Many homeless women have a very robust relation-ship with the "Guy upstairs," although this does not necessarily mean church membership. Spirituality is hardly ever discussed by the helping professions, but it could be a strong factor in helping women if it were more widely rec-ognized and supported in ways respectful of the women's beliefs.

People who can barely read will never find well-paying jobs, yet too many homeless women have come through school without acquiring basic literacy skills. They end up blaming themselves for being slow learners, or for having an attention deficit disorder, rather than questioning why school didn't meet their needs. School systems have to be more aware of the effects of poverty and violence on students, and the public has to be prepared to invest in education.

We also have to be more vigilant about the kind of care we provide for children when families cannot look after them. Women are asking for a less adversarial system and for more support in their parenting rather than hav-ing to fight with social workers who literally grab their children from their arms. Many of the mothers have experienced "care" themselves and know all too well that it produces adults who yearn to love and be loved, but for whom the day-to-day actions of parenting are as alien as herding camels. Should a woman be lucky enough to hang onto her children and to find a job, then comes the problem of good affordable day care—a commodity sadly lacking. Like so many of the changes suggested, uniform nation-wide day care standards and access are vital investments that would bring the very tangible results of more productive women in the labour force and children better equipped to face the world.

In the meanwhile, we have large numbers of women for whom even the basic homeless shelter system isn't working. There aren't enough safe beds nor enough programs to help them on the arduous road back into the community. The Mavis/McMullen Place in Vancouver provides a paradigm of what could be done and should be done for homeless women across the country.

The Mavis/McMullen Place provides co-op housing in the Downtown Eastside of the city on a noisy street where people in extreme states of misery hang out. A female Buddha figure looks benignly on the green central court-yard sprinkled with children's toys. The 34 attractive suites, opened in 1988, are for hard-to-house women with children and for senior women, which in this neighbourhood means those 45 and older. "I think there should be housing for women and children everywhere," says one 53-year-old resident. "As soon as you come into the entrance of Mavis/McMullen Place there is peace, safety, and family."

The residents had a voice in the design and development of the guidelines for operating the centre, and they are responsible for security and maintenance (Brooke interview). In fact, the rules are very few. There is zero tolerance for violence; children can't be left unattended; residents don't allow anyone in who is not their guest, and they are responsible for their own guests. The women are allowed to have male live-in partners, but the leases are all in the women's names. "If the relationship breaks down, the man goes, the woman stays," says Cynthia Brooke, coordinator of the complex. She counsels the women on the advisability of moving in with a boyfriend, pointing out that if his contribution to the rent has been an issue before, it will continue to be an issue at Mavis/McMullen. Many relationships endure but not under the same roof.

The sense of community, a large factor in the success of the project, works only if people are allowed full expression of who they are, so Mavis/McMullen is not a "dry" building. Women can do drugs and alcohol in their suites, as long as their activity doesn't spill out into the corridors; this cuts down on women ratting on each other to the Children's Aid. Most behave responsibly. One of the worst problems arose when an elderly woman, who tried to detox by herself, became quite ill. It was suggested that, considering her age and health, she should consume small amounts of alcohol, which she continues to do discreetly.

One of the women's problems, says Brooke, is that they have moved over and over again, but once they find the security of Mavis/McMullen their lives start to change for the better. "When you give people that basic access to housing ... it's everything. All of a sudden they have breathing room. It's a place to feel safe, and for human beings, that's everything."

If the Mavis/McMullen experience could be duplicated in major cities across Canada, the tragedy of homeless women's desperate lives would be largely alleviated and it would help their children, the next generation, find their way out of poverty, which in the end costs all of us in so many different ways.

Sources

BC Government and Service Employees' Union. 2004. *Budget Works Like a Slot Machine*. News release (17 February).

Donner, Lissa. 2002 (rev.). *Women, Income, and Health in Manitoba, An Overview and Ideas for Action.* Winnipeg: Women's Health Clinic, July. <http://www.womenshealthclinic.org/resources/wih/wih.html>.

Kappel Ramji Consulting Group for Sistering. 2002. *Common Occurrence, The Impact of Homelessness on Women's Health.* June. <http://www.sistering.org/issues.html>.

Mayes, Alison. 2004. "Poor Women's Needs 'Invisible.'" *Winnipeg Free Press* (12 February).

McCracken, Molly, and Gail Watson. 2004. *Women Need Safe, Stable, Affordable Housing: A Study of Social, Private, and Co-op Housing in Winnipeg.* Winnipeg: Prairie Women's Health Centre of Excellence, February. <http://www.pwhce.ca>.

Scott, Susan. 2005. "In the Spirit of Scrooge." *Fast Forward* (2 December).

Interview

Brooke, Cynthia. Coordinator of Mavis/McMullen Housing Society, Vancouver. 2004.